Changing Pedagogical Spa
in Higher Education

Higher education is in a current state of flux and uncertainty, with profound changes being shaped largely by the imperatives of global neoliberalism. *Changing Pedagogical Spaces in Higher Education* forms a unique addition to the literature and includes significant practical pointers in developing pedagogical strategies, interventions and practices that seek to address the complexities of identity formations, difference, inequality and misrecognition.

Drawing on research studies based across California, England, Italy, Portugal and Spain, this book analyses complex pedagogical re/formations across competing discourses of gender, diversity, equity, global neoliberalism and transformation, and aims:

- to critique and reconceptualise widening participation practices in higher education
- to consider the complex intersections between difference, equity, global neoliberalism and transformation
- to analyse the intersections of identity formations, social inequalities and pedagogical practices
- to contribute to broader widening participation policy agendas
- to develop an analysis of gendered experiences, intersected by race and class, of higher education practices and relations.

Changing Pedagogical Spaces in Higher Education will speak to those concerned with how theory relates to everyday practices and development of teaching in higher education and those who are interested in theorising about pedagogies, identities and inequalities in higher education. Engaging readers in a dialogue of the relationship between theory and practice, this thought-provoking and challenging text will be of particular interest to researchers, academic developers and policy-makers in the field of higher education studies.

Penny Jane Burke is Global Innovation Chair of Equity and Director of the Centre of Excellence for Equity in Higher Education at the University of Newcastle, Australia.

Gill Crozier is Professor of Education and formerly Director of the Centre for Educational Research in Equalities, Policy and Pedagogy in the School of Education at the University of Roehampton, UK.

Lauren Ila Misiaszek is Associate Professor in the Institute for International and Comparative Education in the Faculty of Education at Beijing Normal University, China.

The Society for Research into Higher Education (SRHE) is an independent and financially self-supporting international learned Society. It is concerned to advance understanding of higher education, especially through the insights, perspectives and knowledge offered by systematic research and scholarship.

The Society's primary role is to improve the quality of higher education through facilitating knowledge exchange, discourse and publication of research. SRHE members are worldwide and the Society is an NGO in operational relations with UNESCO.

The Society has a wide set of aims and objectives. Amongst its many activities the Society:

• is a specialist publisher of higher education research, journals and books, amongst them Studies in Higher Education, Higher Education Quarterly, Research into Higher Education Abstracts and a long running monograph book series.

The Society also publishes a number of in-house guides and produces a specialist series "Issues in Postgraduate Education".

• funds and supports a large number of special interest networks for researchers and practitioners working in higher education from every discipline. These networks are open to all and offer a range of topical seminars, workshops and other events throughout the year ensuring the Society is in touch with all current research knowledge.

• runs the largest annual UK-based higher education research conference and parallel conference for postgraduate and newer researchers. This is attended by researchers from over 35 countries and showcases current research across every aspect of higher education.

SRHE

Society for Research into Higher Education
Advancing knowledge Informing policy Enhancing practice

73 Collier Street
London N1 9BE
United Kingdom

T   +44 (0)20 7427 2350
F   +44 (0)20 7278 1135
E   srheoffice@srhe.ac.uk

www.srhe.ac.uk

Director: Helen Perkins
Registered Charity No. 313850
Company No. 00868820
Limited by Guarantee
Registered office as above

Society for Research into Higher Education (SRHE) series

Series Editors: Jennifer M. Case, University of Cape Town
Jeroen Huisman, University of Ghent

**A full list of titles in this series is available at:
www.routledge.com/series/SRHE**

Recently published titles:

Digital Technology and the Contemporary University: Degrees of digitization
Neil Selwyn

*Stepping up to the Second Year at University: Academic, psychological
and social dimensions*
Edited by Clare Milsom, Martyn Stewart, Mantz Yorke and Elena Zaitseva

Culture, Capitals and Graduate Futures: Degrees of class
Ciaran Burke

*Researching Higher Education: International perspectives on theory,
policy and practice*
Edited by Jennifer M. Case and Jeroen Huisman

*Freedom to Learn: The threat to student academic freedom and why it needs to
be reclaimed*
Bruce Macfarlane

Student Politics and Protest: International perspectives
Edited by Rachel Brooks

Theorising Learning to Teach in Higher Education
Edited by Brenda Leibowitz, Vivienne Bozalek and Peter Kahn

Access to Higher Education: Theoretical perspectives and contemporary challenges
Edited by Anna Mountford-Zimdars and Neil Harrison

Changing Pedagogical Spaces in Higher Education

Diversity, inequalities and misrecognition

Penny Jane Burke, Gill Crozier and Lauren Ila Misiaszek

Routledge
Taylor & Francis Group

LONDON AND NEW YORK

First published 2017
by Routledge
2 Park Square, Milton Park, Abingdon, Oxon OX14 4RN

Together with the Society for Research into Higher Education
73 Collier Street
London, N1 9BE
UK

and by Routledge
711 Third Avenue, New York, NY 10017

Routledge is an imprint of the Taylor & Francis Group, an informa business

British Library Cataloguing in Publication Data
A catalogue record for this book is available from the British Library

Library of Congress Cataloging in Publication Data
A catalog record for this book has been requested

ISBN: 978-1-138-91721-7 (hbk)
ISBN: 978-1-138-91722-4 (pbk)
ISBN: 978-1-315-68400-0 (ebk)

Typeset in Galliard
by Apex CoVantage, LLC
Printed inGreat Britain by Ashford Colour Press ltd

Contents

Acknowledgements   viii

Introduction   1

1   Higher education, difference, diversity and inequality   11

2   Reconceptualising pedagogies and reimagining difference   29

3   Pedagogical methodology   49

4   Diversity, difference, inequalities and pedagogical
    experiences   59

5   Pedagogical identity formations: student perspectives   76

6   Gendered formations in pedagogical relations and spaces   91

7   Pedagogies of difference: 'race', ethnicity and social
    class in higher education   108

8   Theorising the early career experience: towards
    collective engaged pedagogies   121

    Conclusion: Changing pedagogical spaces: reclaiming
    transformation   131

    Appendix one: Formations of gender and higher
        education pedagogies (GaP)   143
    Appendix two: Fulbright   153
    Appendix three: Table of student information (GaP project)   154
    References   160
    Index   172

Acknowledgements

This book draws from the Formations of Gender and Higher Education Pedagogies (GaP) project, which was funded by the National Teaching Fellowship Scheme (NTFS) project strand initiative funded by the Higher Education Funding Council for England (HEFCE) and managed by the Higher Education Academy (HEA). It also draws from an extension project funded by a US-UK Fulbright Commission Fulbright Scholarship and the London Paulo Freire Institute, Centre for Education Research in Equalities, Policy and Pedagogy (CEREPP), Department of Education, Roehampton University.

This book is the result of a collaborative and participatory process, which involved the invaluable contribution of many participants, including the research participants, both students and teachers, who participated in interviews, focus groups, workshops, discussions and seminars. We are enormously appreciative of the time and thought they committed to the project.

This collaboration involved a strongly committed, perceptive and outstanding research team and we deeply thank and acknowledge the most important contribution to the GaP project of Dr Barbara Read, Professor Becky Francis, Professor Julie Hall, Jo Peat, Professor Louise Archer and Carolyn Gallop. The team collaborated across all stages of the project and we have benefitted in this book from the rich discussions we had with all team members. We also thank the excellent research assistance to the GaP project provided by Dr Andrew Wilkins, Dr Ada Mau, Michele Westhead, and of this book, provided by Dr Georgina Ramsay. We would also like to thank the significant contribution of our GaP Steering Group Committee members, who provided invaluable feedback throughout the life of the project: Professor Monica McLean, Professor Mairtin Mac an Ghaill, Professor Glynis Cousins and Professor Miriam David. Thank you very much to Dr Anna Bennett for her insightful feedback on the book manuscript. Thank you to the Book Series Editors Professor Jenni Case and Professor Jeroen Huisman and to Director of SRHE Helen Perkins, as well as the SRHE Publications Committee for their support. Many thanks as well to Bruce Roberts of Routledge for his support in getting the book to production.

Chapter 7 is based on the published article from: Crozier, Gill, Burke, Penny Jane & Archer, Louise (2016) 'Peer relations in higher education: raced, classed and gendered constructions and Othering', *Whiteness and Education*, 1 (1): 39–53. Parts of Chapters 2 and 6 draw from: Burke, Penny Jane (2015) 'Re/imagining higher education pedagogies: gender, emotion and difference', *Teaching in Higher Education*, 20 (4): 388–401.

Introduction

Higher education is currently in a state of flux and uncertainty, with profound changes being shaped largely by the imperatives of global neoliberalism. The impact of global neoliberalism intersects with a range of other potent forces, changing the higher-education landscape in contemporary times. This includes the forces of globalisation, neoconservatism, corporatisation, new managerialism, neocolonialism, neopatriarchies and enduring forms of institutional racism. In this contemporary and changing landscape, there is increasing pressure for universities to position themselves as 'world-class', and to compete in a highly stratified field driven by discourses of 'excellence' and league tables. Within such a frame, quality is often in tension with equity because it is reduced to neo-liberal principles and limited measurable outputs.

Against this highly competitive and hierarchical terrain, a policy focus on widening participation (WP) in higher education (HE) has emerged, emphasising neoliberal notions and outcomes mostly concerned with the types of employability and development of skills and competencies that promote an efficient and competitive workforce in the context of global knowledge economies. Widening participation policy has been dominated by debates about 'fair access' and has tended to be preoccupied with 'raising aspirations' of those individuals from disadvantaged backgrounds deemed to have potential and ability. Such debates tend to overlook the interconnecting structures, systems, practices, discourses and cultures of higher education that are complicit in the social, economic and cultural reproduction of inequalities and exclusions in and through higher education.

The increasing levels of instrumentalism and utilitarianism shaping discourses of widening participation have been challenged for failing to engage significant and complex questions relating to the right to higher education, not only about who has access, but also about the purposes of participation, and what it means to participate, in higher education in the twenty-first century. The notion of 'diversity' has been embraced to some extent. However, this notion fails to problematise the ways that diversity is intertwined with difference, misrecognition and inequality, and raises key challenges for academic practices, identities and frameworks, including higher education pedagogies. Researchers have pointed out that much of the widening participation policy agenda focuses on access in relation to entry routes into higher education, projecting the problem as 'out there'. Although we agree that questions of who has the right to higher education are deeply entangled in the inequalities that are produced and reproduced through compulsory schooling systems, we are concerned to bring attention to the ways that higher education pedagogies might also be complicit in the reproduction of inequalities even after entry to higher education has been achieved.

Indeed, we argue that there has been a lack of attention to the challenging question of *participation*, and how it is conceptualised across different pedagogical contexts, including the different and contradictory spaces of universities. This book explores those questions and considers the ways that universities themselves might support the participation of diverse groups, or might be exclusive – in terms of being subtly, but powerfully, exclusionary – of difference through their standardising and homogenising practices. Although there has been increasing attention to questions of 'inclusion' in higher education pedagogy, a deeper analysis of pedagogical experiences reveals that 'inclusion' itself often acts as a form of symbolic violence, as the individual is expected to fit and conform to the dominant values, identities and practices of pedagogical participation. This tends to value some dispositions and exclude others, an approach that is often framed by particular ontological perspectives that reproduce the 'subject' of participation in ways that misrecognises those constructed as 'Other'.

In the book, we look at these processes of exclusion and marginalisation through the lens of difference in relation to formations of gender, class and race, drawing on our research data to illuminate our analyses and arguments. One of our concerns is the remedial nature of the initiatives designed to widen participation in higher education, which are couched in the problematic language of 'support' and 'need'. Although we acknowledge the importance of identifying ways to support students from marginalised and/or under-represented backgrounds with their university studies, we argue that the way this is imagined and enacted is fraught with taken-for-granted assumptions about who 'the participant' in higher education is and should be. The focus tends to be on transforming the individual student subject, which is constructed through discourses of 'neediness' and connected assumptions of lack and deficiency, to become a particular kind of (neoliberal) participant that is 'independent', 'resilient', 'confident' and 'employable'. The problematic nature of each of these concepts for the production of pedagogical identity is left unexplored, while the pedagogical practices historically embedded in social exclusion are also not subjected to examination. The limited and limiting forms of support that are provided to university students tend to be remedial in nature, outside of the programme of study and designed to re/form those students identified as 'non-standard' into legitimate student-subjects of hegemonic discourses that frame what a student is and should be. This requires the 'non-standard student' to participate in processes of self-transformation and self-regulation, to become 'fixed' and to become a 'proper' university student, fitting in to the hegemonic discourses and frameworks (although these themselves are complex, shifting and contradictory). Support also tends to be peripheral to the programme of study with structures and mechanisms designed to change *the student rather than the pedagogical spaces and practices that are (re)productive of multiple forms of inequality.*

The target groups that have been constructed through equity and widening participation policies according to gender, class and race and other intersecting differences such as age, ability, family background, migration/refugee/asylum status, gender identity and sexual orientation, religion/or lack thereof, inter/nationality and so forth, and which are different in different countries (see for example Burke and Kuo, 2015), are useful but are also problematic as the politics of recognition and misrecognition play out across multiple differences and intersections across, between, within and against policy and official discourses and systems. It is important to raise awareness about the complexity of these issues around targeting and subjective formation in the development of pedagogies for social justice.

We develop the concept of pedagogic participation to consider the relationship between formations of difference and higher education participation in and across contested pedagogical spaces. Drawing on Nancy Fraser (1997, 2003), we consider possibilities for creating 'parity of participation' in relation to the social justice struggles of redistribution, recognition and representation. How might higher education pedagogies create spaces for the parity of participation across and between these three inter-related social justice domains and complex formations of inequality and difference but in ways that acknowledge the lived and embodied 'cultural politics of emotion' (Ahmed, 2004) that play out in pedagogical spaces?

This book argues that widening participation necessitates the social and cultural transformation of higher education structures, practices and discourses that have been produced over time by those in privileged, authoritative and powerful social positions. Although we need to understand the histories by which certain higher education pedagogies have formed, such as lecturing and teaching, we also need to pay close attention to the ways contemporary political influences are impacting on pedagogical identities, reframing to some extent, depending on the particular university context, what it means to be a university student. The call to diversify student constituencies in higher education requires serious attention to current cultural, pedagogical and educational practices because they are deeply embedded in the very structures, values and perspectives that are reproductive of social inequalities and injustices in the first place. However the reproduction of inequalities becomes more complicated to map as pedagogical spaces are textured, reformed and reshaped by complex intersections of difference. This is multilayered within a globalised HE landscape that contains increasing and contextually varied forms of neoliberalism, corporatisation and shifting political forces that create increasingly complex forms of inequalities within pedagogical spaces.

Widening participation requires a deep and sustained engagement with questions of difference and the ways that difference is continually reconstructed in and through pedagogical spaces, as well as unequal power relations. Therefore, drawing on the wider body of work on teaching in higher education, the book makes a unique contribution to the development of HE pedagogies, aiming to:

- critique and reconceptualise widening participation practices in higher education through a focus on changing pedagogical spaces;
- consider the complex intersections between difference, equity, global neoliberalism and transformation;
- in relation to this, analyse the intersections of complex formations of difference, subjectivities, inequalities and pedagogical practices;
- contribute to broader widening participation policy agendas, paying close attention to pedagogical issues beyond 'raising aspirations' and 'fair access';
- develop an analysis of gendered experiences, intersected by race and class, of higher education practices and relations, with attention to the complex formations of masculinities and femininities in pedagogical relations and practices.

This book draws on and pulls together two recent qualitative projects on higher education pedagogies. The first was an in-depth participatory research project, 'Formations of Gender and Higher Education Pedagogies' ('GaP'), conducted in England and funded by the UK's Higher Education Academy (Burke et al., 2013). The second was an expansion project of GaP, funded through a Fulbright fellowship (Misiaszek nee Jones) (supported by the Paulo Freire Institute-UK and the Centre for Educational Research in Equalities, Policy and Pedagogy, University of Roehampton), examining pedagogical relations, identities and experiences across the European contexts of Spain, Portugal and Italy as well as the US context of California. Details of the GaP project are included in Appendix One and details of the Fulbright project are included in Appendix Two. A table outlining the student participants' pseudonyms and demographic information is included in Appendix Three.

Drawing on critical and feminist post-structural concepts of pedagogy, both projects set out to challenge hegemonic discourses of teaching and learning, to identify the complex ways that identity formations of gender and other social differences (such as class, ethnicity and race) profoundly shape pedagogical experiences, relations, subjectivities and practices. Both projects explored the ways that inequalities, exclusions and inclusions operate at the micro level of classroom practice, as well as wider macro contexts of global neoliberalism and higher education.

Book structure

Chapter one presents an analysis of the international context of higher education, difference, diversity and inequality. It interrogates the hegemony of globalisation, neoliberal frameworks and other key political influences currently re/shaping HE policy and practice. We argue that the increasing emphasis of higher education policy on economic concerns has majorly influenced the discursive rationales and understanding underpinning many policies of widening participation, equity and social inclusion; universities are expected to contribute to global economic competitiveness within a frame that is increasingly marketised. In such frameworks, universities must compete in the global market of higher education for 'world class' students, staff and resources. Whilst higher education teachers[1] and students become increasingly subjected to surveillance cultures through modes of assessment, evaluation and performativity, inequalities of gender, class and race are assumed to be eradicated by the market of higher education, in which individual consumers are perceived to freely exercise their 'choice' to participate in higher education or not. Notions of choice are tied in to discourses of meritocracy, in which the right to higher education is understood in terms of individual ability, efficacy, potential and hard work rather than as shaped by structural, cultural and institutional inequalities and misrecognitions, as well as the ways some families mobilise inter-generational privileges, resources and networks. This chapter provides an overview of research and literature in the field, to shed light on the complex operations of inequality in higher education and to explain the significance of a focus on pedagogies for developing a richer understanding of inclusion and exclusion. It also considers and critiques current and key narratives at play in the field, which reinforce patriarchal, neocolonial and racialised inequalities whilst concealing these from view. The narratives of 'a crisis of masculinity', 'the feminisation of higher education' and 'lowering of standards' are examples of such processes, making inequalities increasingly insidious and difficult to dismantle.

A detailed discussion of the theoretical resources available to challenge hegemonic and instrumentalist discourses of teaching and learning in higher education and academic, teacher and student identity formations is discussed in Chapter two. We draw on critical and feminist pedagogies to explore lived, relational and embodied practices in higher education, which are deeply interconnected with ontologies, epistemologies and the politics of mis/recognition (Freire, 1970; Lather, 1991; Fraser, 1997; Burke, 2012). The dynamics, relations and experiences of teaching and learning are conceptualised as intimately tied to the privileging of some forms of knowledge over others, the recognition and legitimisation of hegemonic subjectivities and the exclusion of 'Others', often problematically constructed as 'undeserving' of HE participation. Reductive language that frames teaching and learning largely as 'styles', 'provision', 'needs' and 'delivery', operates to hide complex power relations within pedagogical spaces, which are constituted and productive of gendered interactions, performatives and subjectivities. Feminist post/structural concepts of gendered subjectivity (e.g. Butler, 1993; Flax, 1995) shed light on the multiple, contradictory and shifting sense of self that unsettles hegemonic versions of the individual as a coherent, rational, knowable and stable self. Importantly, the stroke (/) in post/structuralism signifies the negotiating of structuralism and poststructuralism in our work.

Such conceptual frameworks aim to reveal the multiple layers of injustices that operate around processes of identity formation and subjective construction, in relation to embodied intersections of age, class, ethnicity, gender and race. In addition to these theoretical frameworks we recognise the existence and impact of structural formations and realities. Whilst this may seem contradictory to some, we believe that within the ever-shifting context of a globalised and neo-liberal world this diversity of ideas is necessary in order both to make sense of the emerging complexity and to engage with appropriate tools, which could contribute to developing change. In fact the utilisation of these seemingly contradictory sets of ideas works well within a framework of praxis.

Chapter three explores methodological issues in conducting research on higher education pedagogies and presents our concept of 'pedagogical methodology'. This concept reframes participatory methodologies as creating a pedagogical space to engage participants in research and reflexive processes, collaboratively exploring the complex interrelationship between teaching, learning, diversities and differences. Key themes explored in Chapter three include epistemological perspectives and debates, developing participatory approaches, feminist methodologies, contesting hegemonic evidence-based discourses, the relationship between pedagogy and methodology in participatory methodologies and research on pedagogies and the ethics of researching higher education pedagogies. The possibilities of creating critical spaces of reflexivity and praxis, through participatory research and pedagogical methodology, will be considered as a potential resource for widening participation in the processes of creating new practices, spaces and frameworks in higher education. A feminist, post/structural and critical engagement with Freirean concepts will be developed as a way to re/imagine different ways of doing research and pedagogy, bringing these together for social justice work in higher education. The specific detail of the process and methods used in the two projects is described briefly in the chapter, with more information included in the Appendices One (GaP) and Two (Fulbright).

Chapter four explores the data from both the GaP and the Fulbright projects to bring to light the key themes of diversity, difference, in/equalities and higher education pedagogies in relation to staff identities and experiences. We foreground the perspectives of the academic staff in considering their pedagogies and experiences as HE teachers within the context of widening participation in relation to these issues. We explore and analyse the different pedagogic approaches teachers take and the various influences they feel impact on these. In relation to this we also discuss the different subject disciplines that we researched and consider the internal and external dynamics that disciplinary cultures may have on discourses of pedagogy.

Chapter five explores the accounts generated through the research, expressing contradictory sensibilities about student identities in higher education, drawing specifically on the GaP data. This is framed by wider regulatory discourses of what is expected of an academic or student in contemporary higher education, mediated by the subject or disciplinary area. The individual is caught up in the complex sets of competing demands and expectations of the specific disciplinary context, the overarching and standardising frameworks of academic and research excellence and quality assurance and the ethos, missions and strategic plans of different institutions with unequal status. This affects all academics and students but in different ways in a highly stratified and competitive sector.

Students associated with widening participation (WP) policies, are often labelled as inadequate and or unready for university study. In Chapter five, we explore their experiences of university through their accounts, their perspectives and choices. Identity is about the self and as Sibley (1995) argues the construction of the self involves social, cultural and spatial contexts. Although we take the view that the students arrive at the university with varying amounts of experience, resources and capital in the Bourdieusian sense, these are only effective resources if they mesh with the 'field' they find themselves in. In other words identity formations are constrained by interweaving social, material and structural inequalities (Reay, 2009). In this chapter we explore this interweaving in relation to the students' identity formations and the implications for their university experiences. The key themes that we address in this chapter include: encountering the university – students' expectations and the expectations on them; space and place; pedagogical relations and geographies of exclusion;[2] pedagogies of in/exclusion: power, identities, practices and constraints.

Chapter six examines the narrative of a 'crisis of masculinity' and argues that this narrative presents an over-simplistic analysis of the increasing numbers of women accessing higher education in some parts of the world. It also rests on patriarchal and misogynist assumptions that women's position should always be in a minority (Morley, 2010). In the context of higher education, this has reduced complex gendered inequalities to a presumed battle of the sexes, failing to engage with the intricate ways that formations of gender are produced and performed in different pedagogical spaces and disciplinary contexts, privileging particular kinds of practices, knowledge and identities whilst excluding others.

The research projects illuminate the ways that academic and student subjectivities are gendered and this is enmeshed in the gendering of subject areas, practices and disciplines. However, such insights do not reinforce the wider hegemonic view that contemporary higher education has become a 'feminised' space. Rather, that data show that masculinities and femininities play out in complex ways to shape pedagogical experiences, relations, subjectivities and practices, both influenced by and challenging to hegemonic discourses of gender and masculinity. Pedagogies are conceptualised as constitutive of gendered formations through the discursive practices and regimes of truth at play in particular pedagogic and disciplinary spaces. Chapter six will show that pedagogies do not simply reflect the gendered identities of academics and students but pedagogies themselves are gendered, intimately bound up with historical and masculinised ways of being and doing within higher education.

Detailed attention to formations of gender within pedagogical relations reveals the important ways that gender intersects with other, pathologised identities that inflame problematic anxieties about 'lowering of standards' and the neo-liberal imperative for higher education to produce disciplined subjects, or in Foucault's terms the way that neo-liberalised institutions seek to produce 'docile bodies' (Foucault, 1977). Indeed, gender is always embodied, and although masculinities can be taken up by different kinds of bodies and selves, only certain bodies can be positioned as legitimate and authoritative by and in relation to hegemonic patriarchal discourses of masculinity (which play out differently across different pedagogical contexts). This poses a challenge for the inclusion of men from 'Other' kinds of social backgrounds, in terms of the often-derisive constructions of working-class and Black masculinities, which reinforce inequalities in pedagogical spaces and problematic subjective positions of both students and lecturers. Higher education pedagogies thus require reformation to address such complex issues and concerns but in ways that reject the highly problematic claim that masculinity is in crisis due to the feminisation of higher education.

Fitting in and belonging has been a central theme in studies of widening participation in HE and is explored in Chapter seven with a particular focus on formations of ethnicity and race. Most often this has been discussed with respect to social class and accessing the necessary capitals in order to get to university and progress when there (Read, Archer and Leathwood, 2003). Crozier, Reay, Clayton and Colliander (2008) found that 'fitting-in' for working-class students had different implications in the social field and academic field depending on their educational histories and learning dispositions and the different social and academic milieu they found themselves in. For Black and Minority Ethnic (BME) students in a White-dominated setting there are additional issues. Adapting and assimilating are all forms of symbolic violence, which run throughout the evidence from students. The BME students in our GaP study respond to these pressures in different ways at different times. Frequently BME school students have been accused of not mixing (e.g. Crozier and Davies, 2008), rather than White students separating themselves off. There are similar echoes of this from many of the White students at Riverside University (our case study university). Concerns about cliques amongst students are an ongoing theme and typically White students allege that these are based on ethnicity, together with an accusation that 'Black people stick together'.

Chapter eight considers the struggles and processes of forming an academic identity in the wider context of global neo-liberalism and notions of crisis, with a specific focus on the Fulbright project. Pedagogies are shaped by different and competing power relations, together with the changing contexts in which teaching and learning takes place and the gendered and professional identities and experiences that teachers bring to pedagogical processes. Teachers in higher education are caught between, on the one hand, the imperatives of the neo-liberal market: to ensure success often defined by limited parameters; to ensure retention; to ensure positive student evaluations; to cope with the demands of large groups at the same time of ensuring personal support/feedback and so on. On the other hand, are the desires and sensibilities they bring to their teaching in terms of their own identifications as academics and the desire for fulfilment and recognition. The chapter examines the lived contradiction of ideal practice and practices evoked by the harsh realities of interpersonal relations, which profoundly resonate across the accounts of different academics.

In the chapter, we argue that precariousness in higher education disrupts higher education teachers' identity formation and pedagogies, leading to misrecognition and inequality. Precariousness is often a term connected to the newness of early career. As Gill (2010, p. 232) notes, 'Precariousness is one of the defining experiences of contemporary academic life – particularly, but not exclusively, for younger or 'career early' staff (a designation that can now extend for one's entire 'career', given the few opportunities for development or secure employment)'. To explore this, we adapt bell hooks' concept of 'engaged pedagogy,' theorising how a 'collective engaged pedagogy' might promote well-being and spaces for reflexivity beginning at a personal level but beyond that to the collective sense, which we argue ultimately promotes social justice. We contend that precariousness significantly constrains opportunities and possibilities for early career teachers (ECTs) to be engaged with their colleagues, their students, and perhaps more significantly, with themselves. We ask, what higher education spaces do ECTs have in order to cultivate engagement? We argue that these spaces for engagement are increasingly restricted, and without these spaces, the potential for knowledge creation by ECTs, as well as the trajectories they can forge, are also constrained. This in turn perpetuates patterns of inequality and misrecognition that are in danger of persisting in middle and later career.

We present a conceptual exploration of temporality as it relates to the ECT experience, further exploring 'newness', a concept interwoven with precariousness. Then we engage in a conceptual and empirical exploration of precariousness as it relates to ECTs' identity formations and pedagogical experiences. We conclude with a reflection on how collective engaged pedagogies can offer ways forward for work by and with ECTs.

Finally, the Conclusion chapter summarises the key arguments made in the book and recaptures the significance of critical theoretical resources and insights for challenging hegemonic pedagogies and discourses. The chapter will reiterate the argument that hegemonic pedagogical practices work to silence and make difference and inequality invisible, often through references to social inclusion, widening participation and diversity. Difference tends to be reduced to the marketing images of happy university students from 'Other' kinds of backgrounds (Leathwood and Read, 2009). Diversity is often constructed as unproblematic and desirable, whilst difference is to be controlled through standardisation and disciplining processes. The anxiety about closeness of the 'Other' to those deemed to be legitimate university participants is often expressed through narratives about the 'dumbing down' of HE pedagogies and the lack of discipline, passion for learning and aspiration associated with students constructed as nonstandard from 'Other' social backgrounds. Connected to such anxieties, social inclusion compels those deemed to be 'different' in practices of self-correction. Those seen as deserving of higher education must conform to and master the normalising and disciplining practices of HE pedagogies.

The research projects discussed expose how mainstream teaching and learning practices in higher education do little to challenge exclusionary classist, sexist and racist imaginaries. Indeed, the research demonstrates that HE pedagogies are deeply implicated in the perpetuation of a politics of misrecognition. In times of austerity and crisis, increasing student fees and profound moves towards the marketisation of higher education, students and academics are prone towards risk-averse practices in the pedagogies and identities they engage, unwittingly reinforcing conservative tendencies towards the exclusion and fear of difference.

Throughout the book we argue that changing pedagogical spaces to become more inclusive is constrained by the lack of resources, both material and conceptual, available to support the development of pedagogies that embrace and engage difference, at both the ontological and epistemological levels. We argue that a post/structural reworking of critical and feminist pedagogies and methodologies has the potential to open up interventionist spaces that work towards the development of inclusive and critical pedagogies in higher education for social justice. This requires reflexive attention to the affective, cultural, subjective and symbolic dimensions of pedagogical experience and meaning-making, as well as questions of material redistribution.

Notes

1 We use the descriptor of 'teacher' intentionally throughout the book to foreground the practices of teaching. Although some might identify more readily with descriptors of 'lecturer' or 'tutor', which we also sometimes use, we point out that the practices of 'lecturing' and 'tutoring' are more specific than the broader notion of 'teaching' that we are exploring in this book. The term 'teacher' also connects practices of and in higher education to other educational contexts (in which these inequalities, misrecognitions, pedagogical challenges may also be present).
2 We have borrowed this term from Sibley's book 'Geographies of Exclusion: Society and Difference in the West', 1995. London & New York: Routledge.

Chapter 1

Higher education, difference, diversity and inequality

This chapter presents the international context of higher education (HE), considering difference, diversity and inequality in relation to pedagogical questions and concerns. Interrogating the hegemony of neo-liberal discourses, we consider the ways global forces are profoundly reshaping the policy and practice of teaching in HE across different international contexts. Higher education reforms are often justified in relation to the drive for 'excellence' for all students but largely ignore deeply embedded and complex histories of misrecognition, creating new forms of inequality, stratification and exclusion. Gendered, classed and racialised subjectivities and epistemologies, as well as other intersecting inequalities, are made unspeakable through technologies of performativity, regulation and 'datafication' (Sellar, 2013) yet are deeply felt through lived experiences of misrecognition. The increasing emphasis of higher education policy on the economic realm drives the rationalities underpinning policy discourses of widening participation and equity, with universities expected to contribute to business, innovation and industry, moving increasingly to the logics of the market. In such frameworks, universities are positioned as competing in the global market of higher education for 'world class' students, staff and resources, based on the 'quality' of their institutional profile in relation to research and teaching.

Providing an overview of policy, research and literature in the international field, this chapter aims to shed light on the complex operations of inequality in and through higher education and to explain the significance of a focus on pedagogies for developing a richer understanding of inclusion and exclusion. Although we are critical of a homogenising and monolithic analysis of neo-liberalism, we argue that neo-liberalism is a key force in relation to the politics of higher education reform in the contemporary landscape. We understand neoliberalism as a political and hegemonic discourse that has gained increasing momentum since the 1980s, placing significant confidence in markets as a way to restructure the public sector, including higher education. The logics of neo-liberalism have increasingly led to the substitution of public funding with private individual fees across multiple national contexts. This has also included greater moves towards deregulation, and strong austerity measures to significantly reduce public spending with significant shifts towards the privatisation of the public sphere. New public management is a feature of neo-liberalism and the 'age of performativity' (Ball, 2003). This has led to a dramatic proliferation of new data infrastructures and new accountabilities in the governance of education systems (Sellar, 2013). However, we also argue that neo-liberalism is not the only force at play in understanding the landscape of higher education, and complex pedagogical relations within it. We must understand neo-liberalism as an intersecting political force with other powerful dynamics including, but not exclusively, neocolonialism, institutional racism and contemporary forms of patriarchy.

In this chapter, we will trace the trans/formation of higher education policy across different international contexts, and the ways this is crystallised through particular discourses of 'excellence', 'choice', and 'social mobility'. We will consider the particular implications of this for changing pedagogical logics and the ways this imposes particular regimes of truth on teaching and learning. Our underpinning concern is the impact of such transformations on questions of equity and social justice in higher education, with a focus on themes of difference, diversities and inequality.

The global market of higher education

We must understand that the move towards a global market of higher education is itself intimately bound up with complex international social inequalities, injustices and oppressions. Higher education is an institution constituted through its relationality with other social institutions and organisations with multiple and often contradictory political forces and impulses, and of course wider social, cultural and economic inequalities. Naidoo explains that 'the creation of a global market in HE is of course a rigged market which is twisted with strong protectionism to create an unequal playing field' (Naidoo, 2015) but she also points out that:

> The blame for pervasive poverty, growing unemployment and social unrest is laid at the door of HE rather than seen as an outcome of policies related to predatory capitalism. HE plays a part here but it would be a grave error to believe that HE in isolation can contribute to global wellbeing. It is therefore very important to link HE to wider development and global wellbeing strategies.
>
> (Naidoo, 2015)

The creation of a global market of higher education means that a smaller group of influential players are shaping the direction higher education takes, although of course this takes shape in different ways across different national, regional and local contexts. There are multiple contestations, interests, agendas and impulses at play across and within the field of higher education and yet there are specific patterns of influence, power and transformation that can be traced internationally. Hotson (2012) provides a detailed and provocative analysis of the influence of large, transnational corporations who he argues are now manoeuvring their economic power, networks and resources to reform higher education policy in the interests purely of business and profit. Presenting an analysis of the particular influence of the World Economic Forum (WEF), he argues that neo-liberalism is a smoke screen that conceals from view the power and immense influence of global organisations. He argues that the changes to higher education policy witnessed in localised national contexts are patterns that can be identified across the world. These include: withdrawal of public funding and its substitution with private student fees; viewing universities as service providers and students as consumers; commodification of education; vocationalisation with a strong emphasis on training; exponential growth of the for-profit sector; corporatisation; decline of academic governance; growing casualisation of staff; the commercialisation of research; increasing managerialism; and the move for higher education programmes (teaching and research) to meet the needs of business and industry.

Hotson (2012) claims that we are in the midst of a global higher education crisis and warns that what is driving these changes is not simply a neo-liberal ideology, although this plays a key role; rather it is the imposing demands that large, transnational corporations place on governments with the ultimate goal of maximising profits that also drives policy. He identifies a number of anomalies in higher education policy that lead him to question why such reforms are being made. He gives the examples of the apparent commitment to increasing student choice whilst reducing the range of degree programmes being offered and the fact that despite higher education being key to national competitive advantage, for which an economic rationale would then support public investment, the government is drastically reducing investment in higher education. Anomalies such as these might be explained by understanding that the economy is now a global force, leading to public reform being shaped by external forces. He traces such external forces to the WEF, whose membership is constituted of large, transnational corporations who each generate about five billion US dollars annually. Hotson suggests that decisions about national higher education policy reforms are increasingly being driven by the objectives of external organisations such as the WEF, of which universities are becoming increasingly subordinate. In this way, higher education is no longer being underpinned by academic judgments, principles and values (although these of course are not themselves homogenous but are contested), but by the needs of business to maximise financial advantage.

Hotson's analysis is sobering; however our position is that although we need to keep sight of such an analysis and reveal how such global economic forces are reframing pedagogical spaces, experiences and practices, we argue that there are multiple political forces at play, and there remain spaces where academic-oriented and pedagogically driven values and perspectives are in force, albeit through contradictory and contested processes. Paul Ashwin argues powerfully that:

> The danger of the increase in global information about higher education is that the individual, durable and stable elements of higher education that can be easily measured are given a greater value than those that are collective, complex, changing and country-specific. As higher education researchers, we need to engage with such tensions critically, constructively, collectively and courageously. Critically because we need to challenge the tendency to value only what is measurable and carefully identify the ways in which different simplifications, including our own, offer a partial picture of the world's complexity. Constructively because we need to respect and take seriously the concerns of those both inside and outside of higher education research with whom we may strongly disagree. In doing so, we need to offer alternative ways of addressing these concerns rather than simply dismissing them through critique. Collectively because we need to recognise and emphasise that the value of higher education research comes from the communal bodies of knowledge that it produces rather than individual researchers or projects. Courageously because our contribution to higher education research is always in the process of becoming. This means that our successes and failures are temporary and, as a community, we need to continually work to show the value of what higher education research can offer. This requires us not to underestimate the challenges involved in offering all students a transformative higher education experience but also not to forget the possibilities offered by the power of higher education to transform students' understanding of the world and their position within it.
>
> (Ashwin, 2015)

Ashwin's argument has important implications for pedagogies in higher education, resonant of Freire's concepts of the *inédito viável* (which will be further explored in Chapters three and eight) and of reading the world. Against the pernicious forces of global capitalism, neo-liberalism and the demands of transnational corporations, we must create spaces of refusal in which broader meaning is collectively reconstructed about the world and our contextualised orientations to it. Robert Rhoads and Katalin Szelenyi eloquently argue that universities are:

> One of the few remaining spaces in which unchecked global capitalism (neoliberalism) and the kind of citizenry it advances may still be challenged. We need academics, students and graduates of universities who possess the dispositions and skills to resist the present movement towards corporate-driven self-interest and who see themselves as part of the struggle for a broader, more globally responsive citizenship. As Bakan astutely noted, we

are headed down a pathological path toward our own destruction. What we need more than ever is not the elimination of the public sphere but its strengthening.

(Rhoads and Szelenyi, 2011, p. 28)

However, part of this process of creating pedagogical spaces of refusal is to analyse and uncover the hegemonic discourses at play that are weakening such processes. A key discourse that is contributing to the forces that place the economy and profit-making as the central aim of higher education is the hegemonic discourse of 'excellence'.

Reshaping higher education through 'excellence'

The recent publication of the United Kingdom's Green Paper entitled *Teaching Excellence, Social Mobility and Student Choice* (BIS, 2015) is indicative of the hegemony that 'excellence' has gained across the international field of higher education. The Green Paper, published by the UK's Department of Business, Innovation and Skills, arguably cements a marketised system of higher education, engraining those concepts emerging from a neo-liberal imagination. The Green Paper aims to create a framework in which teaching in higher education might be 'improved' through evaluating teaching through comparative methods across the UK. The Green Paper intends this to lead to better-informed student-consumers of the research and teaching 'quality' of individual higher education institutions; providing greater transparency to student-consumers as the main funding source to Higher Education Institutions (HEIs); enabling student-consumers to evaluate what they are paying for; providing a system by which potential employees (graduates) can be assessed by employers on the basis of the quality of the institution from which the qualification was attained. As well as this, it is seen to empower taxpayers, who continue to provide at least partial funding for HE in England and Wales, to assess the benefits generated though HE.

Concerns about diversity and equity are articulated in the Green Paper as a way of ensuring that all those with the prerequisite potential and talent can enter the marketplace of HE, and thus to 'encourage excellent teaching for all students'. The aims of the Green Paper are embedded in a range of assumptions that are produced through the particular logics of marketisation, evidence-based policy and practice, meritocracy and human capital theory. The overarching framework is economic rationalism: widening access is a way of 'empowering' the student-'consumer' to become the neo-liberal aspirational socially mobile choice-making subject. The Green Paper sets this out explicitly in describing the creation of the Teaching Excellence Framework (TEF):

Prospective students will be able to use the TEF results to help inform their decisions about which institution to attend, and employers can consider it in their recruitment. The TEF will increase students' understanding of what they are getting for their money and improve the value they derive from their investment, protecting the interest of the taxpayer who supports the system through provision of student loans. It should also provide better signalling for employers as to which providers they can trust to produce highly skilled graduates.

(BIS, 2015, pp. 12–13)

Although the framework places student choice as a central theme, it does so through the metaphor of education as a set of products that student-consumers choose in relation to their individual assessment of the quality of that product (Reay, David and Ball, 2005). There is no sense of how the 'quality' will develop equitable frameworks to support student participation and educational outcomes, nor any space for considering the meaning of 'quality' beyond economic rationalism – becoming an employable, resilient consumer-worker who has the capacity to be continuously flexible in the wider context of turbulent economic and employment conditions. In fact, this focus on external indicators to measure teaching quality may reduce equity initiatives because these will not take into account that students do not pick up 'learning gains' as neutral subjects; social and cultural advantages differ in and within student populations across and within different universities. This means some universities may appear to have better 'teaching quality' through an excellence framework, but may in fact just be reproducing disparities in terms of student populations and equity (Tatlow and Phoenix, 2015).

The discourse of 'excellence' has increasingly gained traction over the past fifteen years or so, underpinned by new public management. This has led to increasing attention to external accountability, organisation of quality, and efficiency of resource use in HE with large-scale policy movements such as the Bologna Process epitomising this shift (Froumin and Lisyuktin, 2015). The Bologna Process might be seen as part of an attempt to create a consumer market of higher education that is global in scope (Ramirez and Tiplic, 2014). Transnational and global agents of globalisation, such as the European Commission (EC), the OECD, the World Bank and UNESCO have determined such shifts, with an increased focus on economic growth and innovation as a normative discourse around education policy (Lingard, Rawolle and Taylor, 2005). Teaching is seen as valuable largely in terms of 'developing graduate skills and competences necessary for a career in a globalised knowledge-based society' (Sin, 2015, p. 333). 'Excellence' relates primarily to market-driven competitiveness, not intrinsic value from the institution.

Under a logic of utilitarianism, performance and efficiency teaching and learning is exhorted to align to market needs and to develop employability and entrepreneurship.

(Sin, 2015, p. 328)

Excellence-driven policies then are about competitiveness in a global HE market. The focus on excellence at a global level has reshaped HE systems internationally, with effects such as stimulating new competition, changing financing patterns, and promoting the 'Research University' as the most desirable model, which has had profound effects on teaching and those institutions that are positioned as 'teaching-intensive'. This is exacerbated by institutional success in widening participation as students from under-represented groups are seen to signify a lower standard, largely because those students often enter HE through nontraditional routes and qualifications, often assumed to be inferior to traditional entry qualifications.

'Excellence' is increasingly interconnected with discourses of 'diversity', couched in a neo-liberal logic that foregrounds the market as the key architectural device to create contemporary higher education spaces. However, the meaning of teaching 'excellence' is often left abstracted and obscured, as the following quote from the Green Paper shows:

> There is no one broadly accepted definition of 'teaching excellence'. In practice it has many interpretations and there are likely to be different ways of measuring it. The Government does not intend to stifle innovation in the sector or restrict institutions' freedom to choose what is in the best interests of their students. But we do think there is a need to provide greater clarity about what we are looking for and how we intend to measure it in relation to the TEF [Teaching Excellence Framework]. Our thinking has been informed by the following principles:
>
> • excellence must incorporate and reflect the diversity of the sector, disciplines and missions – not all students will achieve their best within the same model of teaching;
> • excellence is the sum of many factors – focussing on metrics gives an overview, but not the whole picture;
> • perceptions of excellence vary between students, institutions and employers;
> • excellence is not something achieved easily or without focus, time, challenge and change.
>
> (BIS, 2015, p. 21)

The UK's 2015 Green Paper articulates 'excellence' in explicit relation to diversity, using the example that students learn in different ways. However, there is no recognition of the ways that politics of difference plays out in pedagogical spaces and 'excellence' often leads to increased levels of surveillance, performativity and regulation of both teachers and students. Teaching to address diversity is often reduced to identifying individual learning 'styles'. Diversity is structured into the 'excellence' framework unproblematically, without attention paid to the ways the diversity of the sector, disciplines and missions might be complicit in the reformation of social hierarchies and stratification that reinforce rather than disrupt social, cultural and economic inequalities.

After receiving 618 responses to the 2015 Green Paper, from a wide and diverse set of communities across the sector (including HE providers, students' unions, professional and representative bodies, business and employers, charities, trade unions and individuals) the Government published their 2016 White Paper (BIS, 2016), 'Success as a Knowledge Economy: Teaching Excellence, Social Mobility and Student Choice', setting out their decisions, summarised as the following key points:

- making it easier for high-quality new providers to start up, achieve degree awarding powers, and secure university title status
- requiring all universities to publish detailed information about application, offer and progression rates, broken down by gender, ethnicity and disadvantage
- publishing employment and graduate earnings data to provide prospective students with the best possible information
- establishing the Office for Students (OFS) as the new regulator for all higher education providers
- implementing the Teaching Excellence Framework which, for the first time, will link teaching funding to quality and not just quantity, a principle long established for research
- establishing new safeguards to protect students and the sector's reputation, with a risk-based approach to regulation so the OFS can focus attention where it is most needed
- establishing a single, strategic funding body that enables the UK to lead the world in multi-disciplinary research – our plans ensure that each Research Council and Innovate UK keep their identities and separate budgets, with the dual-support system protected for the first time.

(gov.uk, 2016)

The White Paper indicates that the excellence agenda has gathered such momentum in policy that it could be described as becoming a 'regime of truth' (Foucault, 1977) that 'operates to discipline (institutional and individual) practices and subjectivities, restricting conceptions of teaching, and limiting opportunities for critical pedagogies' (Burke, Stevenson and Whelan, 2015). Brusoni et al. (2014) explain that the excellence discourse signifies a breaking away from traditions of egalitarianism in Europe:

> The search for excellence is no longer a new phenomenon in European universities strongly attached to the egalitarian culture of their training and research mission and to recurrent public funding. The excellence initiatives set up in Germany, Spain, and France have been implemented, above all,

to ensure the emergence of a limited number of institutions, laboratories, or doctoral schools of a global nature capable of competing with the best Anglo-Saxon universities. This competitive approach has mobilised a very large number of players within universities who see this as an opportunity to increase both their funding and their reputation. It remains difficult to assess the full impact of these new public policies on the overall system, on university strategies, and on the quality of future graduates, researchers, and teachers.

(Brusoni et al., 2014, p. 16)

They argue that this shift to the promotion of a more competitive market for institutions is motivated by the belief that market forms of competition will improve standards and quality. 'By recognising the "best" providers, it is expected that standards will be established for the sector as a whole' (Brusoni et al., 2014).

The excellence discourses pose serious challenges for equity and social justice as the focus of excellence tends to be on the recruitment and selection of the 'best' and 'brightest' in the wider context of the prestige cultures being firmly embedded through league table rankings, metrics and measurements. This also points to recruitment of the 'best' teachers in order to drive up the 'excellence' of teaching in higher education. The logic is that this is about exercising meritocratic principles to ensure representation of the best and brightest with representation across all social groups. Yet the assumption about what is perceived as the best and brightest is usually not problematised or critiqued.

Sociologists of higher education have drawn extensively on Bourdieusian concepts to expose that what is often being measured is *social privilege* not intrinsic potential, talent and ability. Indeed, those who occupy privileged positions are often able to powerfully leverage family portfolios of capitals and networks and thus to manoeuvre the systems of selection, ensuring their sustained privileged position through the prestige cultures of higher education.

Bourdieu (1986) has highlighted the role of social and cultural capital in enabling and restricting engagement with education. He used the term 'cultural capital' to mean forms of privilege, specifically in terms of education and broader cultural taste, passed down through families. In studies of contemporary education it is often used when considering how affluent parents "play the system" and get their children into the most prestigious secondary schools. The combination of well-informed, educated parents, high achieving schools and a peer group with similar expectations tends to result in higher attainment. Alongside that is social capital, which crucially includes social networks that can be drawn upon to perpetuate privilege.

(Whitty, Hayton and Tang, 2016)

Policy discourses of equity and diversity in this drive toward excellence are largely in terms of the new 'consumer markets' they represent, rather than on widening participation (Hunter, 2013).

Students as consumers and choice-makers

Inequalities of gender and other intersecting structural differences are assumed to be eradicated by the market of higher education, in which individual consumers exercise their choice to participate in higher education or not (Reay, David and Ball, 2005). If they choose to participate, student-consumers then exercise their choice in relation to market principles. Thus, the stratification of institutions and its relationship to teaching and widening participation is concealed. Notions of choice are tied in to the discourses of meritocracy and individualism, in which the right to higher education is understood in terms of individual ability, efficacy, potential and hard work rather than as shaped by structural, cultural and institutional inequalities and misrecognitions.

> Overall in the policy literature on social markets, particularly the education market, the emphasis is on the demand side, on choice. What gets glossed over are the mechanisms of institutional survival in the market – most crucially competition. . . . It is again idealistically assumed that educational values will remain unblemished by the demands of responsiveness and survival.
>
> (Ball, 1993, p. 6)

Critiques of students as consumers and choice-makers emerged during the 1990s, articulating concerns about the ramifications of the marketisation of HE, and remain a key feature of debate in the international field of teaching in higher education. In Australia, Symes argued in 1996 that as universities are being oriented toward market rationalisation, students-as-consumers is a key aspect of that shift. In England, Carole Leathwood warned in 1998 that the marketisation of HE reproduces dangerous discourses of individualism and othering, centred on the student-as-consumer. Baldwin and James in 2000 examined the disjuncture between the 'consumer' model and equity goals of HE (with a note that this has since changed with the lifting of the student cap, moving to increasing levels of marketisation):

> On the face of it, there is no justification for universities to spend large sums of money marketing themselves to local students. They have an agreed quota of government funded places and receive the same funding whatever the entry scores of the students. At present, there is a relatively small demand for the full fee-paying places (. . .) it tends to be in "niche" areas. So, to some extent, the institutions have "manufactured" a competition for high-achieving students. . . This competition cuts across one of the central aspects

of government higher education policy – a commitment to equity and opportunity for all. Australian higher education is no longer supposed to be for an elite, but for the whole population. These deep tensions between competition and equity, between individual choice and the public good, are major fault lines running through the system at present, and at times seem to threaten its stability.

(Baldwin and James, 2000, p. 141)

Joanna Williams (2013) argues that it is important to resist pedagogic strategies underpinned by consumerist impulses. She articulates her concern that the student-as-consumer discourse and the 'relentless promotion of employability' has placed greater value on gaining skills than on processes of learning and understanding:

If studying an academic subject cannot be justified because it makes an essential contribution to our collective understanding of what it means to be human and the nature of the society we live in, it must instead justify its existence in the more mundane sphere of employability.

(Williams, 2013, p. 89)

A crucial point that Williams develops is that the 'demand for [student-as-consumer] satisfaction may be antithetical to education and the development of positive pedagogical relations'. The fundamental problem of a student-as-consumer model is that there is little space to challenge assumptions because it is void of an intellectual process of transformation, which demands sustained commitment (Williams, 2013, p. 100). This viewpoint is also shared by Sharrock (2000), who explains:

Students can't just be given what they want. They don't passively consume their education, they actively co-produce it. Staff don't just feed them information. . . So whether students pay fees or not, calling them customers obscures the fact that 'going to university' isn't the same as going to McDonald's. . . The analogy doesn't work because in the marketplace there's no-one at the door to assess whether you're qualified to eat those fries. . . .

(Sharrock, 2000, p. 151)

In her analysis of the effects of a student-as-consumer model of higher education, Williams also traces the way that accountability becomes seen as the 'hub' of education, rather than knowledge or learning (Williams, 2013, p. 53), stating that there is a 'risk that the focus on measuring the worth of education fundamentally alters that which is important about its content' (Williams, 2013, p. 54). This creates greater levels of surveillance for staff and students in higher education. Concerns about the ways in which everything is being subjected to measurement through 'datafication' (Sellar, 2013) includes the measuring of our desires to become aspirational subjects of higher education.

Pedagogies of desire: creating aspirational and future-oriented selves

Policies of widening participation (WP) are increasingly problematic for teaching and teachers in higher education, as WP becomes part of the wider mechanisms of the 'neoliberal opportunity bargain' (Sellar, 2013). As widening participation shifts further away from the social justice imperatives many teachers have committed to, this raises dilemmas for teaching, with widening participation serving as a policy device to create individual opportunities for social mobility rather than with broader social justice concerns for *social* (as well as the individual) transformation. Teachers must negotiate a number of tensions and contradictions within intensified workloads and often under precarious work conditions, including casualisation and technologies of performance management. Addressing the demands on individual subjects to perform the motivational, aspirational and future-oriented subjectivities being idealised under neo-liberal labour market imperatives, pedagogical spaces might also provide opportunities for critique and even refusal of these mechanisms that seek to measure 'all that we are' (Sellar, 2013). The current modes of performativity at play that compel both teachers and students towards particular forms of personhood for and of the market, are actively reducing the purpose of participating in higher education to increasing the earning power of individuals over a lifetime. A very literal translation of social mobility is being taken up in which desire for career success is seen as the golden aspiration. This is problematic on multiple levels, not least because the promise of high-income graduate employment through gaining a degree is increasingly being broken (Brown, Lauder and Ashton, 2011). This is the case for all graduates, however research also shows that graduate employment and income continues to be tied to wider social structures of gender, class and race. For example, on a global scale, women earn about 77% of what men earn, and this gap widens for higher-earning women (International Labour Organisation, 2016, p. 2).

Aspiration-formation has been at the heart of widening participation policy for the past two decades, based on the assumption that children and young people from backgrounds that are socially and educationally disadvantaged suffer not only from material poverty but also from a so-called poverty of aspiration. This is a highly problematic assumption and a form of gross misrecognition of those communities. Our starting point is that students from backgrounds that are under-represented in higher education have high aspirations but often do not have access to the networks, resources, academic practices and symbolic forms of capital and ways of being that facilitate high levels of educational attainment. Furthermore, we argue that pedagogical practices, which are located in educational structures that privilege certain subjectivities, ontologies and epistemologies above others, are reproductive of educational disadvantages. We also want to take issue with discourses of success that focus individual students on narrow pathways and ignore the richness of human experience of which learning and intellectual and emotional development is a seminal aspect.

Aspiration and other such affective dispositions, such as motivation and being future-oriented, are being regulated through new modes of measurement, datafication and accountabilities. Sam Sellar (2013) argues that human capital is no longer seen only in terms of skills, competencies and knowledge but has expanded to include a whole range of dispositions, including across the affective domains of human capacities and subjectivities. There is an attempt to measure affect as well as the more conventional skills and competencies associated with human capital theory. Our desires and our motivational and aspirational dispositions are thus now being subjected to technologies of measurement and performativity. Sellar argues that there has been an intensification of economic and educational policy around motivation, quoting Lindsay:

> The future of human capitalism may well hinge on . . . motivating the middling and lower ranks of society . . . what ultimately will matter is the strength of purely internal, personal motivations.
>
> (Lindsay, 2013, p. 115 quoted in Sellar, 2013)

The ways that the affective realm is being pulled into the machine of neo-liberalism through widening participation, and the kinds of pedagogical relations being encouraged, raises significant and ethical questions for teaching. Indeed Sellar argues that the attempt to measure human capital has expanded to 'everything that we are – nothing is off limits' (Sellar, 2013). This has implications for the pedagogical relations that are promoted and fostered in higher education and its relationship to questions of social justice. Furthermore, it might be argued that in policy terms, social justice has been reduced to a project of social mobility.

> What matters is the capacity of a high participation system (HPS) of higher education to provide a broad pathway for social mobility, so that students/graduates' opportunities and trajectories are not determined by their social backgrounds. We can call this capacity of higher education to make a difference to the social mix, "the allocative social power of higher education".
>
> (Marginson, 2015)

In effect, social justice has now been co-opted into a hegemonic discourse of social mobility, driven by marketisation and the regulation of subjectivity through new forms of accountability, measurability and datafication. Higher education pedagogies become coerced into a narrow framework to produce human capital that not only measures a person's worth in terms of skills and competencies but extends this to judgments about a person's affective value as aspirational, motivational and future-oriented subjects. This book attempts to bring such discourses to view, to challenge and critique these and to reframe higher education pedagogies in relation to social justice imperatives. Such reframing is concerned to understand the ways that pedagogies are gendered, classed and racialised and to identify spaces of possibility for refusal.

Teaching and learning in higher education: hegemonic frameworks

In the contemporary shifting landscape of higher education policy reform, the rise of marketisation and its league table culture is profoundly shaping academic practice, including teaching. This has led to an emphasis on student evaluation, but this is not driven by a critical concern with student participation, voice and empowerment. Student evaluation practices and discourses are shaped by a regime of performance management. The results of student evaluation are part of a wider set of technologies of regulation in which not only individuals but ultimately institutions become ranked and stratified through marketisation techniques, including a range of evaluation and assessment measures. Evaluation and assessment regimes have become a normative and taken-for-granted part of academic life and are a primary tool of embedding a culture of performativity (Ball, 2001), rather than a way of developing deeper and richer pedagogical understanding and praxis (Burke and Jackson, 2007).

The forms of evaluation being foregrounded by institutional frameworks create mechanisms for the regulation of teaching, learning and identity. Evaluation is another counting device, in which our worth is reduced to dehumanising modes of measurement. Feminist scholars writing collectively explain that:

> Counting culture leads to intense, insidious forms of institutional shaming, subject-making, and self-surveillance. It compels us to enumerate and self-audit, rather than listen and converse, engage with colleagues, students, friends and family, or involve ourselves in the meaningful and time-consuming work that supports and engages our research and broader communities (Pain, 2014; Schulte, 2014).
>
> (Mountz et al., 2015, p. 9)

Teachers and students operate in a context in which 'evidence' is the dominant discourse – if it can't be measured it does not count. Hence the lived, emotional and embodied experiences of inequality and misrecognition go unnoticed and we are unable to develop appropriate policies and practices to address such inequalities. Policy-makers often end up perplexed – because it is difficult to identify or understand why inequalities are being reproduced despite significant policy attention to equity, inclusion and WP. Yet derogatory discourses that place the gaze outside of pedagogical practices and firmly on individual students seen as lacking capability manipulate anxieties tied in with aspirations to be counted as excellent.

Student evaluation sits in a narrow and rigid framework of 'quality' of teaching and learning and creates mechanisms for the regulation of academic labour and identity. It could be seen as a panoptic device (Foucault, 1977), with invisible forms of surveillance operating to regulate and discipline academic behaviour and sensibility. For example, Rosalind Gill (2014) cites the example of one HE institution in which any academic who is rated poorly by her or his students will be subjected to a series of formalised disciplinary procedures, intensifying forms of surveillance and marking that individual academic out as requiring correction and registering that person as a potential threat to the standards upheld by the institution and ultimately to the institution's standing in the market. Taken on face value, this might appear a wholly rational way of ensuring that students receive good quality education for their money, as fee-paying consumers who have the right to expect certain standards in exchange for their investment. However, the evaluation instrument is crucial in terms of the kinds of 'results' that might be produced, which includes how 'quality' and 'standards' are being conceptualised in relation to 'teaching' and 'learning'. A decontextualised, homogenised, performative and skill-based conceptualisation of teaching and learning translates into particular forms of 'quality' and standards'. Indeed, what counts as a 'quality' education will greatly differ across any one student's perception (although perceptions are formed through social discourses, identities, values and perspectives) as well as the ways the evaluation tool is structured and framed.

In relation to this, and as we will argue throughout this book, pedagogical experience is dynamic and complex and is experienced at multiple levels. The same person might simultaneously experience a particular learning experience in a range of ways. It could be experienced as a struggle, as unfamiliar, as exciting, as rewarding, as disconnected or as transformative and compelling. Learning is a process and often a pedagogical moment might become significant for the student long after the moment took place. It often takes time to make sense of new ideas, or to begin to feel a 'mastery' of a body of knowledge, and the process of learning might feel uncomfortable or unsettling. In other words, pedagogical experience cannot be straightforwardly measured, not least because it is entangled with identity formations, processes of becoming and is necessarily emotional. Learning is a process of change and transformation, encountering new and challenging ideas, thinking about complex problems and issues, making connections between experience and disciplinary knowledge, and learning can be painful as well as pleasurable, as we will show through our data analysis in Chapters four to eight. Pedagogical experiences are not only personal or individual; they are connected to social differences, habitus and cultural expectations and are shaped by earlier pedagogical histories and memories, which include residues of emotion and feelings of shame.

Although we take a critical view of hegemonic discourses of teaching and learning, we also want to acknowledge that the foregrounding of teaching and learning in the contemporary higher education landscape has had some benefits, even if situated in a corporatised and marketised framework. It has led to a whole raft of mechanisms, measures and resources geared to support teaching in higher education. This has put a spotlight on teaching, including a number of rewards for the recognition of teaching excellence (although these in themselves are problematic we argue), in an attempt to foreground teaching as an important dimension of academic labour and challenging assumptions that research is more important than teaching in the formation of successful academic identity. The emphasis on teaching quality driven by the marketisation of HE has generated significant investment in the provision of services, resources and training to support teaching and learning. Professional development programmes have been created, and teaching has been recognised as part of a body of professional knowledge, which requires learning, research, resources and development. Teaching is no longer a taken-for-granted practice but is seen as an important aspect of professionalism in higher education, now supported, managed and led through distinct structures, with senior leadership posts dedicated to teaching and 'academic development'. There has also been significant investment in research on teaching in higher education, through agencies, for example, such as the UK's Higher Education Academy (HEA) and Australia's Office of Learning and Teaching (OLT). Such research has been important in contributing to a body of pedagogical knowledge, further raising the profile of teaching. However, 'pedagogic research' has often been seen as sub-standard compared to 'academic research', and associated with small-scale 'practice-based' projects conducted by professional rather than 'research-active' staff.

Despite the ways that teaching has been repositioned as a valued aspect of academic labour, the focus has often been on developing *professional skills* and *techniques* to improve 'quality' and practice, rather than a part of academic and disciplinary knowledge. Such mechanisms lead to increased forms of performativity and might contribute to disrupting deeper-level engagement with the complexities of pedagogical practices. In the UK a national 'Professional Standards Framework' has been established (UKPSF) by the HEA, on behalf of the UK higher education sector, Guild UK and Universities UK, which aims to 'benchmark success' within teaching and learning support and to 'improve quality and recognise excellence' (HEA, 2011). Such frameworks can be important for highlighting the important work of teaching in HE. Yet, such frameworks also tend to reinforce a misunderstanding of teaching and learning as a theoretical set of practical methods, or styles, that are part of a wider raft of professional skills development packages and detached from research. Courses have been established to ensure that all new lecturers in higher education receive quality *training* in teaching and learning, but these tend to lack attention to the *theoretical* dimensions, with a strong focus on 'practical' issues. This often reinforces a 'how to' approach to teaching, rather than a more nuanced orientation that examines the complexities of pedagogical relations, identities and experiences in higher education. Teaching is thus constructed, not as a field of knowledge, but as an aspect of professional practice that requires some training and development. The knotty questions related to higher education reform, including diversity, equity and knowledge formation and the subjective and affective layers of this, have largely been overlooked in the professional development of teaching.

Towards a social justice framework

This book argues for a social justice framework to guide the development of 'inclusive' and 'transformatory' pedagogies. However, we insist on reconceptualising 'inclusive' as hegemonic concepts of inclusion tend to ignore power relations and difference, by demanding that students conform to the dominant ontological frameworks in order to be included. The hegemonic discourse of inclusion reduces 'transformation' to the individual student who is subjected to forms of symbolic violence in having to 'fix' herself to fit into the expectation of the values, judgments and perspectives of privileged bodies and communities within pedagogical contexts. As Keevers and Abuodha (2012) explain:

> The discourse of social inclusion implicitly binarises the "included" and "excluded" and promotes an insider-outsider metaphor (Levitas, 2005). Such conceptions tend to characterise social exclusion as a "state" in which people or groups are assumed to be "excluded" from social systems and relationships (Popay et al., 2008). Further, a discourse of social inclusion that focuses on integrating excluded individuals into higher education often fails to acknowledge the ways in which exclusion, inequality and inaccessibility are created and maintained by higher education institutions and processes (Nevile, 2006). However, neither the broader conception of social inclusion/exclusion as a "state", nor the three discourses argued by Levitas (1998, 2005) to shape its meaning offer adequate guidance for transforming higher education into a more inclusive experience for all students.
>
> (Keevers and Abuodha, 2012, p. A45)

Our view of transformative pedagogy involves broader processes of change driven by a social justice framework. This involves examining how perceived attributes of people or practices are either valued (recognised) or devalued (misrecognised). Social justice pedagogies consider ways of addressing the impediments to equal participation and alerting students to the possibility of destabilising institutionalised cultural patterns through deconstructing binary categories (Leibowitz and Bozalek, 2016). Inequity is perpetuated in teaching pedagogies that fail to recognise forms of privilege, normalisation, and compulsory heterosexuality, gender conformity, and whiteness; whilst these forms of inequity can be addressed when teaching strategies specifically aim to develop social justice and disruptive encounters with students (Case, 2013). A transformatory pedagogy framed by social justice imperatives demands the creation of collaborative spaces designed to enable deep connections that foreground teacher and learner relationalities.

In relation to this, Anderson and McCune (2013) reframe the concept of 'learning communities' (a concept that has been used in multiple contexts including academic, professional and business) to describe the 'spaces of the in-between' in which students are not simply provided with a fixed academic vocabulary, but are enabled to unpack decontextualising learning experiences using their own experiences and understandings within the conventions of their discipline. Anderson (2014) argues for the need to move beyond communities of practice as a heuristic device, to consider their potentiality in explicit equity, inclusion and social justice practices in the specific context of undergraduate learning. This requires a sharing of meaning between lecturers and students and a greater sense of connection in the learning environments between staff and students, from the outset. Anderson explores how complex histories, geographies, and identities of students in this age of diverse and internationally mobilised student cohorts might be brought into HE pedagogies. In exploring this, she describes how more opportunities for connection would be a way to facilitate students' communicative confidence and to develop shared understandings: for example through extracurricular activities and space for social activities in shared spaces through classes, lecturers, tutorials, and departmental activities (Anderson, 2014, pp. 637–652).

Developing a framework for social justice pedagogy recognises the need for critique, action and change. In such a framework difference and disagreement are seen as valuable elements to harness and drive change (McArthur, 2010). We argue for a praxis-based framework throughout this book, which we view as crucial for social justice pedagogies. Praxis foregrounds the need for critical reflexivity in dynamic spaces constituted of complex relations of power and difference. In order to create spaces of refusal against hegemonic frameworks that are complicit in insidious inequalities and misrecognitions, teachers and students must engage in critical processes of reflection/action/action/reflection. We develop the concept of a praxis-based framework throughout the book in terms of both pedagogies and methodologies. In the book we argue that we need to engage pedagogies of difference that embrace power as an inevitable aspect of pedagogical relations, whilst always keeping sight of a broader social justice framework.

Chapter 2

Reconceptualising pedagogies and reimagining difference

This chapter presents a detailed discussion of the theoretical resources available to challenge hegemonic and instrumentalist discourses of teaching and learning in higher education and pedagogical identity formations. Moving away from hegemonic discourses of teaching and learning, we explore the potential of pedagogies of difference to explore lived, relational and embodied practices in higher education, and their interconnection with ontologies, epistemologies and politics of mis/recognition (Freire, 1970; Lather, 1991; Fraser, 1997; Burke, 2012). The dynamics, relations and experiences of teaching and learning are conceptualised as intimately tied to the privileging of some forms of knowledge over others, the recognition and legitimisation of hegemonic subjectivities and the exclusion of 'Others', often problematically constructed as 'undeserving' of HE participation. Reductive language that frames teaching and learning largely as 'styles', 'provision', 'needs' and 'delivery', operates to hide complex power relations within pedagogical spaces, which are constituted and productive of gendered interactions, performatives and subjectivities. Feminist post/structural concepts of gendered subjectivity (e.g. Butler, 1993; Flax, 1995) shed light on the multiple, contradictory and shifting sense of self that unsettles hegemonic versions of the individual as a coherent, rational, knowable and stable self. Such conceptual frameworks aim to reveal the multiple layers of injustices that operate around processes of identity formation and subjective construction, in relation to embodied intersections of age, class, ethnicity, gender and race.

Theorising difference, inclusion and misrecognition in pedagogical spaces

Misrecognition sheds light on the subtle ways that different students and teachers are unequally positioned, constructed and mobilised across higher educational spaces. Discourses of 'inclusion' often work as a form of symbolic violence through the ultimate requirement that the person must fit in to the dominant framework, or be excluded, either through self-exclusion or through institutional exclusion, and through practices of standardisation to ensure the regulation of difference.

The discourse of 'inclusion' coerces those seen as 'excluded' to conform to the conventions, expectations and values of hegemonic frameworks and identities and to participate in a process of 'transformation' into normalised personhoods. This includes for example becoming 'flexible' and 'adaptable' to volatile market conditions and thus being recognised as an appropriately 'resilient' pedagogical participant. Thus, inclusion often perpetuates problematic deficit perspectives that place the responsibility on those individuals who are identified as at risk of exclusion through their lack of confidence, adaptability or resilience. Inclusion might also be seen as a discursive space in which the politics of mis/recognition play out in ways that are experienced as individual shame and not being the 'right' kind of person or higher education participant.

We draw on Nancy Fraser's (1997, 2003, 2008) theoretical framework of social justice to understand the complex relations of inequality that are produced in and through pedagogical spaces. Fraser argues that social justice requires attention to 'redistribution', 'recognition' and 'representation', and we argue that holding these three dimensions together is crucial for developing pedagogies for social justice. Following Fraser (2003), it is important to shift attention away from deficit discourses to directing attention on transforming institutional spaces, systems and practices, which are implicated in reproducing exclusions and inequalities at cultural, symbolic and structural levels. Fraser explains:

> When misrecognition is identified with internal distortions in the structure of the self-conscious of the oppressed, it is but a short step to blaming the victim (. . .) Misrecognition is a matter of externally manifest and publicly verifiable impediments to some people's standing as full members of society. To redress it, means to overcome subordination. *This in turn means changing institutions and social practices.*
>
> (Fraser, 2003: 31, emphasis added)

Such a framework illuminates that transforming pedagogies for social justice relies on equitable distributive recognition and representation processes that work with and through difference. This challenges conceptualisations of equity that rest on oversimplified notions of treating everyone the same. Rather it is important to redistribute resources to those groups and communities who have experienced material and structural disadvantages, whilst valuing the different experiences, histories, values and cultural practices of those heterogeneous groups and communities. It is vital to challenge constructions of 'equity groups' as homogenous rather than recognising differences within those groups and the intricate ways that differences intersect in formations of identity and subjectivity. It is therefore crucial to create institutional mechanisms of representation *across* different groups and communities, whilst recognising differences *within* those groups and communities. For example, it is important to redistribute resources and opportunities to those communities who have been denied such opportunities. It is also important to recognise and value the different perspectives and knowledges marginalised communities bring to higher education and to provide genuine opportunities for representation of their perspectives.

However, targeting a particular community through an explicit policy focus tends to reinforce homogenising constructions and stereotypes, thus perpetuating a pathologising neocolonial gaze whilst ignoring the differences within and between communities. Thus the pedagogical frameworks available must be highly sensitive and fine-tuned to the formations of difference within and across different communities and to understand this in relation to the complex intersectionalities that form subjectivities, ontologies and epistemologies. For example, in the Australian context, 'Indigenous knowledge' is not a homogenous and unchanging body of knowledge; rather it is dynamic, changing over space and time and in relation to different political forces and influences, such as neocolonialism. 'Indigenous knowledge' is a contested space and so pedagogical (and curricular) approaches must be developed in such a way as to deal with difference in all its shapes and forms. Although there are differences *across* and *between* groups targeted by higher education policies to widen participation, there are also differences *within* target groups. Target groups constructed by policy are also different and changing across time and space, and this is problematic and open to contestation. Policy target groups such as: 'Black and Minority Ethnic', 'Students of Colour', 'Indigenous students', 'mature and part-time students', 'students with disabilities', 'lower socioeconomic status', 'working class', 'regional and remote' are all entangled in the politics of redistribution (i.e. which groups will benefit from specific widening participation resources, opportunities and funds) and recognition (the implications for individuals, groups and communities of being categorised as a specific 'equity' group).

Drawing on Fraser, parity of participation in higher education depends on having the means and resources to develop participation in ways that a person might be recognised as a legitimate participant within particular disciplinary contexts. Becoming a participant requires representation within that space. Having access to certain material and economic resources such as a computer, internet, transportation and books are important in developing the forms of 'participation' that might be recognised by university lecturers and that enable representation of different student perspectives, histories and values.

Participation is more complex than simply having access to financial and material resources or cultural and social capitals, as important as these are. Nancy Fraser sheds light on the ways that misrecognition and misrepresentation deeply undermine *parity of participation* within social institutions such as higher education and generates the insight that the processes of misrecognition are about institutional values and judgments that are imposed on the misrecognised person in ways that effectively exclude her/him from parity of participation. In order to have parity of participation, the person must be *recognised* and have *access to representation* as a fully valued member of the community.

However, we also agree with Lois McNay (2008) that although such perspectives of recognition and representation are highly significant, Fraser's theoretical framework might not fully capture the affective, subjective and lived experiences of misrecognition and misrepresentation, that are felt in and through the body as forms of symbolic violence and injury on the self (McNay, 2008, p. 150). Such experiences often lead to feelings of shame and fear (Ahmed, 2004). Institutional fields such as schools and higher education are sites in which subjectivity is formed and personhood is constituted. Recognition is formed through the dual processes of mastery and submission of the discourses at play within a particular field (such as higher education) (Davies, 2006). The discourse of 'participation', which is multiple and contested, itself formed through the social practices and values at play within a subject field, constitutes the student in particular ways through the politics of mis/recognition and mis/representation. The concept of 'performativity' (Butler, 1993) sheds light on the ways that subjectivity is formed not through who we *are* but through what we *do*; through social and cultural practices.

Burke et al. (2016) examined such issues in pedagogical contexts in Australia through the lens of 'capability'. They argue that:

> To be seen as a 'capable' student in higher education, the student must act in certain ways. For example, being recognised as "academically capable" depends on performing "academic capability" through body language, literacy and communication practices, analytical and critical practices (which might differ across and within disciplines), demonstrating certain skills in particular ways (such as time management and organisation skills) and so forth. Each of these aspects of capability are shifting discursive practices.
>
> (Burke et al., 2016)

They argue that the politics of 'belonging' are deeply entwined with such questions of recognition and representation (Burke et al., 2016). Our research shows that sensibilities of 'not belonging' are partly about the internalisation of shame and shaming experienced by groups through pedagogies of 'misrecognition', a theme we explore in greater detail in Chapter six.

Reconceptualising pedagogies: complex relations of difference

In this book we theorise pedagogies as relational, and as always tied to complex formations of power that circulate fluidly across and between pedagogical spaces. However, we also take the non-relativist view that structural and material inequalities matter and continue to characterise pedagogical spaces, which are structured by gendered, classed and racialised formations and inequalities. The concept of 'pedagogies' pushes our thinking beyond the hegemonic notions of teaching as 'delivery' of educational programmes, to capture the ways that subjectivities and meanings are formed *through* pedagogical participation. Formations of knowledge/power shape our subjectivities and sense of being in and of the world. Knowledge and power are indivisible, which challenges the oversimplified concept that 'knowledge is power'. Rather knowledge-making is an ongoing site of struggle, and powerful forms of knowledge are only constituted as powerful through institutional validation as related to historical processes of colonialist, imperialist and patriarchal histories of knowledge production and legitimation.

Drawing on two sets of Bernstein's (2000) concepts in his work on pedagogic discourse helps to illuminate the above, further. These are classification and framing and the redistribution and recognition rules. These key related components, which are fairly well known, are concerned with the organisation of knowledge and the control of knowledge. As Bernstein says: '. . . control establishes legitimate communications, and power establishes legitimate relations between categories' (2000, p. 5).

For Bernstein 'classification' refers to relations between categories and is concerned with the boundaries around that category. Bernstein (2000) explains that a category can only be a category in relation to another different category. Classification constructs the nature of stratifications, distributions and locations. Bernstein argues that classifications disguise the arbitrariness of power relations and construct imaginary identities. Classification can be strong and weak. Framing is the means by which communication in pedagogic relations is regulated and legitimised. 'Framing is about who controls what' (p. 12). In the teaching context framing is about the decision of the means of communication, the sequencing and pacing of the transmission of knowledge together with the criteria on which selections are based. Framing also can be strong or weak. In the GaP study we looked at subject disciplines, which according to documentary sources and from our observations, were strongly classified such as Classics and English Literature and weakly classified such as Business Studies and Creative Writing. Both strong and weak framing existed across all of the subjects depending upon the teacher's individual approach, although strong and weak framing was used variously by individual teachers. The importance of weak framing is that whilst it is often associated with the opportunity for greater creativity of teaching and learning and student engagement, in fact weak framing adds to the mystification of knowledge and imposition of power (Crozier and Reay, 2011) or what Bernstein referred to as 'invisible pedagogy' (Bernstein, 2000, p. 14). In order to make sense of the context the individual needs to have access to the recognition rules. These are affected by strong and weak classifications. The weaker the classification the more nebulous and ambiguous are the possibilities for recognition, rendering the student silent: 'Power is never more fundamental as far as communication is concerned than when it acts on the distribution of recognition rules' (Bernstein, 2000, p. 17). However, even if the individual, and student in our case, does recognise the context, 'the power relations', s/he may not possess the 'realisation rules' to engage in the 'legitimate pedagogic code' (Bernstein, 2000). It is in this way that control is maintained and the student is positioned.

It is in this way that control is maintained and the student is positioned. We argue for the political imperative of redistributing access to those forms of knowledge that are institutionally validated as 'powerful'; including those knowledges produced through the disciplines. Indeed, we argue that such disciplinary knowledges provide intellectual capital for privileged groups to reassert their powerful position and so *the redistribution of access to those disciplinary forms of knowledge is a social justice imperative.* It is important to note that such intellectual capital is always combined with other forms of capital in the perpetuation of social privilege and esteem. As part of a framework for pedagogies of difference, we also argue for the *inclusion of knowledges emerging from communities who have experienced historical oppression and marginalisation and whose knowledge, experience and wisdom has suffered denigration, exclusion or marginalisation.* Drawing on Freire's notion of the 'circle of knowledge' (Freire, 2009) helps us to reconceptualise pedagogies in higher education *as spaces for the cyclical and reciprocal reformation of knowledge.* Such reformation of pedagogical space is the participatory process of bringing together disciplinary knowledge with the heterogeneous knowledge of those groups, communities and societies that have often been denied representation in higher education curricula.

'Space' is an important concept in thinking through pedagogies in all of its complexities and intricacies. 'Space' might be physical or virtual; drawing on a concept of 'pedagogical spaces' helps to consider how the architectural or the technological make possible certain forms of pedagogical practice in relation to questions of space and time. Physical and virtual spaces in higher education generate complex pedagogical relations that are related to formations of difference and power in time and space. Other researchers in the field have identified the significant role that space plays in structuring student experience (Radcliffe, Wilson, Powell and Tibbetts, 2008; Ahlefeld, 2009; Neary et al., 2010; Souter, Riddle, Sellers and Keppell, 2011). Recent research into pedagogical spaces has emphasised the need for the physical spaces in which learning takes place to be adaptable and flexible, so that students can engage their learning environments and transform them as they see necessary (Jamieson, Fisher, Gilding, Taylor and Trevitt, 2000; JISC, 2006; Temple, 2008; Powell, 2014). Yet, this research primarily treats the student population as a homogenous entity, whereby the capacity to access, engage and transform the flexible potentialities of pedagogical spaces is assumed to be neutral (Ahlefeld, 2009; Neary et al., 2010; Scholl, 2012) and not conditioned by the diversity of the student body in terms of gender, class, ethnic or cultural background. Research has emphasised the need for physical spaces that are designed to support inclusive pedagogies and foster diverse student engagement (Ahlefeld, 2009) and reveals that many students find the physical spaces of colleges and universities intimidating, alienating and marginalising (Burke, 2002; Burke, 2012). This body of research also reveals that belonging and inclusion are closely related to spatial relations and structures and that students are far more likely to succeed in higher education when they experience a sense of belonging in pedagogical spaces as valued and fully recognised participants (Burke, 2012).

We need to consider the ways that we take up, embody and move through the different spaces in higher education that produce unequal pedagogical relations; for example, the ways the lecturer might position her/himself at the front of the lecture hall with the students in rows of seats listening to the lecturer speak. The physical and virtual spaces, in which we position our bodies and in which our bodies are repositioned, profoundly shape our practices, experiences and emotions within that space. We might be able to subvert those spaces but this is constrained by the physicality and/or technology of those spaces. Space therefore is not only about the physical, technological and/or architectural 'reality' of universities but is also about our embodied, lived and emotional experiences of those spaces – how we feel in and about those spaces, how those spaces position our embodied selves, how mis/recognitions play out within those spaces and how we might reconfigure those spaces in ways that contribute to pedagogies for social justice. The spaces are also discursively constituted and open to refashioning; we can find possibilities for articulating difference and different ways of being and knowing across and between hegemonic pedagogical spaces. Spaces are also deeply tied in with temporalities; the ways that time is structured within and across those spaces as well as our different relationalities to time across structural and symbolic inequalities.

Pedagogies in higher education are complex spaces, and thus a range of conceptual resources is required to think about the possibilities of creating pedagogies for social justice and difference. Throughout this book, we draw on an eclectic set of intellectual tools to think through pedagogies as complex relations of difference in which power is dynamic, fluid and generative but also shaped by structural, cultural and material inequalities. We understand pedagogies as always entwined with the politics of knowing and knowledge and thus ontological and epistemological questions are also key in theorising pedagogies for social justice. In thinking through these challenging issues, we bring into the frame the work of a diverse community of theorists including Foucault, Butler, Fraser, Bourdieu, Freire and Bernstein. Rather than this creating an 'incoherent' theoretical framework, we argue for the necessity in reconceptualising pedagogies of difference to bring to work a broader range of theoretical perspectives in order to think through the complex spaces and relations that form our experiences and understanding of pedagogies in higher education.

Pedagogy and difference in higher education

Underpinning the hegemony of performative and marketised constructs of teaching in HE is the continual reformation of normalised academic and student identities, with a focus on standarisation. Yet, within this, diversity is increasingly constructed as a positive characteristic reflecting an institution's commitment to equity, usually accompanied by a discourse of assimilation and acculturation. 'Difference' on the other hand is not a part of hegemonic marketising discourses, often triggering anxieties connected to pathologised identities, associated with widening participation and those students (and staff) attached to under-represented groups (particularly those associated with working-classed and Black-racialised subjectivities). Those who are different are often viewed as 'high-risk' and threatening to academic standards.

Pathologising identity constructions are held in place through institutional categorisations and structural inequalities of social differences. The agenda to widen participation has raised some challenging dilemmas and tensions in relation to this. On the one hand, universities must identify structural inequalities, which are tied in with relations of power and difference, such as race and ethnicity. This requires methods of targeting. However, this must be nuanced in terms of the ways structures of inequality are recognised as *intersecting sets of social and structural differences*, rather than one-dimensional homogenising identity constructions of a targeted group. HE institutions committed to widening participation, and receiving public funds to support this, must be held accountable for ensuring that resources intended for widening participation are appropriately targeted and not exploited by those who already benefit from multiple forms of social and cultural privilege. It is our view that such accountability should be applied particularly to those selective institutions that are not demonstrating any progress in providing access and participation to students and staff from under-represented backgrounds.

However, and at the same time, it is important to interrogate and challenge pathologising constructions associated with policy and institutional (and research) categorisations, such as 'Black and Minority Ethnic'. This is a tension policy-makers, institutions and teachers are compelled to address within a framework of equity and widening participation. Categorisations help us to decide how to redistribute resources whilst simultaneously categorisations require interrogation of the ways they become mechanisms to homogenise, standardise and pathologise. The category of 'Black and Minority Ethnic' is both a useful device to identify an appropriate target group for the redistribution of resources but it also contributes to the perpetuation of social divisions and hierarchies through reducing that person or group to one aspect of identity. We must make visible the ways such constructions are entangled in cycles of exclusion and unequal power relations and devise inclusive, reflexive and participatory frameworks that challenge misrecognition.

'Excellence' has become a central goal for higher education institutions to strive towards, as already discussed in Chapter one. Difference (and by association widening participation) is posed as potentially dangerous and contaminating, because 'excellence' ironically requires conforming to an idealised set of standards and homogenising practices that signify 'quality'. Excellence is measured through a variety of benchmarks and key performance indicators and is couched in a wider culture of performativity. A university might brand itself as offering a distinctive educational experience but simultaneously must be ranked according to hegemonic discourses of excellence, which depend on evaluations such as student surveys and evaluations or research assessment exercises. Thus, teachers and students are subjected to homogenising and neutralising processes via technologies of managerialism and assessment and through the fixing of socially constructed categories. Such manoeuvres are deeply bound towards hyper-individualism in which specific performative and instrumentalist models of success are being mobilised. They are also connected to the production of a restrictive view of identity, which:

> Encourage separation and decrease our obligations to the world by making believe that we only belong to one corner of the world. Instead of defining ourselves in relational connection with the people around us, we place ourselves in sealed boxes.
>
> (Chawla and Rodriguez, 2007, p. 704)

In an age of performativity (Ball, 2003), neo-liberalism and its connected discourses of 'excellence', 'quality' and 'standards', increasingly restricts our pedagogical imaginations, concealing the ways that educational encounters form subjectivities, ways of being and doing. However, it is important to trace how neo-liberalism works in complex ways with other oppressive forces, such as patriarchy and institutional racism, to limit our conceptualisation of 'diversity' and 'difference' and how these dynamics reinforce our complicity in the politics of misrecognition, even when we strive towards social justice approaches. Furthermore, we need to consider how the emotional shapes such processes – the ways that the emotional works on and marks out different bodies.

Sarah Ahmed (2004, p. 10) explains that emotions 'produce the very surfaces and boundaries that allow the individual and the social to be delineated as if they are objects'. Pedagogies are formed through intersecting and embodied classed, gendered and racialised subjectivities, intimately bound up with historical ways of being a teacher or a student in higher education. Neo-liberal imperatives reemphasise techno-rationalist discourses of human capital and individual responsibility. New formations of patriarchy within neo-liberalism ensure that characteristics associated with difference in HE, such as 'being emotional' or 'caring', are regulated and controlled through a range of disciplinary technologies, including teaching. Pedagogical relations are thus deeply implicated in the gendered (and classed and racialised) politics of (mis)recognition, and profoundly connected to the impact of the emotional on the body and the self (Ahmed, 2004) and to the politics of difference and dividing practices.

As described above, 'diversity' has been embraced as a way to improve the image of a university in its commercial projection, in order to attract students from a range of backgrounds. However, and ultimately, diverse students must take up a particular set of performatives and discourses that enable their recognition as 'academic', 'bright' and 'having potential' within the restrictive disciplinary contexts in which they need to be recognised. Diversity is often represented visually on websites and in glossy marketing material, with colourful images of happy university students from 'Other' kinds of backgrounds. Such images construct *diversity* as unproblematic and desirable, whilst *difference* is to be controlled through standardisation and assessment processes. However, Mayuzumi, Motobayasho, Nagayama and Takeuchi (2007, p. 585) posit a more nuanced conceptualisation of diversity, which encompasses the politics of difference and recognition:

> Diversity in higher education, from a subjective point of view, is never a random blend of bodies with different skin colors, or, of bodies speaking in various accents. Nor is it a one-way process of assimilation to the established norms. Instead, diversity allows shifting modes of subjectivities.

Their insights raise issues about the tensions between recognising fluidity in processes of becoming, and structural inequalities that reposition persons and institutions in relation to more fixed notions of difference (for example gender or ethnicity, in relation to persons, and teaching-intensive or research-intensive, in relation to institutions). Chawla and Rodriguez (2007, p. 701) explain that diversity is 'ontological, epistemological, and ecological' and make a distinction between concepts of 'diversity' and concepts of 'plurality'. They argue that plurality 'constitutes the bleaching of diversity' and highlights normalising discourses of 'tolerance' and 'accommodation' reminiscent of discourses of multiculturalism that claim to be apolitical (Troyna, 1993; Stevens and Crozier, 2014).

Pamela Barnett considers the task of addressing diversity in relation to fear, which often stems from the desire to be accepted by those who are different from us. Although she notes that university student bodies in both the US and the UK are increasingly diverse, 'students are not actually learning about and from diversity' (Barnett, 2011, p. 671), yet:

> Given the entrenchment of racism globally expressed in all kinds of structures, sometimes in violence and even genocide there is a tremendous need for people to know about and understand each other, to learn how to live together and solve common problems.
>
> (Barnett, 2011, p. 671)

She argues that students are not learning from diversity due to a fear of difference, explaining that we tend to 'project all that is bad onto those who are different' (Barnett, 2011, p. 673). Barnett argues that 'we must address the emotion that holds us back from true dialogue and allow productive conflict' (p. 674) in order to address difference through pedagogical spaces. In our view such fear also stems from the threat to the position of power held by powerful groups. In a social justice framework, participants engage in processes of reflexivity to acknowledge, unsettle and interrogate such fear, engaging in critical discussion about their 'distrust, fears and needs' (p. 675), thus contributing to recognition and representation of difference through HE pedagogies. Such themes of working *with rather than against* emotion challenge the instrumental discourses at play, encouraging participants to work with a pedagogical imagination that is deeply attuned to emotion as part of HE learning (e.g. Leathwood and Hey, 2009, p. 438). Judith Butler (2014) speaks about the impact of disconnection and explains poetically the need to use emotion as a way to create non-violent spaces:

> We are from the start both done and undone by the other and if we refuse this we refuse passion, life and loss – the lived form of that refusal is destruction; the lived form of its affirmation is non-violence.
>
> (Butler, 2014)

Leathwood and Hey (2009) analyse the ways that emotion often becomes a disciplinary technology of neo-liberalism in the context of producing particular kinds of (employable) subjects. They emphasise that it is important to 'work with 'emotion' but in a way that 'critically engages with the neo-liberal (and any successor) projects which use a discourse of feelings and personal skills in an effort to micromanage the educational trajectory of subjects' (p. 436). This involves feminist analyses that 'socialise' emotion. This includes attention to the seductions of emotions, in some contexts, and the fear of emotion in others. However, and importantly, this requires refusing the binary divisions that lock us into an either this or that mindset. Rather we need to develop analyses and practices that recognise 'emotions as about control *and* resistance, as relational and circulating, and as productive of social relationships and identities' (p. 436).

We understand pedagogies as lived, relational and embodied practices in higher education that are closely connected to identity formations and subjectivity, as well as the emotional layers of pedagogical experiences. We draw on notions of 'identity formation' to consider the ways that structural differences and inequalities of gender, class, race and ethnicity intersect to form our sense of self. The concept of 'subjectivity' captures the post/structural insight that we are constituted discursively, through the politics of recognition and through the dual process of mastery and submission of hegemonic discourses. Drawing on Foucault (1982), we understand such processes to be generative, with possibilities of remaking the self always part of our 'becoming' recognised subjects. We also draw on feminist insights, to understand the ways that identities and subjectivities are formed through the affective layers of our lived and embodied experiences, which deeply shape our sense of personhood and our understanding of our 'place' in and our relation to the world and others. Drawing on Butler, we argue for pedagogies that are embedded in notions of connectivity that seek to develop our capacities of empathy. Our stance is that higher education has a deeper relation to the world than the labour market, business and industry. Rather than restricting our imagination to the realm of employability, we struggle for pedagogies with richer imaginations that consider the relation of higher education institutions and subjects to the world and society. In thinking about questions of global well-being, social justice and struggles for peace, our position is that higher education pedagogies provide spaces of critical reflection of our position in and of the world.

One of the most powerful ideas we ourselves encountered as university students is that our personal experiences are central to the development of our critical understanding of the world and our contribution to it. In developing our humanity and critical awareness we need to make rich and textured connections – to understand ourselves as situated in and with the world and society, and as formed in relation to others. To deepen our understanding of ourselves, others, our values and worldviews we need to make connections between our personal histories and the wider histories in which we are a part – to trace our beliefs, understanding, perspectives in relation to wider debates, histories and social relations (Miller, 1995). Drawing on Freire (2009), we also need the capacity to dream – as he says, 'to dream is to make' – and part of our humanity is our capacity to dream and remake the world. Higher education should always provide such spaces – to dream of other ways of being, doing and thinking about ourselves and our deep relationality to others and to the world. This requires a self-reflexive interrogation of our complex relation to power, in terms of structural inequalities as well as symbolic forms of misrecognition.

Although hegemonic discourses at play in higher education policy construct largely instrumentalised notions of teaching and learning, the dynamics, relations and experiences of teaching and learning are intimately tied to the re/production of particular identity formations and ways of being/becoming a university student or teacher. As argued above, discourses of teaching and learning frame teacher and student experiences and identities largely in terms of 'styles', 'provision', 'needs' and 'delivery' and such language tends to be couched in a market-oriented perspective that often constructs teachers as service providers and students as consumers. Although some attention might be paid to issues of power, this is often framed in terms of simplistic notions of student 'voice' and 'empowerment'. Concerns with 'diversity' are often associated with the individualising need for 'personalised', 'differentiated' and/or 'independent' learning. We argue that such perspectives ignore the ways diversity is always tied to complex relations of power and difference and the ways that inequalities are very often insidious, subtle and difficult to capture through the technologies of accountability and governance that currently shape higher education.

Teaching as an interdisciplinary field of praxis

> The requirements of praxis are theory both relevant to the world and nurtured by actions in it; theory that emerges from 'practical political grounding.
>
> (Lather, 1991, pp. 11–12)

In this book we argue that teaching and learning are not just about acquiring key skills but is a dynamic and complex field of praxis. This helps us to reconceptualise teaching and learning from a broader perspective that aims to capture the complex relations, power dynamics, identity formations, subjectivities and politics of difference that form and reform pedagogical spaces and experiences. Praxis is a critical dialogic framework that requires reciprocal processes of reflection/action/action/reflection, creating reflexive pedagogical spaces that are underpinned by the core principles of equity, ethics and pedagogies of difference. This requires teachers and learners to develop reflexive approaches that open up difficult questions around power and difference and the relationship between teaching, learning and meaning-making. It also insists that teaching is not only a professional *practice* but that teaching practice should be formed in dialogue with *critical theories* if it is to be fine-tuned to complex and intricate relations of power, difference and inequalities.

The concept of praxis demands that teaching practice is shaped by a strong theoretical framework that offers the analytical resources for the project of disrupting deeply entrenched inequalities in higher education. Pedagogy is seen not only as a space of teaching and learning practices but of struggles over meaning and the validation of particular bodies of knowledge. Pedagogy then is deeply connected to relations of power and authority in which the professor has historically been positioned as the expert knower. However, although we acknowledge the significance of expert and disciplinary knowledge in the pedagogical interaction, we also argue that the HE professor and the student must work together collaboratively to create meaning and 'truth' in order to engage in the 'circle of knowledge' (Freire, 2009, pp. 169–170).

Freire's concept of the circle of knowledge facilitates the creation of opportunities for exclusive forms of knowledge and practice to become accessible, inclusive and participatory through processes of redistribution, as well as to subject these to critique and to the possibilities of change and transformation. In the processes of redistribution and critique, the forms of knowledge and practice will evolve, transform and change and, at the same time, those groups who have now become included will contribute to the development of alternative forms of knowledge and practice in higher education. This will open up the possibilities for other ways of doing, thinking, studying and knowing. However, it is important to strongly emphasise that this is not about lowering of standards or creating sub-standard courses and degrees. Indeed, it is about *strengthening* standards and quality, as it requires all participants in higher education to develop deeper levels of criticality and reflexivity, bringing together theory and practice through a commitment to praxis. The impact of such approaches will not only be to widen participation in higher education, but to transform higher educational spaces in dedicated projects of creating dialogical spaces of ethical, inclusive and participatory meaning-making for collective well-being, social justice and more peaceful societies. The circle of knowledge helps to focus on developing pedagogies that nurture, enrich and fully recognise the importance of diverse forms of knowledge, subjectivity and practice (Burke, 2012).

An ethical and reflexive framework of praxis involves the teacher in critically exploring connections between research and teaching, disciplinary knowledge and the knowledge students bring to their learning in a process of reforming knowledge through reflection/action/action/reflection. In this framework, pedagogy is developed through an understanding of the relationship between, pedagogy, ontology and epistemology. This creates spaces for and of transformation; including transformation of power relations, identity formations, subjectivities and knowledge construction. Pedagogical praxis aims to create challenging, imaginative and creative spaces for teachers and students to work collaboratively and dialogically to critically reflect on, interrogate and further develop understanding and meaning. This poses the urgency of creating spaces of dialogue to inspire the pedagogical imagination in ways that explicitly challenge inequalities, misrecognitions and exclusions.

Teaching, we argue in this book, is an interdisciplinary field of praxis. We share the perspective with other critical scholars, that:

> Interdisciplinarity is premised upon a notion of "disciplinarity" – just as interstate collaboration is based on a notion of 'statehood' or interpersonal relationships on a notion of "personhood". From this perspective interdisciplinarity does not obliterate disciplinary and subject-specific frames, but asks us to see those frames as permeable, negotiable and inter-dependent.
>
> (Nixon, 2015)

In taking this position, we invite academics from across the disciplines to explore teaching and pedagogy in higher education in dialogue with us, within an ethical and reflexive framework of praxis. This recognises the contextual nature of pedagogy; teaching is embedded in the power relations and disciplinary and institutional contexts in which learning, meaning-making and identity and subjective formation takes place. However, the ethical, reflexive framework of praxis enables us to pay close attention to the exclusionary aspects of power and disciplinary contexts that are entangled in the re/production of inequalities and misrecognitions. At the same time, drawing on feminist post/structural critiques, we argue with Foucault that power is generative and productive as well as potentially exclusive and destructive. Power is not a dynamic to be overcome, as this is an impossibility; human relations will always involve complex webs of power.

However, the aim is not to ask teachers to relinquish power and 'give it' to their students, not least because as Foucault points out power is not a 'thing' that we 'have' to 'give' to our students. Power is not a tangible object but is a dynamic and fluid force that circulates in unpredictable and shifting ways. It is not something we can simply 'locate' and 'remove'; it is complex in its multiple and fluid formations. However, our focus in this book is to develop an understanding of the ways that power is exercised, generated and (re)produced in and across higher education and pedagogical spaces, considering also what this means for participation, equity and inequality. We are also concerned to acknowledge the ways that power continues to be exercised in relation to structural inequalities and in this book we pay particular attention to this in relation to gender and its intersections with class, ethnicity and race, although we recognise that there are multiple other structural inequalities at play. In relation to this, pedagogy is not only shaped by complex power relations but is also a key dimension of epistemology; the forms of knowledge that constitute the curriculum are deeply entwined with pedagogical frames, how, what and why we teach and what this means for the constitution of inter/disciplinary knowledge and wider concerns about social justice.

Drawing on Foucault we theorise power as re/shaping pedagogical relations and experiences in and across changing social, cultural, spatial and (micro) political contexts. Power is not an oppositional force that predictably benefits one group above the other but rather moves fluidly across and between differently positioned subjects. The teacher is not seen to 'have the power' to give to the students but rather power is generated, exercised and struggled over within lived social spaces such as classrooms and lecture theatres. Furthermore, power is not tied to one single source, but is interconnected to multiple dynamics, including space, place, time, context, identity and inequality. Power shapes pedagogical relations in profound and unexpected ways and this is inextricably tied to questions of knowledge, authority and representation. As such, pedagogy, curriculum and assessment are not separate entities but *overlapping* and *intersecting* dimensions of educational practice in which power plays out in different ways, depending on context, relations and identities. Pedagogies are thus profoundly shaped by the different power relations at play, the changing contexts in which teaching and learning takes place and the identities and subjective relations of teachers and students. Simultaneously, pedagogies are constitutive of subjectivities, discursive practices and regimes of truth at play in particular pedagogic relations and spaces. Pedagogies both shape and are shaped by complex identity formations, epistemological frameworks and processes of recognition, as well as notions of 'right' to participate in higher education. Pedagogies do not simply reflect the classed, gendered and racialised identities of teachers and students but *pedagogies themselves are classed, gendered and racialised*, intimately bound up with historical and masculinised ways of being and doing within higher education spaces. Pedagogical relations are thus deeply implicated in the processes and politics of identity, recognition and misrecognition.

As Freire (1972) argues a praxis-oriented pedagogical framework counters the destructive and oppressive forces of 'banking education', in which 'knowledge' is a one-way process of deposit from the teacher/knower to the student/passive recipient. Freire argues that the essence of dialogue is 'the word' constituted by the interactive dimensions of reflection and action. His 'pedagogy of the oppressed' involves the dialogic process of reflection/action in the transformation of the world through seeking 'truth' through praxis. This helps us to understand the importance of a praxis-based approach to pedagogy; Freire explains that reflection without action is simply verbalism and action without reflection is simply activism (1972, p. 87).

The project of humanisation that Freire compels us to participate in, is not one of simply developing ideas and theories but to develop ways of doing, acting, being in the world that counter the destructive forces of oppression in all the myriad forms that these might take. Praxis is necessary in any project for social justice. This is a key message of Freirean pedagogy and is a loud call to academics who work across disciplines and fields and are committed to developing social justice and equity approaches to their work. The words we write are valuable as part of a project of social change and transformation – not only *what* we write but *how* we write and *what and who we intend our writing to be for*. However, words, as important as they might be, are only part of a process – and this is why the concept of praxis is so profound in projects of social justice – we need to attend to the continual interrelationship between our reflections and our actions and our actions and our reflections – it is only through this praxis that we can move forward in our collective and individual journeys towards social justice. This requires the space of respectfully living together and this is the link with ethics, with the notion of sustainability and with the question of violence, in all its myriad formations.

However, such orientations must also acknowledge the complex dynamics and operations of power, which are reworked and reformed in ways that often surprise, perplex and collude in relations of exclusions, misrecognition and forms of symbolic violence. The spaces of praxis that we develop must be sensitive to the multiple, interconnected and insidious inequalities that are often unnoticed not only by those we might name as the 'oppressor' but indeed, by us ourselves. We are all complicit and embedded in complex forms of inequality, power and marginalisation. We must therefore continually engage an ethical reflexivity in our everyday practices and relationships with others and in the ways in which we reconstruct our identities, relations and practices.

Re/imagining difference through critical and feminist pedagogies

In this section we explore possible interventions and strategies for disrupting misrecognition, by re/imagining difference and attending to the emotional levels of pedagogic identity and experience. Post/structural, critical and feminist re/

workings of difference draw on emotion and difference as critical resources for remaking selves within pedagogical spaces. In such spaces, selves are explored through difference as relational, as situated within complex histories and as committed to a collective process of (re)making meaning. The processes of meaning-making are tied to reflexive and collective projects of critical engagement with the curriculum, which allow spaces for engaging with disciplinary/subject knowledge through the perspectives of diverse student insights, experiences and histories. The aim is to generate different forms of higher education pedagogic practice, embedded in a framework of connectedness with one another/ the 'Other', addressing that we are both 'made and unmade' by the 'Other', in Butler's (2014) evocative words. The remaking of selves is bound up with a co-commitment to practices of refusal, with freedom and identity seen as sites of struggle rather than as endpoints to be achieved (Ball, 2014).

Such approaches draw on, rather than regulate, the tensions, contradictions and problematic nature of difference. As post/structuralism illuminates, processes of learning are never straightforward and linear but are necessarily tied in with complex relations of power, difference and subjectivity (Gore, 1993). The rational and emotional are viewed as inseparable and there is a firm commitment to an ethical framework in which pedagogical participants share the responsibilities of creating inclusive and equitable spaces. At the same time, there is an understanding that 'inclusion' and 'equity' are problematic aspirations that require ongoing, reciprocal and reflexive forms of critical consideration through pedagogical processes. In such a framework, participants reject the model of inclusion that insists on fitting in and/or conforming to the hegemonic and normative frames, but rather takes an approach to 'inclusion' that emphasises being committed to exploring meaning through the inclusion of the (contesting) perspectives of relational Others. Although difference is embraced, a commitment to challenging misrecognition, connected to structural and symbolic inequalities, is an underpinning principal that guides practice.

Drawing on Boler's concept of 'pedagogy of discomfort' (Boler, 1999; Zembylas and Boler, 2002; Boler and Zembylas, 2003) Macdonald (2013) examines the practices of such a pedagogical frame, in which the ethical goal underpinning the pedagogical space is to 'inhabit a more ambiguous and flexible sense of self' (Boler, 1999, p. 170 in Macdonald, 2013, p. 675). She 'examines the potential and limitations of pedagogy of discomfort in a post-apartheid yet heavily racialised South Africa, where higher education institutes were, and continue to be, seen as vitally important in the transformation process, both as a vehicle for transformation in reconstituting South African society, and in need of transformation in and of themselves' (Macdonald, 2013, p. 671). Drawing on the 'pedagogy of discomfort' in a second year course on citizenship, the state, forms of exchange, colonialism and development, she asked her students to:

> recognise and embrace discomforting emotional investments as moments to
> interrogate rather than as a result of intuitive inference, even if this simply

meant to park the discomfort for better time with which to name it and work with it towards conceptual shifts in understanding.

(Macdonald, 2013, p. 675)

She found that discomfort was 'produced in ways that reflected the "diversity of lives, experiences and identities shaped and refashioned within the classroom, a fractal of the wider world"' (Mills and Spencer, 2011, p. 1 in Macdonald, 2013, p. 680). Key issues for the teacher to embrace included a sense of 'unsafety', interrogating one's teaching practices and to relinquish control in the classroom and encourage students to find their relationships not only to the teacher but to their own knowledge and how it has been produced and emotionally embodied (Macdonald, 2013, p. 680).

Similarly, Barnett (2011) speaks in terms of 'productive conflict' within a 'pedagogy of difference'. She argues that 'trust' is an important characteristic of the relationship to be developed amongst pedagogical participants because trust 'can provide a sense of security' for surviving in contexts of 'high ambiguity and uncertainty' (Six, 2005, pp. 2–3 in Barnett, 2011, p. 674). However, Barnett admits that 'trust' is a problematic concept and argues, drawing on Rojzman, that there is no single strategy for building trust. Rather trust is understood as a shared principle within an ethical framework of pedagogical practice in which participants 'become aware of their own distrust, fears and needs in ways that lead them to change themselves' (Barnett, 2011, p. 675). Such arguments highlight though an ongoing dilemma for critical and feminist pedagogies, which is the partial nature of our knowledge, including knowledge of ourselves and our practices (Ellsworth, 1996). We can never fully know ourselves or the Other. This points to the problematic nature of 'reflexivity' and other forms of critical consciousness-raising associated with critical pedagogies. However, we argue that acknowledging that such orientations are problematic and necessarily partial is an important dimension of developing pedagogies that re/imagine and re/work difference. This requires finding comfort in our discomfort; we must continually work through the making of meaning as an ongoing process of refusal and resistance and as a site of struggle. An explicit engagement with emotion is an important dimension of such processes.

Chawla and Rodriguez (2007) write movingly and powerfully about new imaginations of difference 'rooted in the complexity of relationships rather than in the socially constructed categories of gender, race, ethnicity, sexual orientation' (p. 700), urging an exploration of difference outside categories. This is about moving towards solidarities and reimagining 'identity in ways that enlarge possibility' (p. 702) 'with the aim of destroying categories' (p. 703) and thus challenging 'dividing practices' that produce misrecognition. Chawla and Rodriguez highlight the ways our fixation on specific identify categories deeply limit understandings of our cultural selves (p. 704).

They trace Chawla's pedagogical practices, in which she works with such 'imaginings of difference' together with her students. Using various exercises to open up new ways of thinking about difference and identity, she and her students work towards 're-create[ing] selves in writing, narrative, memories, and performance' (Chawla and Rodriguez, 2007, p. 705). In engaging her students in a collaborative process of rethinking and reimagining, Chawla engages her students in the study of 'human identity/s in all their anxieties, vulnerabilities, and im/possibility/s wherever they may be' searching together for 'an opportunity to resist the forces that stop us from re-imagining more worlds' (p. 707).

A post/structural re/working of difference helps to nuance our understanding of pedagogy as related to complex power relations, in which power is exercised rather than 'had', disrupting binary divisions that imagine difference in binary terms: rational/emotional, independent/dependent, active/passive, powerful/powerless and so forth. This also helps to examine how the emotional profoundly shapes pedagogical experience, including the experience of fear in pedagogical contexts. It is important though to not only examine fear *as* emotion but also fear *of* emotion (Leathwood and Hey, 2009) and how this is deeply connected to those 'dividing practices' that operate to recover the hegemony of rationality and the exclusion of emotion from higher education pedagogical spaces. It also helps to re/imagine difference not as a problem to be regulated for neo-liberal processes of standardisation and homogenisation but as a critical resource to reflexively develop collective and ethical participation in pedagogical spaces. Such collective participation is not based on a notion that we can *overcome* power relations, but an understanding that power is complex and fluid and an inevitable dimension of pedagogical relations in which *difference is and should be part of the dynamics in which we create meaning and understanding.*

Conclusion

This chapter has explored ways of reconceptualising pedagogies with a view to develop praxis-oriented and ethical approaches to teaching and learning that recognise difference and create spaces for representation across difference. We have explored constructions of difference in order to consider the complex operations of power in higher education and its relation to questions of equity and social justice in pedagogical relations and practices. Pedagogy is relational and tied in with the micro-politics of misrecognition, in which recognition as a 'proper' student or academic depends on particular performatives and discourses. In the contemporary university, such performatives and discourses are embedded in the imperative and aspiration to be constructed as 'excellent'. Indeed, 'excellence' is a prerequisite for being positioned at the top of the league tables as a 'global university'.

However, as discussed in Chapter one, 'excellence' in higher education is a problematic discourse. The meanings behind it are often vague and left largely undefined, although they are formed through the attributes and criteria that constitute league table measurements and rankings. Together with moves towards the marketisation of HE, this has led increasingly to an age of performativity, which tends to narrow possibilities for recognition and practice. It moves us further away from the social justice aims to widen participation because difference is associated with the Other, the pathologising contaminating subjectivities that are seen to 'lower standards' and 'dumb down' higher education. Thus, a reductive view of diversity is upheld, as a way to project a positive image of 'inclusivity' whilst a range of technologies are in place to regulate difference.

Chapter 3

Pedagogical methodology

This book draws on and pulls together two qualitative projects on higher education pedagogies, both of which were framed by 'pedagogical methodology'. This chapter describes the framework of 'pedagogical methodology' (PM), which aims to cultivate spaces of praxis and critical reflexivity for 'research that makes a difference'. After setting out the two research projects, we will then briefly discuss and critique the concept of 'research that makes a difference' within the current research climate, as well as the problematic process of translating research and theory to practice (Clegg, Stevenson and Burke, 2016). The chapter will focus on exploring PM in depth as a way of creating counter-hegemonic spaces in higher education for social justice pedagogies of and for difference.

Background: our projects

This book is based on one large-scale study and a smaller-scale project. The large-scale study, Formations of Gender and Higher Education Pedagogies (GaP), was a result of the National Teaching Fellowship Scheme (NTFS) project strand initiative funded by the Higher Education Funding Council for England (HEFCE) and managed by the Higher Education Academy (HEA). The small-scale project [funded by a Fulbright Scholar Award and an award from the School of Education, University of Roehampton's Centre for Education Research in Equalities, Policy and Pedagogy (CEREPP), was designed to complement the efforts of the larger study and explore them in new country contexts, employing one component of GaP: focus groups with university teachers. Here, we will first briefly introduce the projects; further description of the projects, design and process can be found in Appendix One (GaP) and Two (Fulbright).

GaP

This two-year project makes a unique contribution to the development of higher education (HE) pedagogies by exploring their relationship to complex identity formations of gender, and other social identities and inequalities. The project also makes an important contribution to understanding broader widening participation policy agendas by paying close attention to pedagogical issues beyond mainstream discourses of 'raising aspirations' and 'fair access'. Connected to this, and with consideration of the recent panic about men's HE participation (HEFCE, 2005; Bekhradnia, 2009), the project provides a qualitative account of gendered experiences, intersected by race and class, of higher education, with attention to the complex formations of masculinities and femininities in pedagogical relations and practices.

The project adopted participatory approaches, framed by a pedagogical methodology (which we will explore further in a moment), which involved methods of qualitative data collection about HE teachers' and students' experiences and perspectives of HE pedagogies (through in-depth and detailed interviews) and of their practices (through observations of classroom practice). Additionally, the project sought to enhance participation in consideration of pedagogical relations, experiences and practices through a range of participatory methods including workshops, forums, seminars and discussions. The research was designed to create dialogic spaces of reflexivity in which HE teachers and students critically discussed and reflected on their pedagogical experiences and practices in a wider social context that explored the relationship between HE pedagogies, complex inequalities and exclusions at the micro-level of classroom experiences and the significance of identity formations in shaping HE pedagogies and spaces. The project aimed to provide pedagogical spaces through the research process, with all participants, including the research team, engaged in pedagogical relations to reflect critically on the ways these formed through gendered intersections of and with diversity and difference, including race and class. The research team was intentionally constituted of those of us positioned institutionally as 'academic staff' and those of us positioned institutionally as 'academic developers'. The framework was designed to include those researching with us: the HE teachers and students who participated in the forums, workshops, seminars and discussions.

Fulbright

In order to sustain the work of GaP, a 2012–2013 UK Fulbright Scholar Award Project entitled 'Gender and Higher Education Pedagogies in a Comparative Perspective' was undertaken. The project focused on participation in HE across four country contexts – Italy, Spain, Portugal and the USA.

The aims of conducting this project were three-fold: (1) to examine gender-sensitive and inclusive teaching practices across four country contexts; (2) from the results of this examination, to develop an agenda for research on HE pedagogies and gender within a large international network (the Paulo Freire Institute [PFI] network) and to expand and strengthen this area of research in the UK, Europe and the USA; and, more broadly, along with this agenda, (3) to promote the development of gender-sensitive and inclusive pedagogies in HE with the goal of expanding these studies – critical to expand the field of comparative social justice education – within the UK, Europe, the USA and beyond. In response to the latter two aims, Lauren and Penny Jane have created the International Doctoral and Post-Doctoral Network on Gender, Social Justice and Praxis. The Network emphasises the creation and dissemination of inclusive pedagogical work by cross-trajectory, university–community relationship–centred teams of experienced and early-career academics.

Having briefly introduced the projects, we move now to a brief discussion of the research climate in which these projects were conducted.

Background: 'research that makes a difference'

Before introducing the idea of a PM, it is useful to contextualise the research climate in which we are working. We also recognise the problematic process of translating research into practice (Clegg, Stevenson and Burke, 2016). We argue that it is a crucial time to explore the concept of 'research that makes a difference' as we are at the beginning of a new and understudied wave in higher education. In the UK for example, the requirement to assess 'impact' was introduced into the 2014 Research Excellence Framework (REF), the system of assessing research quality in UK higher education institutions, and the notion of 'impact' is taking hold in a range of other international contexts. Importantly, measuring 'impact' is a trend shaping higher education reform worldwide, although this is arguably underpinned by the neo-liberal move towards 'datafication' (Sellar, 2013) rather than the concern to make a difference driven by social justice considerations. Caress (2014) provides a concise overview of this new assessment criterion:

> [E]xactly what constitutes a good example of "impact" is *still evolving*. REF guidance defines "impact" as follows: "For the purposes of the REF, impact is defined as an effect on, change or benefit to the economy, society, culture, public policy or services, health, the environment or quality of life, *beyond academia*" (HEFCE et al., 2012a). . . . Researchers are now required not just to demonstrate ways that their research is highly regarded by fellow researchers, but also how it is *"making a difference"* more broadly.
>
> (Our emphases)

The quality of research is thus being judged in relation to 'impact beyond academia'. This has generated significant uncertainties amongst researchers – with contested meanings circulating around 'impact' from 'evidence-based' and 'large-scale' to 'close-up research' with 'transformatory social justice aspirations'. 'Social justice' itself is a contested discourse. It could be seen as being co-opted by neo-liberal forms of governmentality with foci on auditing, outcomes and performance measurements (e.g. UK's REF; other measures such as the Times Higher Education University League Tables), which often seem at odds with critical concepts of social justice (e.g. Freire, 1970; Fraser, 1997, 2003; Fraser and Honneth, 2003).

However, this paradoxical moment ('still evolving' impact criteria and ambiguous pursuits for social justice) presents opportunities for 'making a difference' through research. This is a challenging task not least because 'impact,' in the sorts of assessments described above, must be supported by evidence and it is a problematic task to 'evidence' 'making a difference', as it is 'fraught with contradictions as the translation from research to action is far from straight forward' (Clegg, Stevenson and Burke, 2016b). Clegg, Stevenson and Burke (2016) have problematised Burke et al. (2013) research to show that 'the real contradictions of the world in which students and staff find themselves constrain and limit the translation of research into practice'. They further note that 'the connections between even carefully designed and critically theorised 'close-up research' – research that examines the micro-level practices and experiences of higher education – and making a difference is a hard road to navigate and one which requires something beyond individual agency' (Clegg, Stevenson and Burke, 2016).

Thus, this climate both requires and is ripe with, possibilities for reimagining research methodologies. It is within this climate that we have developed the concept of a 'pedagogical methodology'.

Introducing a 'pedagogical methodology'

As we explore the idea of PM, we discuss what has actually worked in our own research. We argue that PM creates possibilities for 'research that makes a difference' but that there are many nuanced challenges and dilemmas within this process.

The GaP project aimed to create participatory approaches through the research. A major theme of this was the imperative to create spaces of reflexivity through the research process in which teachers and students had the opportunity to reflect critically on the complexities of pedagogical relations, experiences and practices, with a particular focus on its relation to formations of gender and other intersecting social inequalities and differences. We sought ways to embed the continuous, iterative, reciprocal learning-teaching praxes (processes of action and reflection) in our research frameworks. Conceptualising this as 'pedagogical methodology' (PM) foregrounds those key dimensions of our methodological approaches. PM is premised on the aim to provide parity of participation (Fraser, 1997), but it goes beyond participation and beyond the traditional boundaries of what a methodological framework might consist of. It is a framework for creating and opening up collaborative, collective, dialogical and participatory methodologies and spaces which, through the research processes, engage participants in pedagogical relations. PM provides opportunities to talk about pedagogical experiences and expectations, pedagogical frustrations, and identity that would never happen in formal and bureaucratic committee meetings, driven by performative and regulatory governance frameworks. These are counter-hegemonic spaces of refusal, resistance, and of doing things differently.

PM begins with us as the researchers. The process of carrying out and writing about our research at all stages, including this book, necessarily involves negotiating the (dis)connections between our theoretical and methodological (auto) biographies. These (auto)biographies are fluid, complex, and include subdisciplinary differences and intertwined theoretical and methodological differences. The 'auto' in '(auto)biography' acknowledges that the ways in which we represent/position ourselves may differ from the biographies that others ascribe to us; these differences between autobiographies and others' biographies of us also must be negotiated. These negotiations then extend into the participants' (auto) biographies. It also acknowledges the ways politics of recognition play out in sites of power and discourse and the ways that institutional positionings (professor, lecturer, academic developer, teacher, student and so forth) intersect with mis/ recognitions in the formation of self and other.

PM requires broadening how we conceptualise 'pedagogies'. 'Pedagogies' is a concept that allows us to think not just about what we do but about the relations that are created and recreated through the pedagogical process. Developing pedagogical spaces through PM attends to the complex ways in which (iterative) processes shape our sensibilities of self and personhood through meaning-making. The meanings we produce are part of a circle of knowledge, enabled through participation in the research process and through the inter/relationships between pedagogy, identity formations and difference. PM frameworks allow for meaning-making to be refined through participatory practices, creating spaces of praxis both through and *beyond the research*. Whilst the research is about 'findings', it is as much about generating spaces for critical reflexivity and praxis and new ways of knowing and understanding that otherwise might be unavailable and/or closed down. In PM frameworks, research *becomes* a form of pedagogy, as part of the process of meaning-making, learning and making sense of ourselves and our relation to others. This engages research participants in relational processes in which we, as the researchers, learn and in which the participants in our study also have opportunities to learn; this ultimately is manifested in the way the research is iteratively understood, and how it is shaped/ formed/developed.

PM draws on feminism and post/structuralism, which involves negotiation of material inequalities, social structures and cultural and symbolic misrecognitions. Importantly, the stroke (/) in post/structuralism signifies the negotiating of structuralism and poststructuralism in our work. Thus, we insist on recognising the material realities that structure lives, as well as the social inequalities that reproduce gendered formations. We understand the material and structural as deeply entwined with the discursive, affective and symbolic, so that inequalities are lived, felt and embodied, often in subtle ways, within pedagogical spaces. PM also draws on liberatory pedagogies, which seek to engage in processes of humanisation, drawing particularly on the work of Paulo Freire. Humanisation is characterised by valuing empathy, connection and care, which we have argued throughout the book is being eroded through neo-liberalism, managerialism, technologies of regulation and governance and intensified forms of performativity.

In constructing PM, the Freirean concept of the *inédito viável* – a concept that refers to 'that which has not been realised,' possible dreams, and utopias – is generative. The concept of *utopistics* is a guiding tool in relation to this. Here, utopia is seen, to quote Galeano in Torres (2014, p. 132) as:

> A distant horizon, a horizon that one always wants to reach but can never approach. One takes two steps toward this horizon and it recedes another two paces. What then, is the advantage of utopia, we might ask? As a rational and spiritual model guiding our desire, it helps us to keep moving.

Thinking about those horizons and the contributions of humanism to our thinking, PM is concerned with new ways of working with people and of developing new knowledge formations that are able to grapple with questions of difference, power and contestation. There were moments in which we did not agree with each other during the research but creating spaces of understanding and having patience, empathy and compassion to work with people through differences was central to our process. Our thinking shifted through working together as a team and our participants have expressed similar experiences. The participants often commented on the significance of having spaces of critical reflection of their pedagogical experiences for rethinking and reshaping their assumptions.

As we live in cultures of individualism/performance management in which we are isolated, overworked, highly regulated and managed subjects, in order to carry out PM we must be strategic and subversive and understand the meanings and implications of these terms in the context in which we are working. The tensions between structure and agency and the ways subjectivities are formed in relation to practices of the self – the remaking of self through ongoing critical reflexivity and praxis are the kinds of questions that participants of PM might explore collaboratively. We draw on an eclectic set of conceptual resources to think through such questions throughout this book.

In the GaP project, the data collected through more conventional methods (interviews and observations) was used as a resource for generating thoughts, reflections, and ideas in discussion with the research participants. The data was used as a prompt to get people to talk, share, and feel comfortable putting their views forward about sensitive issues to do with pedagogical identity formations and subjectivities – the same kind of process that you'd want to achieve in a learning situation. Engaging in these PM processes is a way of challenging established power relations in research and pedagogy. PM facilitates the sort of engagement that allows people to contribute to meaning-making and knowledge production through research and pedagogical spaces. This might be named a form of 'empowerment', although we are also mindful of the problematic nature of 'empowerment' as a pedagogical aspiration, not least in its over-simplistic conceptualisation of the circulation and dynamics of power in pedagogical relations.

Questions around 'empowerment' surface in PM. In post-structuralism, power is generative. Through the processes of engaging people with us, we work to shift the power relations so that participants are questioning their relation to power and ways that power is exercised in and through institutional contexts and positions in order to 'develop inclusive practices'. In other words, PM allows us to think about power explicitly and reflexively and to understand that we are all complicit in complex relations of power. In discussions with the teacher participants, many expressed how they valued this space through the research as there were no other spaces in higher education that teachers engaged in such deep considerations about questions of power, gender, identity formations and difference. Drawing on Foucault's argument that power is positive and generative helps to convey how such spaces provide an important resource to create possibilities for counter-hegemonic structures and discourses that either ignore unequal power relations or fail to acknowledge the ways that power is an inevitable and central dimension of pedagogical identities and experiences.

Critical reflections on 'empowerment' highlight the restrictions around the language we use and require us to think about how to move beyond 'empowerment'. Empowerment is problematic because it assumes that teachers can 'empower' their students, as if they 'have' power to 'give' to their students. This conceals that power is deeply relational and is not a 'thing' that one group has and another does not. Rather, we all have the capacity to exercise power, although structures and discourses shape the ways we live and experience 'power'. Creating space to critically discuss these linguistic, structural and discursive limitations/boundaries, and to problematise and think through ways to reframe our ideas (in order to create new ideas) with a focus on social justice considerations, is central to PM.

PM involves discussing the principles underpinning our collaborative work and participatory project. Identifying the shared principles that guide the team's work that are not negotiable – agreeing about this ethical framework – is part of PM. Our starting point is developing pedagogical spaces for anti-oppression and the recognition of difference: for example, anti-racist, anti-sexist, anti-classist practices that also recognise the complexities of identity formations that always intersect with multiple differences. This demands continual attention to developing equitable conditions through denouncing these inequalities and announcing what these equitable conditions might look like (drawing on the Freirean dialectical concepts of announcement and denouncement). For example, in the GaP project we embedded a participatory approach throughout the project to create opportunities for ongoing discussion and feedback. We invited students to work with us on the project as Executive Student Consultants (ESC), giving them recognition of their important role in contributing to the project approaches, reflections and analysis. We developed intensive workshops for teacher and student participants across the country (UK) to work with an external facilitator (Professor Louise Archer) with our data, reflecting collaboratively on emergent themes, exploring connections and disconnections with these and feeding into the process of collaborative forms of analysis.

There were moments in the process that the participants' insights both shocked and enlightened our understanding of our own data. For example, a group of women studying history discussed why gender matters in their discipline. The group brought up that they were studying women figures in history that weren't important to them and that they wanted to study the important (male) figures instead. At first, we were saddened that the women did not recognise the importance of these female figures. However, on reflection, we realised the women raised a number of dilemmas. Despite the best intentions to make (feminist and/or anti-sexist) curricular changes, if these changes do not connect to experiences of classroom pedagogy, including explicit discussions about such issues as disciplinary canons, then the changes might be experienced as confusing and disappointing to students who might have different expectations from the teachers. It also raises the question of epistemic access within different disciplinary contexts, and the ways that students expect, and also need, access to knowledge that has status and power in wider society. We are not arguing that disciplinary canons should not be questioned, but rather that students should understand what they are studying and why, and should have access to both 'powerful' forms of knowledge (in terms of social status and legitimacy) and forms of knowledge that have been historically marginalised and or misrecognised.

This relates to the issue of how students, who are all subjected to neo-liberal discourses and expectations, just as teachers are, might desire forms of didactic teaching (versus more critical teaching), and how students might perceive and assess what constitutes 'good teaching'. These under/currents are at play in, for example, a recent BBC 5 Radio survey (BBC, 2015) in which two-thirds of students studying science, technology, maths and engineering – disciplinary fields that require a great deal of practical teaching and staff time – said their courses had been good value, but in which 44% of humanities and social science students, which tend to receive less direct teaching time, said they felt their courses represented good value. How the survey and the students (similarly/differently) understand 'practical teaching', 'staff time', and 'direct teaching time' all come into play. We take these discussions forward in our work.

As well, in interviews, numerous students said that no structural distinction existed in their university setting. Here, 'structural distinction' refers to the influence of structural variables that emphasis 'distinction' ('them' and 'us' (Crozier, 2013 as cited in Francis, Burke and Read, 2014), such as race, class and gender, on students' behaviour and outcomes (for more on this, see the research team's article, Francis, Burke and Read, 2014). These statements made us reflect on how we can apply a sociological analysis and identify structural inequalities of gender, class and race; we are exercising our power in doing so. This illustrates the complex power dynamics at play in the project, as well as in writing this book about how our analysis is foregrounded. However, despite inequalities between researchers and researched regarding decisions about representation of voice and context, we also recognise that any reader of this book, or of other works from the projects, could use these publications in their own way to develop their own project (with frameworks that may differ). In this way, spaces of social justice/socially-just spaces in higher education can be cultivated, and research can become more equitable and participatory. Power always plays out in research and pedagogical relations, but recognising that, thinking through it and creating more equitable practices has the potential to bring about a sharing and potentially a transformation of knowledge and experience. It is about redistributing spaces that we are privileged to have and processes of engaging reflexively and about re/defining our practices to nuance them with social justice aspirations. PM allows for epistemological questions to be raised, such as whose forms of knowledge are privileged in the academy; as Sue Clegg (2011, p. 102) notes, 'the interest in including those who have been excluded from university in higher education, therefore, has an epistemic as well as social dimension. Different groups of students bring diverse life experiences and outsider knowledge that often shakes up an intellectual field. Clegg notes that this requires these students to have 'epistemic access to the curriculum' (Clegg, 2011, pp. 96–97).

These issues bring us back to the broader question: what is pedagogy for? It raises a post/structural critique of critical pedagogy – how do we deal with the way in which our choices indicate that we think our own values are better? These are questions that require us to draw upon critical studies around such issues as 'culture' (Harding, 1991; Bhabha, 1994; Hall and du Gay, 1996) and 'race' (Ladson-Billings, 1998; Delgado and Stefancic, 2000; Bonilla-Silva, 2003; Gillborn, 2005), including Critical Race Theory and Critical Whiteness Studies which disrupt hegemonic values, perceptions and, in particular, White supremacy. Furthermore, these questions require us to ask Carvalho's (2014, p. 102) important question, 'how far are my ideas understandable to readers from other parts of the world?' Carvalho concludes that 'from this question we can reach broader ones about the relevance of our theories and conclusions for all situations – in other words, on their universality'. Thus, generally, we can say that these issues require theory that is sensitive to context and which recognises the traps of uncritically universalising theory. Returning to our team's guiding principles as we explore these issues and questions helps us arrive at a place where we can draw a line in terms of how we understand our work in critical pedagogy. As Torres (2011, p. 180) says, there is a need for 'serious analytical and scientific work' since, 'after all, not all social constructions are equally powerful in their logical configuration, methodological rigour or solid empirical proof'. Indeed, the theoretical and methodological rigour with which we do so will ultimately distinguish the work.

Conclusion

The framework of PM that we have laid out above has discussed a number of methodological nuances. Here in the conclusion we want to highlight that PM requires practitioners to be thoroughly supported at a systemic, institutional, and personal level. It is important here to emphasise notions of sustainability around social justice praxis. For example, through the Fulbright, we have used the data from GaP in order to enable people in other national contexts to engage in some of the debates raised in the UK. The specific strategy of 'social justice networks', in this case, through the Paulo Freire Institutes (PFIs), was employed. The project led to the development of another network under the PFIs: the International Gender Network, discussed earlier. Within these networks, possibilities for capacity building, reciprocity, and funding are strengthened.

Research networks have also opened up opportunities for Gill and Penny Jane, who were invited to lead a number of workshops across the UK and internationally, around GaP. They have reached numerous other audiences through their *Teaching Inclusively* Continuing Professional Development resource (Burke and Crozier, 2013). Clegg (2014) used GaP as a case study in her Higher Education 7 Close-Up paper. Penny Jane has led the development of communities of praxis at University of Newcastle (Australia), which echo many of the themes of GaP. These are all examples of utilising (some high-profile) spaces to engage people in other ways of thinking around research. Through all of these sorts of activities we aim to sustain these frameworks as far as possible in order to develop resources for pedagogic encounters with those in the field interested in refining their practice in dialogue with research.

And even as we aspire to make a 'difference' by cultivating these spaces in which PM can be conducted, we must be aware that the practical can't always embrace all of the nuances raised by post/structural theory. Aspiration for making a difference and reality of what happens and what difference means in practical, grounded work may (and often do) vary greatly. Iterative reflection on the relationship between the concepts of PM and *research that makes a difference* is thus fundamental to the research processes.

Chapter 4

Diversity, difference, inequalities and pedagogical experiences

In this chapter, drawing on both the GaP and the Fulbright projects, we foreground the perspectives of the academic staff in considering their pedagogies and experiences as HE teachers within the context of widening participation together with issues of diversity and in/equalities. We look at the different pedagogic approaches teachers take and the various influences they feel impact on these. In relation to this we also explore the different subject disciplines that we researched and consider the internal and external dynamics that disciplinary cultures may have on discourses of pedagogy.

Immense changes have taken place in higher education in Britain (where the GaP project was located) over the past decade involving, in addition to the increased ethnic, social and gender diversity of the student body, the policy frameworks and expectations on academic staff and the requirements for them to adjust their practices and reorient their approach to their subject (Clegg, 2008). As well as the nature and style of governance and management orientation of HE, the question of the purpose of the university has been raised (see for example Collini, 2012). Indeed the purpose of higher education has taken on a narrow, more pragmatic, view of learning outcomes, focusing more on vocationalism and the employability of graduates (Mann, 2008; Clegg, 2015).

At Riverside there was an expectation that new members of staff undertake the then Higher Education Academy postgraduate higher education teaching qualification, which arguably provided some support to prepare for these changes but at the same time the teachers, in the GaP project, explained that the changes represent a significant departure from their own experience of HE. This may be a positive development, giving rise to creativity and critical engagement with change and a challenge to historical elitist practices but the changes also represent disruption and risk. We found from our interviews with participants that these changes present challenges, not only to the teachers' practice, but also to their identities as academics and subject specialists. In this chapter we explore how the teachers in our study negotiated this.

As we have indicated in Chapter one, the British Government is currently devising a framework for evaluating teaching in higher education (TEF). There are various speculations about the main purpose of this but one of our concerns relates to the impact that this initiative will have on HE pedagogies. As in all such evaluative measures, tight criteria are applied which tend to force the participants to adapt and change in order to meet these. This can have negative as well as potentially positive effects and consequences. Whilst the TEF was not an issue during the period of our research, other effecting conditions, such as the impact of marketisation, were apparent. For some teachers, these included the socially and ethnically diverse students themselves (perspectives about whom we will discuss below and also in later chapters). Many teachers already felt under surveillance, particularly regarding the need to 'keep the students happy' and achieve good teaching evaluations, as part of the pressure to ensure measurable indicators of 'the student experience', and some teachers spoke of the resources and teaching conditions and environment as impeding how they 'would really like to teach'.

The pedagogical methodology involved teachers and students re-examining some of the data as it emerged, which resulted in some disquiet amongst the academic staff when reading (anonymised) extracts of the GaP data of student experiences of their pedagogic practices. The data revealed a sense of disjuncture between the aims of their pedagogy, the tacit knowledge and assumptions, which underpinned their practice, and how these were experienced on the ground by students. Some academic staff appeared anxious about asking for advice and sharing concerns and seemed constrained by normalising discourses of academic identity which constructed what an academic should be, in ways which were felt to be sometimes marginalising.

As Ros Gill (2009) has said, in spite of the interest in reflexivity, the experiences of academics within the context of their institutions have been neglected. Following Gill, we also explore academic staff experiences and teaching within a context of neo-liberal discourses that increasingly heighten competitiveness and the focus on particular performativities. Alongside or possibly arising from this, in part, is the emergence of writings on the emotions and the emotionality of teaching and working in higher education.

The anxieties, lack of confidence and sense of pressure to perform in prescribed ways identified in our study, echo Gill's (2009) work. However, additionally in our project, a central concern is the widening participation agenda and how teachers' perspectives, attitudes and practice relate to BME and working-class students and learning/teaching experiences. We are also of course interested in the interrelation of gender within the expressed views, their practice and its impact. These are the key themes discussed in this chapter.

Constraints and collusion in pedagogical practices

Both the internal and external contexts of HE created competing and often contradictory demands on the teachers, which we found also challenged their pedagogic principles. The institutional focus on retention, student satisfaction and maintaining student numbers for example, led some academic staff to feel that their identity as an academic, intellectual leader or disciplinary expert was valued less. There was a sense that this had been displaced and challenged by an expectation that pedagogic practices should be more focused on support, more orientated towards meeting student learning needs in a pragmatic, functional way and 'keeping students happy'. Most staff found the drive-by external forces (Deem and Brehony, 2005) oppressive, whilst at the same time aiming to maintain their pedagogic principles and do what they felt was best in the interests of their students' learning needs. How they endeavoured to do this and were enabled to, was often in conflict. The perceived emphasis on 'looking after' the students seemed to stand in contrast to developing students' interest in intellectual pursuits and critical engagement, activities which can be challenging and unsettling to students; arguably all part of the learning process. They often felt an expectation on them to ensure emotional well-being and some likened this to a highly gendered description of 'mothering', 'babying' 'caring for' and so on (see Chapter six for a development of this analysis and the problematisation of the feminisation of HE discourse which these sentiments reflect). This is exacerbated by and in relation to, the perception that certain student identities as higher education learners are not fully formed – that there is some kind of deficit that teachers have to remedy.

> I feel because of retention rates and all these systems which are in place when you first . . . I am expected to be caring, more caring than I actually want to be.
>
> (Male lecturer, GaP project)

> I understand we have, to some extent, to spoon-feed them for the first year . . . but I feel that if I have to continue with that in the second and third year, I feel I am not doing my job as a lecturer.
>
> (Male lecturer, GaP project)

Although some blame is placed by the teachers on external policy changes and the institution itself, there is also a view that the student body is not capable of university-level work. As we see above some students are infantalised by staff and purportedly need to be 'mothered' and 'spoon-fed'. This view suggests that university students do not need to be 'cared for' as learners implying a more distant and even pragmatic philosophy of teaching. As others have also written (e.g. Morley, 2003) there is evidence that lecturers regard 'Widening Participation' (WP) students as different from the norm and there is an implication that they are 'not quite good enough'. Or according to the following lecturer, they are not very well equipped or prepared for university, and they often do not know what it is for:

> It's one of these bugbears I have, that students don't know what a university is, and what it's for, and what their role as a student is, and what our role is.

And they, the perception is it's a bit like school, but not quite, so they come with a certain attitude.

(Female lecturer, GaP project)

Similar views emerged in the Fulbright study. This Spanish lecturer for example commented that: students' lack of prior 'appropriate' preparation has implications for how she and her colleagues can teach:

. . . it's . . . like "okay, can't discuss this because you don't have the background knowledge that you'd need because the ideology – the way that you've been taught before – has cut out all of these other possible ways of looking at it, and if you don't have knowledge of these other possible ways of looking at it, we can't begin to discuss the points that we're supposed to cover in this class.". . . . What do you do [if they don't come into the course with the required prerequisite knowledge]? You can't just start in with the course materials. No, . . . you have to start all over.

(Female lecturer [pre-PhD], Fulbright project, Spain)

Amongst some of the teachers there appeared to be a sense of irritation that not all students were of the type they had come to expect. The Spanish teacher complained that she had to change the way she teaches – she had to spend *"the whole summer constructing how I was going to give the class"*. The emphasis and expectation is on the student to adapt and conform; this is resonant of the view that the student is responsible for her/his own failure or inadequacy.

The lecturers expressed a concern with the ways multiple expectations and demands, including wider policy discourses about teaching in HE, as well as their pedagogic practices, amongst other sets of issues, contributed to the instrumental approach to learning they described students engaged in. It became clear that lecturers were often faced with complex and competing situations, which in turn led them at times to decisions about which they were unsure or unhappy. Some expressed a concern that they might be complicit in a pedagogic practice that positioned the students as passive recipients of higher education teaching:

. . . we are giving them too much and so therefore they don't feel they need to listen, and they don't feel they need to engage, because they know they are getting it all anyway.

(Male lecturer, GaP project)

There's something about some courses that's feeding into that passivity, this kind of "I'll just stand at the front and talk and you'll just listen".

(Female lecturer, England)

Others expressed a sense of frustration that they were being thwarted or constrained in fulfilling their role as lecturers and that the university needs to have clearer expectations, explanations and communication strategies:

> I mean there should be a culture . . . from the first year, and expectation from the first year and second year, and second and third year, and that message should be given to the student, you know, they are here, to some extent to learn, some, most of the learning, you know, through their time period in the first year, is to some extent part of that independent study. When I give a lecture, one hour, two hours, that is not the end of the story. You expect, the university expects, as well in terms of their policy and obligation, is to do for every two hours maybe another five hours or six hours that they have to do outside there. They don't do that, you know.
>
> (Female teacher, GaP project)

Some of the Fulbright participants also expressed a disjuncture between students' pedagogical expectations and their own, including in terms of engagement, and the balance of how and what theory/practice is incorporated within the classroom:

> I'll comment on . . . the constant resistance in the classroom to revisions and self-critique – to thinking by the students due to the 'non formal' education (on TV, out on the streets, etc.) they continued to be more used to information that's very processed. That they don't need to think about. So this topic (gender), if you do it well, or even if you do it poorly, it makes them have to think and look inside themselves. So it's there that there's resistance. A very big resistance. More likely with the guys because this [need to] look inside themselves [and] critique themselves as guys who are treating their sisters poorly . . etc. . . . so maybe the guys are more scared of those topics because of this. But generally there's a resistance in all of the topics that let's say [require] critical reflection and this topic is one that there's a lot of self-reflection in.
>
> (Female associate professor, Fulbright project, Spain)

> . . . Some of the students tell us, like "I didn't like this part" or "this was too hard to follow" and stuff like that, but usually they complain about the theoretical part. Like "this lesson . . . we had too much theory. We wanted to do something" because when you show them that there is another way of learning things that is not only theoretical or just lecture in front of the class, they tend to ask for direct engagement. So whenever you try to go back to theoretical and lecture, they say, "Ok, why? I mean, we want the other."
>
> (Male lecturer [pre-PhD], Fulbright project, Italy)

Although, in the GaP project, teachers indicated reflexivity at times, the outcome was often inappropriate or reinforced negative constructions of the 'Other'. There was a tendency to lower expectations; reference to 'our kind of students' and little recognition of the need for enculturation (although this in itself is not without its problems).

The student associated with WP and the challenges they face in higher education are often linked to the discourse of emotion. The emotionality of learning is frequently dismissed and disparaged, implying that the 'emotional learner' is somehow inadequate and inferior. However, there is a growing body of research that points to the significance of the psychosocial in the learning process (e.g. Leathwood and Hey, 2009). The 'fitting in and belonging' thesis is associated with these discourses together with the importance of students' confidence in the learning context that they need to feel a strong sense of identification with the learning context they are situated in. However, we suggest it needs to be recognised that it is the responsibility of the university (in terms of the organisation, ethos and pedagogic practices) to make changes in order to develop an inclusive environment conducive to learning by all its students. As we see from the above, the opposite view prevails.

The issues of identity and performativity discussed above impact on any approach that may appear to be risk-taking. As Ball (2012) observed:

> [N]eoliberalism gets into our minds and our souls, into the ways in which we think about what we do, and into our social relations with others. It is about how we relate to our students and our colleagues and our participation in new courses and forms of pedagogy and our "knowledge production", but it is also about our flexibility, malleability, innovation and productivity in relation to these things. Knowledge has its price.
>
> (p. 18)

The neo-liberal ethos and regulatory discourses seemed to cause teacher confusion and destabilise their practice or principles, leading to a loss of the sense of meaning in what they do (Ball, 2012). Hence, for example, even though teachers were often clearly frustrated that students seemed unable or reluctant to engage critically with academic knowledge, many seemed to find it difficult themselves to employ a range of pedagogic practices that could engage students more fully. Much of their practice involved more 'teacher talk' than student participation. And in many cases student interaction was fairly limited with students remaining quiet. Although many teachers were reflexive about their approaches and critical of unequal power relations, at least in relation to gender and their own role as the teacher, this did not tend to translate directly into inclusive practices.

As Ball goes on to say, one of the impacts of performativity is to reorient the teacher's pedagogy to something that is clearly measureable (Ball, 2012). Ensuring a positive student evaluation at the end of a module is one such key driver (Gill, 2009). Having the knowledge and expertise to change practice is another factor and the more prosaic but nonetheless salient aspects of class size, facilities, room space and time-table slot are all important considerations, all of which the teachers whom we interviewed at Riverside referred to. Inappropriate rooms were a particular concern; the learning space represents a signifier of the value of learning and arguably of the student and teacher. Inadequate or poor rooms suggest a lack of respect and recognition. One teacher, for example, complained that they sometimes had to teach in the chapel and another lamented that:

> I am forced to teach in a space with a little kitchen in it. It's a bit of a junk room. We started in a good room but now squashed in with 30 people and a kitchen and it's not good. Students do get up and use the kitchen during the session.

Clegg (2008) points out the contradiction between international governments driven by global competitiveness and the desire to produce employable and flexible graduates, whilst at the same time they are de-investing in the unit of resource as well as student support.

Moreover, increased student numbers leading to larger class size and or increased teaching loads, leads to less contact with students and the exacerbation of distancing and thus less opportunity to get to know students as individuals and discern their specific needs (Mann, 2008). Arguably where the student body is increasingly diverse socially and ethnically, from the teachers, the need to develop this knowledge and these relationships is all the greater. Whilst teachers referred to 'our kind of students' and gender at times, there were few references specifically to the social class composition of the students and to race or ethnicity from White teachers, as social dimensions and equity concerns that might inform their pedagogy. By contrast the two Black teachers we interviewed spoke about themselves as Black academics and how this had varying effects on the Black, and in one case White, students. Sarah Mann (2005) argues engaging students is not simply concerned with making them feel at ease; she goes on to say that developing communication within the learning environment, rather than a community of practice or focusing on belonging in a learning community, is more important. We take a less polarised view since identification with the learning context and the need for teachers to enable this is part of the pedagogic endeavour to develop better communications. But communication is not simply about giving an explanation or conveying an idea; it is as much if not more about the embedded and implicit nature of that knowledge and the powerful processes that structure teaching. The knowledge has to be 'worth' engaging with; students need to relate to what is taught or otherwise the learning process will be reduced to a perfunctory, surface level, technicist process of learning to pass the course assessment. One of the Black teachers we interviewed talked of an interaction with her group of Black and White students which depicts the importance of meaningful knowledge and ideas but also how existing perspectives and beliefs, and in this case racialised discourses, are brought into the learning space and influence the dynamics. This underlines the importance of teachers thinking through the implications of their practice but also having knowledge of such issues and some kind of support for developing inclusive and robust practice:

> At some point, just because of my personality, it becomes clear across the term that I'm Jamaican, in particular. And as a personality I do identify myself as Black, because I'm aware that some people don't know that I am, it just kind of comes out at some point along the way. But I find then that Black students will particularly align with me. And so there is a dynamic within the group, and it's the subtlest, subtlest thing in the world, often, but one has to be very careful that there is no perception from the whole group that somehow I am showing any favouritism, or any kind of extra layer of understanding, or even mummydom to the Black students in par-ticular. I remember one particular case, we were talking about something we were talking about in life writing, called social languages, just essentially the different positionality of people depending on what kinds of dynamics and who they are and how they meet the world. And people were identify-ing social languages, and a group of Black students had gotten together, and they were identifying social languages that I knew, so I went across and went oh, that's my grandmother, and we all dropped into a different social language around me. And then I became aware of a silence around me, and I looked up, and the larger group of students were all going . . . and looked very unhappy.
>
> I said "hello", what's happening? What is everybody feeling, what's going on? And they were brave enough to say we suddenly thought you had some-thing in common with them that we don't have in common.
>
> And I said oh, that's what happens to people, that's the power of social languages.
>
> I just dropped into my grandma's social language, which they share as well, and what did you suddenly feel? You felt left out, didn't you? And so then we could all come together as students and have another conversation. But I did have a moment of oh, shit, what do I do with this dynamic? Because it is true that I felt on some level closer, but it was a perfect situation.
>
> (Female teacher, GaP project)

This teacher, who identified as Black, had experiences that had resonance with some of the Black students. She responded to this and exploited it for pedagogic purposes. From her account the emerging issues and situation gave rise to some meaningful engagement both positive and potentially negative: lived experiences drawn on to discuss theoretical ideas. She was also sensitive to the White stu-dents' reaction and in turn utilised the themes embedded in this scenario to engage all of the students in the group.

This kind of approach and its value is difficult to 'measure' and is potentially risky. Failure to engage the students makes blaming the students themselves as a more plausible and 'safer' explanation. So often in teachers' accounts of the 'WP subject', ambiguity about his or her authenticity as a university student tended to dominate their perspectives and understanding of the students. In relation to this, the issue of powerful knowledge and knowledge that is owned by the teacher, but not or not yet the student, can render the student silent and afraid. According to the teachers interviewed, students frequently did not contribute to discussions and did not question or challenge. Such silences were regarded as an indicator of a lack of engagement, disinterest, or 'inability' and were seen as representing the passivity of the students. Teachers expressed anxiety about the silence in seminar sessions and the powerful positioning of the teacher in controlling discussion, which in turn often exacerbated the silence. Overall, the responsibility for the lack of participation was seen as lying with the student. Teachers were often aware of the contradictions in what they did and what they expected but there is a sense that they felt faced with an impossible task to motivate the students:

> Actually my experience is thinking about the power dynamics in business studies as well because . . . I don't think any of us would think we have to go in and manage that space because as a lecturer it's not about allowing silences and not allowing silence and telling them when they can speak and when they can't. But there is that dynamic about independent learning and reflective learning – probably you go into a situation and you are the manager, if you have power.
>
> (Male teacher; focus group interview, GaP project)

Teachers' constructions of students as passive did not remain there: teachers also had a concept of the 'good' student. The good student, as Grant (1997) suggests, is what the global and, as she says, 'enterprising' university seeks to develop; the good student is necessary in order to achieve the ambitions of the global/globally competitive university. Conversely, according to Williams (1997), the binary opposite is seemingly the 'bad' student or the 'non-standard', 'non-traditional' student. The 'good' student, Grant argues, is a cultural construction and for some this 'idea' is impossible or undesirable from their perspective, for them to become. Those students regarded as lacking confidence, dependent, anxious or troublesome, in other words not 'good' students, were frequently working class, both BME and male, especially when regarded as troublesome, and female. In a focus group interview one of the teachers described noisy and disruptive Black male students who sat at the back of the lecture theatre, at times arriving late:

> [W]e've got your classic middle-class blokes who performed very well in school, they are quite sporty, they are quite middle-class, quite confident, all of that, they are generally the rugby team. And then we have the footballers

who are a mixture of White and Black, and they are a bit "alright love" . . . you know, and they mix together, and then we've got the Black boys who sit at the back, and they are, without question, giving the impression of being . . . it's going to be uncool, kind of falling asleep. A number of them are incredibly talented, but it's not cool to show that talent. . . .

. . . so they are the dudes, they are down the back, they are coming in late, they are slouching in their seat, and I do quite a lot to engage them, and I've even said to them if you sit up I won't pick on you, but if you slouch like that I will pick on you to make sure you don't fall asleep in my class and things, to try to get them to engage and things. If you try and mix the groups they don't like that at all, they just, they have formed their groups.

(Female teacher, GaP project)

In the same group interview another teacher who had previously taught at a Russell Group University, expressed disquiet at the students at Riverside and also made negative comments about the Black students. In one of his teaching groups of first year students, 70% were Black men. This seemed to be a shock in itself to him:

Race and ethnicity is all that identifies them. I am intimidated by the group of Black boys (sic) at the back. Having the bravery to go back and break up [the talking] that is very difficult. The problem is more that they are Black. And they are at level 1. . . . One or two students arrive 30 minutes late all the time. If you ask them they say they are late and make no apology.

[There are] problems of attendance. We write a letter but they still don't come. If they have to submit a piece of coursework for another module they don't turn up to the lectures that are not having that assessment.

At X [Russell Group University] the writing skills were better. The quality is better. At [another traditional university, where he also worked] there were mainly White middle class blokes but here you have to say WHOAH! I have to think about this. Black lower class blokes here. It's a completely different management style.

(Male teacher, GaP project)

Whilst voice was often seen as the key indicator of participation, here we see that some voices are less welcome. Language is a mechanism of power and in the university it is a 'polished' language that has to be adapted to in order to succeed (Bourdieu, Passeron and De Saint Martin, 1994). In capitalist society it reflects individual's relational position in the field (in the Bourdieusian sense) and it determines who has a right to be interrupted, ask questions, be listened to (Crozier, Burke and Archer, 2016). The Black male students are not complying with the behaviour of the good student and seemingly they have not adapted to using 'the polished language'. They are also not given the respect of being fully fledged adults but rather are described as 'boys' which in the USA, for example, has historical racist connotations. It is the students who are blamed for their lack of engagement, but these Black male students are not positioned simply as passive, but on the contrary, they are perceived here as the 'dangerous' Other. Nirmal Puwar (2004) describes the Black presence in *White spaces as 'space invaders': Black bodies out of place*. She goes on to say:

> They have entered spaces where their bodies are neither historically or conceptually the "norm". For those whom the whiteness of these spaces provides a comforting familiarity, the arrival of racialised members can represent the monstrous. . . .They threaten the status quo.
>
> (p. 50–51)

It is notable that the teacher says in order to teach these students a different management style is required rather than a different pedagogic style. The Black students need to be controlled.

As we have said the teachers are also caught up in regulatory discourses, and thus they are compelled it seems, to take up a position as controller of student voice and student behaviour, suggesting explicit forms of power in teaching in HE and different levels of class, race and gender consciousness. Some teachers expressed awareness of the complexities of unequal power relations. Anxiety, fear of risky situations and experiences, and uncertainty, are pervasive themes amongst the teachers but also the students. In the students' accounts, which will be discussed more fully in the next chapters, significant levels of anxiety were raised in relation to giving voice in the classroom space, blaming fellow students as much as teachers. Seminar contexts, and specific expectations of students within this context, created uncomfortable and disempowering spaces.

Academic identities, disciplinary differences and practices

In spite of these expressed views and doubts, a more complex relationship to the students manifested itself. Teachers' views comprised both negative and positive perceptions; sometimes held simultaneously and in tension with each other. Some individuals, for example, expressed the benefits of working with a diverse student body:

> The fact that you have a kind of range of age groups often, in the class, people from different social backgrounds and so on can be quite an advantage. . . . And increasingly I've found that I absent myself from discussions in seminars, either not talking or actually just going off.
>
> (Male lecturer, GaP project)

Others discussed the pedagogic practices they developed to create a productive and engaging learning environment.

> I would like to push the students more and unattach myself.
>
> (Female lecturer, GaP project)

> When the technology breaks down . . . you just have to give an ad-libbed 50-minute lecture, it turns out the students really like that.
>
> (Male lecturer, GaP project)

One lecturer talked about an elaborate process of peer assessment of student presentations that he had instigated and how he could see its efficacy through the engagement of students who hitherto had been reticent or silent. In these reflections lecturers expressed a sense of excitement and creativity about their pedagogy particularly when they could see the students' intellectual development.

Some disciplinary subjects facilitated close relationships with students partly because of 'class size' but also perhaps because of the way that the discipline was perceived and the identification that arises or was promoted (by the teachers) through this. As we know disciplinary subjects in Western society at least, are hierarchised with some such as philosophy, history and literature being highly valued and interdisciplinary and vocational subjects being less so (Bourdieu, Passeron and De Saint Martin, 1994; Bernstein, 2000). In one of our observations of a Classics/History lecture, we observed the lecturer spending time displaying her status within the disciplinary field and the importance of knowing and associating with other internationally recognised Classics/History academics. She aimed to involve her students in this culture encouraging them to write for a journal which she edits and she had arranged a visit to a conference/workshop where the students were able to meet and interact with these internationally known scholars. This strategy is a mechanism, we suggest, of enculturation and 'educational cultivation' (Lareau, 2003) to engender identity (with the discipline) as well as cultural capital. This has privileging implications for students but also as we are suggesting here, for academics.

The disciplinary subjects were seen to influence the identity of the teachers often presenting different emphases in what is regarded as important and indicating their view of their role as university teachers. This in turn appears to influence or be reflected in their pedagogy. History and Classics is quite varied in terms of the kinds of identities the lecturers construct and practices they reflect on in the focus groups. They present themselves as highly academic, which in a sense is reflected in the example above. Unsurprisingly therefore, the teachers responded to the discourses of student deficit as posing a major problem for their pedagogical practices.

Creative Writing lecturers tended to construct themselves primarily as 'writers' rather than 'teachers' or 'academics', although they claimed that their students wanted them primarily to be 'teachers':

> It's kind of they need to know that we are writers who, because they also talk about that, how they are convinced by us, because they know that we are writers. But they don't want that to be the kind of primary way that we have a relationship.
>
> (Female teacher, GaP project)

They talked about being misunderstood in the institution and as misrecognised by others as being English Literature's poor, un-academic cousin. However, some teachers expressed a rejection of the identity of 'an academic' because it detracts from the salience of teaching and because of the pressures it seems to entail. These sentiments were expressed in the following focus group interview for the GaP project:

FL1:   I think of myself as an accidental academic.

FL2:   Yes, me too.

FL3:   I refuse to define myself as an academic. The day that I say I'm an academic . . .

FL2:   I never tell people I'm an academic.

FL3:   . . . feels like I will have lost the battle, I will have lost the balance in my life. However I did find myself the last couple of days, last couple of years, you know, you sit next to somebody on a plane and they ask you what you do, and the other day I heard myself saying I'm a teacher. I thought no, no, no, no, that's horrible.

FL2:   Because I feel, you know, on the research, that I'm a disappointment to them, I don't, I am not an academic, because I am not.

FL1:   You are not doing academic things.

FL2:   I'm a lecturer, I'm a teacher, fine.

FL1:   I suppose that's what I mean when I say I am an academic. I mean some people put teachers in university, that's kind of really what I mean by that.

> (GaP staff focus group discussion; FL = female lecturer)

A conflict is being expressed here over the teachers' value of teaching in that to describe yourself as a teacher is, or is perhaps perceived as, undermining one's status or value as an 'academic'. There may also be some significance here that creative subjects are not as highly valued in the pecking order of subject hierarchies.

In their focus group interview they placed significant emphasis on the emotional side of learning and teaching. At times their gaze becomes very introspective and they seem to situate themselves at the centre of their teaching, although they claim to embrace student-centred pedagogies. There is a lot of talk around being creative with and within the space in which they teach. For example:

> . . . when they are writing, so there are periods of times, this is not when there is a formal lecture, but I've asked them to write something, I've also given them the opportunity to leave the room if they want to. Or I say to people, provided there are no health and safety issues, you can lie on the floor if you like. I've done so to give them permission to do so. You know, I've sat on the floor and said I am going to do the exercise with you, this is my easiest position to write, you can get into yours, so long as you are not getting in anyone else's way or whatever.
>
> (Female teacher, GaP project)

By contrast, Sports Science teachers position themselves as science academics, beset by the problems of students who do not appreciate the scientific nature of the discipline. They strongly position themselves as researchers who teach.

> I think there is an enormous pressure on us to become school teachers, and we can't be school teachers and researchers and administrators and all of those sort of things, and I think it would be a disaster if you became a teacher, and other people were researchers. We are very lucky in this university that that doesn't happen, that the researchers are teachers, and we are expected to bring our research into our teaching, and our teaching into our research.
>
> (Female teacher, GaP project)

They also express though, a sense of being beleaguered by institutional demands as well as by the constant changes in the institution. There is much talk of the institution as some powerful and fairly malign force that makes unreasonable demands on them. They strive towards an ideal of collegiality as well as becoming 'more effective' teachers, but feel that the pace of change and overall institutional environment constrains these aspirations. They are conscious about the impact their approaches will have on the students, but do not have the time to pursue this and, when they do, express their frustration that the students seem to just want 'spoon feeding' rather than being encouraged towards independent learning. The deficit discourse of recalcitrant (male and BME) students and the WP student who is 'underprepared' for university education, is very strong amongst this group of teachers.

> When I started lecturing, as I said, you could assume that they'd get it, and now we have to work so hard, and we do some students an enormous disservice, because I'm standing up there telling them that F equals mass times acceleration, means if you know the force, and you know the mass, you can

work out the acceleration, this is how you do that maths. And there are people there just thinking this is ridiculous, I knew this when I was twelve. And then there are people there going I don't know what she's doing. I have no idea, there are numbers flying around on the board and they might as well be airplanes, I have no clue, you know. And so that's what I have found, I feel that I am being pulled in a number of different directions, and I'm pulling myself in a number of different directions. And I don't want you to think that I just stand up there and don't reflect, I do reflect, and often my reflection puts me into such a spin of crisis that the best thing to do is to stop reflecting and to just keep going, until, also until it's all settled, but it will never settle, because it's like everything around, you know, it goes around in cycles doesn't it?

(Female teacher, GaP Project)

Teachers of Dance, also a creative subject, did not indicate the self-consciousness or feelings of misrecognition experienced by the creative writers. Dance teachers embraced the insights of critical pedagogy (Freire, 1970) and attempted to put these into practice. Their identities as teachers are invested in critical pedagogical approaches. In drawing on such insights, the lecturers have a strong sense of the relationship between identity and pedagogy, and talked about the relationship between their own personal histories and perspectives and their pedagogical practices:

In dance we have a lot of assumptions about what dancers are, and their relationship with their teacher, and it used to be a very matriarchal kind of world, the training world, and for us to be in academia there was a lot of thinking, clinical thinking around our roles, so we don't necessarily want to think of ourselves as mothers, teachers, in that sense. But there are moments where I think it is important to consider my biography, and the biography of my students, and I have found that these are the moments you take a risk, you might make a link that might motivate the student, might make them more aware of themselves and their own relationships, but I have also felt that there is a risk there, there is a risk for me, maybe, you know, not having boundaries as a, pedagogical boundaries and professional boundaries, maybe imposing my own understanding of what motherhood, what independence is. But I definitely think that there is, the two should be explored, and they come up organically in class, in conversations, and yeah, that's a recent experience that we had.

(Female teacher, GaP Project)

In conducting the observations, it was notable that Dance as a disciplinary framework presented opportunities, not visible or as visible in other subjects, for the lecturers to teach differently in higher education spaces, and the critical pedagogic framework that shaped the Dance team's approaches supported this. For example, the students were invited to lead different sections of their session and were encouraged to engage in reflexive discussions. Furthermore, the physical space, which included a spacious dance floor, provided a symbolic openness in which the dance students positioned their bodies through movement across space and this disrupted any hierarchical positioning of either the students or the two dance teachers. When the dance teachers presented ideas, they did this in short bursts, then opened up to the whole group for student contributions to develop and build on these ideas. The students observed were all female and White but they were physically and generationally diverse, displaying different levels of dance technique, without any sense of hierarchical ordering. This provided an overall sense of inclusion and of encouragement to creatively express individual differences in what appeared to be a supportive environment.

However, not all teachers held strong identifications with their discipline or perhaps it was a lack of identification with their subject team. Some spoke repeatedly about feeling isolated and having to work alone and how these individualised approaches to pedagogic practice were at odds with the collaborative discourses, which underpinned the design of their degree programmes. Some members of the programme team felt that a solitary and competitive existence lay at the centre of the identity as a researcher in academia. A number of staff described the isolation experienced because of the way teaching and research was organised. Far from feeling part of a disciplinary or pedagogic community and perhaps developing an identity from shared practices and dialogue, one young female member of staff described her existence as solitary and described her work as causing her to feel as though she was 'in a cage . . . '. The respondent described the 'professional bubble' she had created within which she worked with her students in order to 'survive'.

Conclusion

The teachers' accounts expressed contradictory sensibilities about professional and academic identities in higher education. These are framed by wider regulatory discourses of what is expected of an academic in contemporary higher education, mediated by the subject or disciplinary area. The individual academic is caught up in the complex sets of competing demands and expectations of the specific disciplinary context, the overarching and standardising frameworks of research excellence and quality assurance and the ethos, missions and strategic plans of the institution. This affects all academics but in different ways in a highly stratified and competitive sector.

Pedagogic practices of teachers were significantly shaped and constrained by such discourses as well as university systems, strategies and procedures. Some teachers were anxious to admit that they needed advice as though this did not fit with what being an academic 'should be'. The accounts of academic staff raise questions about the possibilities of achieving student-centred pedagogy and enhancing the engagement and learning experience of students who in many cases appear to remain marginalised from the university experience and learning community. They also raise questions about the deficit – racialised, classed and gendered – discourses and the effects of these on the students. In the following chapter we will explore these themes focusing on the perspectives and experiences of the students.

Chapter 5

Pedagogical identity formations

Student perspectives

This and the following two chapters draw on the GaP data to explore the accounts and perspectives of students about their pedagogic identities and the influences on these in their university. Similar to the academic staff discussed in the previous chapter, the students' identity formations and experiences are framed by wider regulatory discourses of what is expected of them in contemporary higher education, mediated by the subject or disciplinary area. The individual is caught up in the complex sets of competing demands and expectations of the specific disciplinary context, the overarching and standardising frameworks of academic and research excellence and quality assurance, and the ethos, missions and strategic plans of different institutions with unequal status. This affects all academics and students but in different ways in a highly stratified and competitive sector. Whilst we take an intersectional approach in our analysis, in this chapter we foreground social class and consider different perspectives across the different class locations as well as recognising the intersections of 'race' and gender. We draw on the ideas of Bourdieu and Bernstein to make sense of how social class plays out and shapes pedagogical identities and experiences. In Chapter six we foreground gender and in Chapter seven 'race'.

As we have seen, students associated with widening participation (WP) policies are often labelled as inadequate and or unready for university study. In this chapter we explore their experiences of university through their accounts, perspectives and choices. Identity is about the self and as Sibley (1995) argues the construction of the self involves social, cultural and spatial contexts. Although we take the view that the students arrive at the university with varying amounts of experience, resources or volume of habitus and capitals in the Bourdieusian sense, these are only effective resources if they mesh with the 'field' they find themselves in. In other words identity formations are constrained by interweaving social, material and structural inequalities (Reay, 2009). In this chapter we explore this interweaving in relation to the students' identity formations and the implications for their university experiences. We also, together with others (Crozier and Reay, 2008; Reay, 2009), identify both the differences but also interconnectedness between social and learner identities. The key themes that we address in this chapter include: encountering the university – students' expectations and the expectations on them; space and place, pedagogical relations and geographies of exclusion;[1] and pedagogies of in/exclusion: power, identities, practices and constraints.

University students' expectations and the expectations on them

Students with poor school experiences (most often working-class and Black and Minority Ethnic students) in the English context where the GaP research was located, frequently come to university with vulnerable learner identities (Crozier, Reay and Clayton, 2009) not because of some deficiency but because the university, whilst opening up access, has failed to change its narrow exclusionary and often elitist value positions and practices. Students from working-class and BME backgrounds have to struggle to assert their authenticity and their right to be at university at all, often struggling with their own perceptions of their learner identity; these students, together with female students, are faced with further issues of, for example, exclusion, stereotyping and discrimination (Leathwood, 2006). Policy has neglected to give attention to the experiences of students once at university in spite of the rhetoric of 'the student experience', which is putatively addressed through the questionable British National Student Survey (Harvey, 2008; Swain, 2009) There is, however, growing research evidence which demonstrates that there are too many taken-for-granted assumptions made of students on first coming to university and the nature and implications of the transition are poorly, if at all, addressed. We also have found that across class locations, students were often daunted with how to perform as 'a university student' and often had little idea of what to do, what cues to look out for or, more implicitly, what Bernstein (2000) called the *recognition and realisation rules*. Bernstein explained that recognition rules are the means by which individuals are able to recognise the particularities of the context and 'recognition rules relate to power relations' (2000, p. 17). He gives the example of a seminar where members who share an understanding – have acquired the recognition rules – of the context compared to those who do not. Those who do not either remain silent or make what might be regarded as inappropriate contributions, talk and behaviours. A key element, together with power relations, is 'classification': the means by which the recognition rules are controlled and directed. The realisation rules are the mechanisms by which the recognition rules can be operationalised; whilst the individual may have the recognition rules – can recognise the power relations and their position in relation to these, but if they do not have the realisation rules then they will not be able to engage, or speak, 'the expected legitimate text' (p. 17). Students' silence, which teachers lamented, and which we discuss in Chapter six, is a key indicator of this. On first going to university, students reported apprehension and fear. Whilst this is the case for most students irrespective of class, in their accounts the working-class students indicate a recognition of this experience as being outside of anything they have had previously and also a strong sense of discomfort about how to behave:

> I thought it'd be like scary at first, like meeting like other people. Just like different cultures as well and like meeting older people. Oh yeah I just found it really nerve racking but I thought it would be like [beneficial] to get a higher education [degree] and just mix and probably help me grow up more.
>   Yeah at first it was like, it's like really hard to go up and talk to people but yeah soon as I started meeting people it's like, it got easier.
>
> (Elizabeth, working-class, female student)

> Well, yeah, I think the combination of nervous and excited, because I was excited at the prospect of actually going to university, because being the only one in my family to go there, but also nervous because, you know, English is not my first language, and the most challenging thing that I'd had to do was the language.
>
> (Sameera, BME, working-class, female student)

> Totally, totally different to college. Totally to where I thought "oh am I going to be able to do this?" I was really hit hard in that, how can I explain it. In college the teachers are much more understandable straight away. Just the way they come across to you and stuff.
>
> (Ayesha, mature student, mixed race,
> working-class, female student)

We sense students' feelings of self-doubt about whether they are capable of actually 'doing it' but also a determination to prove themselves. The contrast with college expressed by Ayesha was a theme recounted by other students. College teachers seemed to be more approachable and connected to their students. This relates to the teachers' accounts in Chapter four where they were on the one hand sceptical of the students' ability to develop independent learning skills and on the other concerned that they were too indulgent of the students, giving them too much 'care' and possibly preventing the development of independent learning. This clearly has implications for the learning experience and perhaps also the generation of student confidence and reassurance that they are 'able'. It indicates a transitional issue and the emphasis on individual and independent learning, which Leathwood (2006) has critiqued as inappropriate for students unfamiliar with university practices. On describing their initial responses to the academic encounters this dislocation with the university teachers, which in turn the students interpret as a reflection of their own inadequacy, stimulates further anxieties:

> And then when I came to uni I sat – I'll never forget it – I sat in – is it the [Name of Building] – sorry – in the big room there and I was thinking,

"what is this lecturer going on about. I'm just going to have to write some of these words down and check what they mean." Sort of thing. . . . Not just the subject. I think just generally most lecturers – not all of them – but quite a lot of them instead of just plain simply speaking, they come out with these words and you think "oh, you know". And then when you realise it meant whatever it meant well why didn't they just say that? I did find that in my first year definitely. And it was very daunting. But you know I stuck at it and now it's, it's helped me so much more with my vocabulary, just so many different areas not just my course. It's opened my mind in a way that I never thought I could open it, just by coming to uni. For me anyway.

(Ayesha, mature student, mixed race,
working-class, female student)

I thought actually the university wasn't going to be this hard, because the access course to higher education that I did before was basically a crash course, two years in one. So I thought the difference between university and that course, you know, which was basically A Levels, I did them in one year, I thought it wasn't going to be that much of a difference, but it kind of was.

(Sameera, female BME, working-class student)

I think at first it seemed like kind of harder 'cause there was quite a lot of subjects all like in first year. Yeah it steadily got harder like the final year is quite hard. . . . I think it's a bit harder than what I expected it would be.

. . . No I didn't really know about how the teachers speak as well. Just quite like more intellectual like and I didn't understand at first some of the words. I'm getting more used to it now . . . it's quite different from high school. . . . I found [submitting a piece of written work] really nerve racking as well – will it be up to standard? And hitting the deadline and the words and everything. Quite scary.

(Elizabeth, White, working-class,
female student)

There are experiences here that overwhelm and undermine the students. The actual space – 'that big room' seemed to intimidate in a building the name of which she couldn't pronounce (and nor could one of us!). This perception together with an abundance of subjects and the language (and others referred to different accents) and some students spoke English as an additional language, underlines the disjunction between what the students bring to their studies and how the pedagogy is presented. It conspired to make the students feel estranged as though they did not belong.

By contrast, middle-class students tend to start their university with the self-belief that going to university is their destiny. This confidence contributes to the resources they tend to have to navigate and negotiate their way through university.

> It was always a thing that I felt like I had to do like my parents had said "well obviously after college, you'll go to university and stuff". So it was a natural thing – I'm the first born out of me and my sister and it just sort of seemed like a natural thing that would happen and I think I would have felt a little bit uncertain with things if I had just left and worked in the big old world straight after school or college. So I think I felt a little bit secure if I went to university 'cause I was still in like education.
>
> (Christopher, male, middle-class student)

> . . . I was like uh uh university. I don't know what it's like. You know but um I found first year quite easy to be honest. I mean the transition from sixth form to first year was OK. I remember the first sort of welcoming we had was daunting. I remember them saying "you've got deadlines. You've got to meet the deadlines". You know it was an information overload. But after that, first year just flew through to be honest. No I wasn't [daunted by the first year assessments]. . . . But year one I don't think I even did it. I probably did it the last minute, the night before. I don't do things like that anymore. So I really wasn't much bothered with year one to be honest.
>
> (Petra, middle-class, female student)

Middle-class students were also more likely to have undertaken preparations for university either through school or through their parents' experiences of HE (Crozier and Reay, 2010) and the additional activities, what we might call 'concerted cultivation' (Lareau, 2003), providing cultural, experiential and social enrichment as Michael explained:

> Most people did a gap year. I did it [Majorca, Spain] and it just makes you grow up a little bit more. . . . I worked for a bit and I went away and I played a bit of tennis abroad as well. I'm really like quite good at tennis. But I would suggest to anyone if they weren't really focussed on going in the first year, I would tell them to get a gap year and do a job or travel a little bit; get a little bit more maturity, it does help. Whereas I think most 18 year olds they go in thinking it's a little bit of a joke. But in fact you are paying like now £9000 a [year] for it.

These experiences show stark contrasts in experiences and resources with, for example, Ayesha who went to college in the evening after a day's work and looking after her children, in order to complete her Access course to gain a place at university. For the middle-class students their experiences at the outset of their university journey, give advantage and position them as the 'good' student, ensuring that they are recognised as the authentic student. The middle-class student is more likely to ensure a smoother transition to university where their fit between their school/home and university is relatively smooth, enabling a greater likelihood of identification of and operationalisation of 'the rules of the game' (Bourdieu, 1990).

Social class is not the only influence on managing this transition and impacting on student identities. Students with disabilities were faced with particular challenges and anxieties. Agda a student from a middle-class background has dyslexia and her start to her studies undermined her confidence:

> In general I feel it's a little bit hard at times to improve like I mean I know that I'm better now than I was at the start of course – if I wouldn't then there would be no point in doing this. But I feel I could improve more if things were a little bit different maybe. I dunno. But I think it's also down to me and maybe – the thing is I get really stressed so I don't feel like I have time to do a lot of extra work. Like now I'm seeing my dyslexia teacher after I get out of this and I brought all the like old feedback so I can go through that and just see what I can work on. So I think in a way it's down to me as well.
>
> (Agda, White, middle-class, international, female student)

Another student who was a mature student explained the challenges she faced

> I was nervous and very anxious. I didn't know what to expect and also I knew at my age it was quite different compared to a lot of people who have just come out of school and straight into uni, whereas I've been out of school for a long time. I mean I have done courses, loads of courses but nothing to a degree level. So I was quite nervous. . . . for me it's been quite a bit different, because I was a pre-school teacher for seven years, and my identity was (. . .) kind of, and a lot of my contact was with pre-school children, so coming to university was a big change, because I lost my identity as (. . .) and starting as a very old mature student, but because yeah, it was quite hard in the first year, I didn't know what to expect, and I didn't know anyone.
>
> (Kate, White, female, middle-class student)

This student talks of losing her identity: all of the experience she had amassed prior to coming to university seemed worthless. Although there is awareness of mature students there would seem to be an implicit assumption that because they are older they can cope. The views of our participants suggest that the youth culture in the university is quite exclusive ('mature' is defined by the university as any age over twenty-one. At Riverside across the subjects in our study over twenty-five-year-olds were significantly in the minority with the exception of Psychology where the ages were more balanced). The difference between social class and these other identity 'constraints' however, relates to the invisibility of the structural organisation which disadvantages those working-class students who do not manage to gain the necessary insights. Whilst disabilities and age often lead to discriminatory behaviour and we are not seeking to privilege one form of oppression over another, they play out in very different ways. Social class discrimination often remains unacknowledged as a structural impediment and as a responsibility for the university to address.

Space and place: pedagogical relations and geographies of exclusion

Reference to youth culture and the mismatch of the older students' needs and desires, points to the issue of the differences between academic identities and social identities. Whilst these are related, an individual can simultaneously feel secure with respect to one of these aspects and insecure with respect to the other.

> I think there's like two groups at university. There's a group of students that live on campus or close to uni so they know each other by going to social events at university. Then there's another group of people who come to university from home so they travel into university and I think they're quite disconnected with the university events and they miss out on making those relationships with other students because we don't really find out about those events.
>
> (Kalini, female, British-born Asian,
> working-class student)

This student sums up well the structure of the relationship between the students and the university showing how students living off campus can feel disconnected from university events and relationships. Amongst BME participants all, except one student in our study, lived at home and the majority of the working-class students also lived at home in their first year, at least. There are various reasons for this 'choice' including financial costs but as Clayton, Crozier and Reay (2009) also say it minimises the risk of exposure, injurious interactions and the potential of being degraded (Charlesworth, Gilfillan and Wilkinson, 2006). Of course given this, it is questionable whether this was a choice at all. We have also found, together with Crozier, Reay and Clayton (2010), as the insightful remarks of the student above stated that living off campus leads to a disconnect. Students who live at home or away from the university at least in their first year, were not able to access or were not in the position to develop networks – generate social capital – or discern the availability of vital information, a form of cultural capital, that could enable their negotiation of the university experience. Some students lacked basic information such as one who was not aware of the availability of one-to-one tutorials, which students needed to request; another already in her second year, was not aware of where the Students' Union building had been relocated to. This is not just about not knowing or not being university experienced, it is about not having the 'right kind' of habitus to know how to navigate this different and unusual environment. Home-based students tended to maintain just their home-based friends who in many cases were not at university themselves and so could not provide that capital. Spending most of their time away from the university meant they were not immersed in the culture of the university. They made university friends but only as 'day-time' friends. Greg explains both the advantages and disadvantages of living at home:

> To me the advantages of living at home are as I get older, I have to chip on bills but I really don't have to pay for much [. . . .] And I always have my family around me so there is no sense of homesickness [. . . .] But the problem with living off campus there is less opportunity to socialise. Like I could go to all these bars but because I don't know anyone its very awkward to go there by myself and try and start a conversation. Whereas people who live in halls they might see someone who lives on their floor in the bar and they will strike a conversation with them like "hi how you doing? We live on the same floor." and then you start like that.
>
> (Greg, Creative Writing student, male,
> Black British Caribbean student)

In effect, they are cut off from opportunities to acquire knowledge and experiences which they do not necessarily recognise as available or relevant. Some students did recognise this but at the same time they felt uncomfortable with that normative 'going out' and implied drinking culture which was prevalent at Riverside and most UK universities but which is also exclusionary.

Being on-campus, accessing a range of social and cultural experiences and also forming friendships are all part of the development of habitus and accumulation of capital both social capital, which can help students develop networks advantageous for their career trajectories amongst other things, and cultural capital. As both Charlesworth, Gilfillan and Wilkinson (2006) and Bourdieu (2000) have said friendships and popularity are important not just for reducing loneliness but for making oneself appear to be worthwhile (Crozier, Reay, Clayton and Colliander, 2008) and to gain status. As Bourdieu said:

> . . . the feeling for counting for others, being important for them and therefore oneself and finding . . . requests, expectations and invitations – a kind of justification for existence.
>
> (Bourdieu, 2000, p. 240)

For working-class students who tended to do part-time work in order to pay for their studies and therefore had limited time, as well as, not being on campus very often, making friends and accessing social experiences was less feasible and unsurprisingly was regarded as less of a priority. By contrast middle-class students attributed substantial importance to this:

> [The] social thing is probably one of the most important parts [of being at university] really I think. Um 'cause obviously the work is important but that is to bring you to the end of your degree. Whereas during the time you are here, people another aim is to sort of make as many friends, meet as many as possible. And it's the sort of thing that gets you through 'cause obviously university is quite a stressful time.
>
> (Gary, male, White, middle-class student)

> I definitely think connecting with people on the first couple of weeks of the course really made – you find your buddy or your friend. I've made a group of friends that have definitely kept me going and without them I don't think – uni has been made more bearable in [terms of having a] coping mechanism.
>
> (Audun, female, White, middle-class, international student)

Audun also points out the support that friends can provide being away from home and feeling lonely and vulnerable. Others spoke of friendships as a coping mechanism. We are not suggesting a polarisation between working-class and middle-class students in terms of these experiences. But it is our view that in these respects middle-class students tend to have more choices.

However, as well as having the right material conditions in which to develop a vibrant social life, students needed to have the self-confidence to do so. Some students talked about how lonely they felt and how difficult it was to 'get into a group'; others talked of exclusive cliques rather like school. As Crozier, Reay, Clayton and Colliander (2008) also found, it was clear that developing friendships at university was influenced by 'race', class and gender in spite of 'the submersion of structural distinction' as Francis, Burke and Read (2014 writing about this project) described it: student denials that any of these social identities were significant in the university (see also Chapter seven where we develop these issues further). The structure of the campus university into colleges, which in turn are subject related, may have contributed to this. At the level of school education there is research that shows the importance of the peer group as an influence on the learning process, experience and the development of learner identities (e.g. Astin, 1999; DCSF, 2010). The organisation of friendship groupings, particularly along gendered dimensions in school education, is thought to have an influence on social interactions in the classroom as well as gendered identities (Archer et al., 2007). This also has implications for the academic and pedagogic experience in the university context.

Clearly the students are not overtly excluded from on-campus experiences but their financial and social circumstances militate to prevent their access. Moreover, the significant point here lies in the importance of such access in order to generate their habitus and accumulate further necessary capitals. What they are missing out on amounts to discerning the 'invisible pedagogy' (Bernstein, 2000).

Pedagogies of in/exclusion: power, identities, practices and constraints

The university experience presents a range of challenges as well as opportunities. Engaging with ideas that should disrupt and trouble can be threatening and disorienting. This can be exacerbated where the social and material conditions are also troublesome and not favourable. Working-class (intersected by race and gender) students, as we have said elsewhere, find they have to struggle for legitimacy, which in turn impacts on their ability to contribute, to be recognised as 'having voice'. Asked about how she felt early on in her studies, Elina for example, explained that she:

> Struggled. Struggled very much. [Why?] I don't know, I think there's just like what was expected like in particular; it was the referencing style – like we didn't have any of that back in school and it was like the Harvard referencing style. My grades were like between the 40s and 50s or I was just scraping 40 in first year and I was like, and 'cause the teachers, I dunno maybe I felt they kept looking down on us. I had several teachers – I don't want to name them – they were literally, like, treat you like they were superior. I know that they are superior and they know everything but it was just the way they showed it. So I was too scared to go and ask for their help. And 'cause my friends were like in the same boat, kind of struggling, it was just like really hard. Second year came, confidence grew a bit, lecturers were all different, all much nicer, treated you more respectfully and so yeah grades went up then.
>
> (Elina, British Sri Lankan, working-class, female student)

As we discussed in the previous chapter, different teachers held different views of their pedagogy and practice, how they identified as academics and or teachers, and indeed of the students themselves. All of this impacted on their classroom practice and how they related to students and the learning environments they created. But none of this seemed to be uniform. We can see this reflected in the students' responses to the teaching and what they felt was expected of them.

Many students complained that lectures were cancelled and often without any notice. They felt aggrieved if they had had to travel in to the university to find that there was no lecture that day and insulted that they hadn't been informed. There were mixed views about whether they had a voice and were listened to. A number of the students in our sample were student reps and one was on the Vice Chancellor's student group. For others, they seemed to experience a kind of dislocation from the life of the university and their home life as we have already indicated. These students seem to see their studies – attendance at taught sessions, their assignments – as their university experience: as a means to an end. The social aspects are incidental rather than pivotal. We suggest that these students would feel less likely to have a sense of voice.

Some students did talk about being passionate about their subject and inspired by their teachers. This seemed to be subject specific and included History, Classics, Dance and Drama. These are subjects, as we have said, where group sizes are relatively small and also where teachers consciously promote the status of their subject by reference to their intellectual standing as academics, which seem to give rise to a strong disciplinary identification.

> I am very very very passionate about it [History]. . . The first lecture we had at university one of my favourite lecturers was on Medieval Europe and completely inspired me . . . to study. . . . I adore talking about History. It's what I love doing at the museum as well. At the moment I'm a volunteer sort of a front of house volunteer so I'm talking to the visitors. When I do my internship this summer, I will be immersed in people of a similar interest to me who happily talk about History for a long time. So it's something I'm massively passionate about. [Talking of the lecturer's inspiration] It's initially it's their excitement about what they're teaching.
>
> (Michelle, White, middle-class, female student)

This student's account also contrasts sharply with Elina's who struggled and felt looked down on, reflecting the uneven playing field and differential positioning. Michelle in her second year has already arranged an internship at a museum. She has a clear view of her future trajectory. Later in the interview she also talks about how she nurtures, implicitly, her relationship with her teachers in order to maximise her experience:

> I've had this lecturer, I had him twice for two modules last year. . . . I've got him this term as well and I will have him next year as well. He's like a secondary Personal Teacher to me. I can go and see him about any of my assessments. He doesn't mind at all. So it's just generally making themselves not a friend to the students 'cause you know, I wouldn't say that I have a friendship with any of my lecturers but as much of a friendship as a lecturer/student should have.
>
> (Michelle, White, middle-class, female student)

In the same way that academic staff felt constrained by university and policy systems, students too were frustrated by some of their pedagogic experiences, which at times they felt did not meet their needs or were inadequate. Similar to the teachers, students were also critical of size of rooms, large group sizes, inadequate library facilities. There were examples of students not feeling engaged or supported, or they expressed a kind of disconnect.

> He was just [such a] bad lecturer. I mean, I think it's obvious if a person . . . they are teaching at university, he must be smart . . . but he was so horrible. I actually tried to listen to what he was saying, but some of his sentences were 5 minutes long! So basically he would just go into this conversation with himself, although he was talking at the class for such a long time.
>
> (Andrew, male, White, middle-class student)

> So if I asked her for some help she would be so vague. Like I've asked her for help this term about how to write a blog which is part of our assignment and she is annoyed with everyone because no-one is putting up their blogs but she is not giving us any advice about it so how are we meant to write it? She hasn't given us any examples. She doesn't really help. She's just like "read other people's and say what they say" . . . So I'm going to probably fail this module because I just haven't got the confidence in her – any confidence in her.
>
> (Mary, White, middle-class, female student)

On the other hand, students also gave examples of pedagogic practice that they valued and that they felt inspired by.

> It's more like a class so we are always contributing when we want to and asking questions and that's really nice and she has slides up so she is actually showing you something and you are engaging with that. And you are coming up with your own ideas and everything.
>
> (Alexia, White, female, working-class student)

> He has like a specific flow in his lectures. It doesn't feel like a bouncing ball. It rolls all the way. If the lecture is actually structured properly you will receive it in the way he structured it. And the way he structures it is really easy to understand.
>
> (Marc, male, White, working-class student)

These are fairly traditional safe pedagogic frameworks. The metaphor of the ball suggests a soporific experience, gliding through the hour or two, making it easy to understand but there are no comments about challenge or expression of a desire to be unsettled. On the other hand, the criticisms about 'bad' lecturers and being bored could be said to be an expression of this but it translates into a desire for something safe rather than challenging and potentially risky. Students of course need to be exposed to critical pedagogy in order to want it and recognise its value. Very few of the student participants in our study seemed to understand what this was. Some students recognised the need for engagement and an exchange of ideas and how this is a more stimulating way of learning.

> When it's the interaction, the engagement between everybody in the class with the teacher, with the lecturer then I learn much better, things sink in much better hearing people's different views rather than sitting in front of a bored projector screen and just the teacher going on and on and on and on. . . . And I've noticed the difference in the different lecturers and their different techniques and I come out so much more and feeling so much more confident when I've learnt in that way where there's a lot of interaction going on and people's different ideas bouncing around the room than the other way.
>
> (Ayesha, working-class, mixed race, mature student)

However, this approach was not consistent amongst lecturers and as Ayesha went on to say she was resigned to that.

Regulatory control becomes more paramount in a neo-liberal system based on heightened competitiveness. Student success and maintaining student retention, as we have said, are both key performance indicators for universities. This implies the need for tighter controls and less risk-taking in the form of critical pedagogies and an emphasis on outcomes rather than process (Mann, 2001). The regulation and surveillance of academics through student evaluations and the focus on 'excellence' are, as we have discussed (see Chapters one and four), additional mechanisms which tend to mean that teachers are more cautious in their pedagogic practice. Likewise in this environment students tend to adapt and conform to the status quo since they too are heavily invested financially but also socially and psychically in the process they find themselves in. Students were often very focused on their marks aiming for a first or 2.1 and keen to identify the necessary cues from the lecturers to achieve this. Some students were quite critical of their fellow students' behaviour, in terms of being late to class, not working hard, not contributing to group activities. As we argue in Chapter seven, this scenario contributed to discourses of antagonism. Arguably these putatively 'difficult' students were the risk-takers, the rebels challenging the status quo. Mann (2001) describes such behaviours as a form of alienation, which it may be, but at the same time it could be said to represent a challenge to control and achieve docility (Grant, 1997).

In most instances the students were not challenging but accepted what was on offer. In most cases they complied with the differential power relationship, which Bourdieu, Passeron and De Saint Martin (1994) described as 'distancing'. This comprised organisation of the teaching space and the relationship in general between student and teacher, which ensured control and eschewed challenge or questioning of powerful knowledge. Instances where teachers tried to stimulate pedagogic practices that could create dynamic and critical praxis were often feared by some students. They saw this as potentially exposing their identities as lacking in some way. Earlier for example we discussed the concerns of students who felt they did not have the vocabulary; elsewhere we discussed the student who was dyslexic and felt too vulnerable to participate in seminar discussions for fear of losing face with other students as well as the teacher. There was a palpable sense of fear and anxiety in relation to who they were. As Mann (2001) suggests the relationship of power between academics and students is not conducive for critical transformatory learning. Pedagogy remains at the level of control and the learning that takes place is frequently instrumental and achievement oriented.

Conclusion

The experiences and perspectives of the students both between and also within social class locations vary and are diverse but there are strong themes of misrecognition, anxiety and competitiveness. We have shown the importance of geographies of space and place and that the context and organisation of the university itself is a strong influence together with the discipline of study and the range of academic practices. This enmeshes or rebuffs the relative 'fit' or not, with what students bring with them to the university in terms of habitus and cultural and social capital. University should be an opportunity both to acquire and develop these capitals simultaneously while challenging their necessity and influence through critical pedagogy and reflexive practice. We have found little evidence that the balance of power at Riverside has shifted to enable students to make such challenges. As others have suggested the university institutional culture/habitus has not been impacted by the diversity of the student body and thus academic culture continues to reflect the dominant discourses of society and of the student learner, as White, middle class and male (Leathwood and Read, 2009; Mirza, 2009).

The hierarchies of knowledge play out in subtle and often in explicit ways. The traditional academic subjects of History, Philosophy, Classics and English were taken by very few BME students. The university interestingly did not collect data on social class. At Riverside there was a high proportion of female students and therefore women were in the majority across all of the disciplines with the exception of Business Studies. Business Studies also had the largest number of BME students. Sports Sciences are grouped by the university under Life Sciences, which do not show the race or gendered breakdown but anecdotally men and BME men, appear to dominate these subjects. Both Sports Science and Business Studies are very popular and hence have large groups of students which in turn lead to accommodation difficulties and constraints on student-staff relationships in terms of lecturers knowing individual students and students feeling comfortable approaching their teachers. This likewise impacts on the subject/discipline – pedagogic identity and identification. For some, middle-class students these identities have been generated already through their schooling. For working-class students they frequently arrive at university with little concrete idea of what to expect or what will be expected of them together with a conflicting sense of their learner selves. The array of teaching styles, course requirements, university procedures and social aspects conspire to disturb and disrupt rather than generate pedagogic identities for these students. In the following two chapters we explore these issues further in relation to gender and race.

Note

1 We have borrowed this term from Sibley's book 'Geographies of Exclusion: Society and Difference in the West', 1995. London & New York: Routledge.

Chapter 6

Gendered formations in pedagogical relations and spaces

The research projects outlined in the book illuminate the ways that academic and student subjectivities are gendered and how this is enmeshed in the gendering of subject areas, practices and disciplines. However, such insights do not reinforce the wider hegemonic view that contemporary higher education has become a 'feminised' space. Rather, our project data show that masculinities and femininities play out in complex ways to shape pedagogical experiences, relations, subjectivities and practices, and are both influenced by and are challenging to hegemonic discourses of gender and masculinity. Pedagogies are conceptualised as constitutive of gendered formations through the discursive practices and regimes of truth at play in particular pedagogic and disciplinary spaces. This chapter draws on both the GaP and Fulbright data to show that pedagogies do not simply *reflect* the gendered identities of academics and students but pedagogies *themselves are gendered*, intimately bound up with historical and masculinised ways of being and doing within higher education.

Feminist insights have contributed rich and textured analyses of the profound relationship between the histories of gendered formations and the vacating of the emotional from the world of the academy. Carole Leathwood and Valerie Hey (2009) have sought to expose the ways that fear of emotion generates misogynistic orientations. We are at a moment in history when more women than ever have successfully gained access to higher education in most OECD countries (OECD, 2012). We will argue that this has led to a desire to reinforce the divisions between the rational and the emotional, subtly reasserting hegemonic masculine dispositions and orientations.

Feminist approaches reveal the multiple layers of injustices that operate around processes of gendered subjective construction, in relation to embodied intersections of difference and the ways that emotion works on and marks difference on and through the body. Such frameworks also point to the subtle forms of inequality that work through the politics of misrecognition in which the Other is excluded, marginalised and often subjected to ridicule, derision, shame or symbolic violence. The affective dimensions of experiences of misrecognition have also largely been ignored or under- theorised in relation to processes of becoming a student in higher education within historically exclusive pedagogical spaces.

Higher education pedagogies require reformation to address such complex issues and concerns but in ways that reject the problematic claim that masculinity is in crisis due to the feminisation of higher education.

As discussed in Chapter two, exploring the emotional layers of pedagogic experiences not only helps illuminate 'fear *as* emotion' but also 'fear *of* emotion' (Leathwood and Hey, 2009). Fear is entangled in multiple political frameworks operating to reform processes of misrecognition and exclusion, even as HE policy is demanding that universities evidence inclusive practice as part of their commitment to diversity. Underpinning the hegemony of neo-liberalism, meritocracy and globalisation, and related undercurrents of misogyny, racism and classism, is the construction of 'difference' through fixing and pathologising identity positions. Difference and emotion are often perceived as dangerous forces that undermine the aspiration for excellence. As such, technologies of managerialism are brought to work to standardise, systematise and thus neutralise difference.

Neo-liberal forces increasingly restrict our pedagogical imaginations. It is important to consider how neo-liberalism works in complex ways with other oppressive forces, such as patriarchy, neocolonialism and institutional racism, distorting the meanings we give to 'diversity' and 'difference'. These dynamics reinforce our complicity in the politics of misrecognition, even when we strive towards social justice approaches. Sarah Ahmed (2004) explains that emotions 'produce the very surfaces and boundaries that allow the individual and the social to be delineated as if they are objects'. Pedagogies are formed through multiple, intersecting and embodied subjectivities, intimately bound up with historical ways of being a teacher or a student in higher education. Neo-liberal imperatives reemphasise techno-rationalist discourses of human capital and individual responsibility.

New formations of patriarchy within neo-liberalism ensure that characteristics associated with femininity in HE, such as 'being emotional' or 'caring', are regulated and controlled through a range of new disciplinary technologies, inclusive of teaching. Pedagogical relations are thus deeply implicated in the gendered politics of (mis)recognition. Indeed, some feminists have argued that contemporary higher education is characterised by a 'careless' culture (Lynch, 2010), valuing those without caring responsibilities and privileging hyper-masculinized subjectivities.

The silencing of gender inequalities in higher education

As we move increasingly towards a neo-liberal, marketised and corporatised framework of higher education, in which technologies of regulation through intensified levels of performance management are becoming taken for granted, relations of difference and inequality become increasingly silenced and insidious.

Universities are increasingly encouraged to develop 'evidence-based' policy and practice but this locks policy-makers and practitioners into constrained and reductive ways of thinking about equity issues. 'Evidence' emphasises generalisability and objectivity, with a strong focus on the tangible, observable and measurable and is often embedded in those technologies of classification that perpetuate rather than challenge polarising discourses and dividing practices (Ball, 2003). Evidence is clearly important in uncovering patterns of inequality but only provides restrictive knowledge and insight. Lived and embodied experiences of inequality are difficult to 'evidence' and measure because these work at the everyday level of lived experience and emotion. Generating knowledge about the ways that insidious inequalities work requires a range of fine-tuned research methodologies that are designed to explore the fluidity of power and social relations, the complexity of intersecting differences and socio-cultural contexts, the ways that social practices and processes might be historically embedded and taken for granted, as well as to trace, map and quantify patterns of inequality that are intersecting, multiple and contextual. The projects, drawing on a pedagogic methodology, aimed to expose the subtle processes in which inequalities of gender and intersecting differences are reformed through and in pedagogical spaces.

Masculinities are multiple and contested formations, challenging common sense understanding of gender that assumes masculinity is connected only to those bodies identified as male. It is important to note that a person, whether identified as male or female, can take up, cite and perform different, competing and multiple discourses of masculinity and femininity. However, subjectivities are embodied and gendered, so that a female performing masculine discursive practices risks being (mis)recognised and 'Othered', often through patriarchal and misogynist discourses that function to reposition the authority of the legitimate hegemonic male masculine subject. Performatives are relational and always made sense of in relation to gendered bodies, as well as discourses and contexts, including the context of social institutions rooted in patriarchal histories, such as higher education.

Furthermore, masculinity is not only a concept that describes ways of being or acting in the social world, it can also be applied to wider social discourses, practices and cultures. In higher education, certain practices are historically associated with hegemonic masculinities, such as lecturing, professing, claiming authority, operating in ways that might be seen as competitive and so on. Additionally, certain practices are embodied in particular kinds of persons; for example discourses of 'the professor' tend to be associated with White, middle-aged, middle-classed male bodies, subjectivities and dispositions. This is tied in with questions about gendered participation, the legitimation and exclusion of certain forms of knowledge and the politics of recognition, power and authority in pedagogical spaces. The embodiment of certain forms of masculinity in higher education is deeply connected to the politics of recognition and misrecognition.

For example, the following young, female Philosophy lecturers (from the GaP project) explain that:

Female Lecturer 1:   None of us fit the image, do we? The old White man . . . you know, like whatever, elbow patches. But I think that's good because it very immediately breaks the stereotype, and then there isn't a problem with that at all, but it's interesting that sometimes you get that preconception. On occasion, somebody comes to your room to see you before you've started teaching them, and they are like – ooh. And also the age thing, because the image is also a very old one, and if you look a bit younger as well, it's kind of like, you know, oh, you are my professor.

Female Lecturer 2:   Yes, one discussion I've heard is that women philosophers tend to stay in history of philosophy, but also in sort of philosophy of science, disproportionately. It's thought to be that perhaps it's because there you can really prove your point, you know, you can go back to the text and prove your point, so people can't undermine you quite so easily, which is . . . apparently there are a disproportionate [number of] men and women doing philosophy of mind and philosophy of science . . .

The data from the two projects revealed the competing ways that gender relations and inequalities are silenced and concealed in diverse pedagogical contexts. For teachers in higher education, there appeared to be a particular silencing of feminist voices and/or of gender studies more broadly. Gender is presented as largely absent from the curriculum and from wider discourses about teaching in the data across the two projects. When asked about how colleagues working on gender are viewed in her university, a female lecturer in Spain explains that the general attitude is:

> Don't come out of there, we'll leave you to work and we'll give you what you need when we can . . . but [just] keep quiet. . . . The feminists are told to pick a course as to not get involved in other courses.
>
> (Female lecturer, Fulbright project, Spain)

A male lecturer in Spain explains that:

> The initial formation that's occurring in the universities is one in which the question of gender/sex is absent or it's treated as not a transversal or current topic.

Another male teacher talks about the difficulty of incorporating gender into teaching:

> There's still people in this country that defend that education is neutral and it was very difficult to incorporate gender. . . . But I've never liked to incorporate it superficially. Let me explain: gender doesn't make any sense if it's not accompanied . . . by interculturality, diversity, and peace.
>
> (Male professor, Fulbright project, Spain)

Such experiences of the marginalisation of gender have significant implications for the ways that gender inequalities might be challenged in and through higher education. One of issues that emerged that we found particularly troubling was the lack of pedagogical and critical spaces for teachers and students to explore problematic assumptions about gender and other discriminatory perspectives. This in effect meant that students attain their university degrees without having troubled the taken-for-granted and often discriminatory perspectives they brought to their studies at the start of their programmes. However, this is not to individualise the responsibility of addressing complex power relations and inequalities. The following extract from an interview with a Spanish lecturer captures the challenges for individual teachers in dealing with such complex gender relations in the classroom:

> [If we're discussing if certain groups had trouble participating, here it's the opposite]: one group gets it great, [seen in their attitudes]. . . they react very viscerally to what they've read. . . . And at the same time the inhibition of the other part of the class that keeps completely quiet like a victim of the others who take all of the power [is] so worrisome to me. . . . They don't listen. . . . I observe [them] having a lot of trouble putting themselves in other's shoes, a reaction – when we are speaking about women – a reaction . . . almost violent, by the guys . . . I get scared! . . . It makes me think that I am missing more tools and resources to be able to work on questions of these guys' emotions . . . how can they stop for a bit to reflect . . . I've told them, but it's not sufficient. . . . Ask [them] why do they react like that? . . . It's unbelievable. . . . I think that I don't have the formation for this. . . . Sometimes it feels like too much for me. . . . The class isn't going badly, I feel like they are enjoying it, they tell me, I get along fine with them but this educational process of being able to manage it in a positive way (like I'd like to – for them and for myself) is hard for me. . . . I see myself with a lot of personal and professional limitations.
>
> (Female lecturer, Fulbright project, Spain)

This points to the need for more systematic attention to the issues around embedding equity and inclusion in institution-wide pedagogical frameworks and strategies. Our position is that it is just as unfair and problematic to place the blame and responsibility for inequality on individual teachers as it is to do so to individual students. The commitment to widening participation and developing more equitable and inclusive higher education spaces must be taken up at the national and institutional levels, with carefully thought through support and resources to facilitate this.

The gendering of voice in HE pedagogical spaces

Voice and silence pose particular challenges for teachers and students and yet 'participation' appears to be largely conceptualised by lecturers as related to student voice (and silence). Museus and Griffin (2011) argue for the need to consider voice in relation to complex intersections of marginality, explaining that:

> Overreliance on one-dimensions categories, even though giving space to the voices of racial minorities and women in higher education, fails to establish adequate space for individuals who are situated at the margins of multiple groups.
>
> (p. 9)

Batchelor (2006) points to vulnerabilities in relation to 'voice' arguing that we need to pay closer attention to the 'vulnerability of certain modes of voice' when students are participating in higher education (p. 787). Our data show the ways that students' different voices reproduce gendered, classed and racialised judgments and misrecognitions, reinforcing Batchelor's important insight about vulnerabilities in relation to student voice. Although voice is often associated in educational literature with student 'empowerment', only particular forms of 'voice' have the potential to be validated through gendered pedagogical relations. It was clear in the data that some voices cause quite significant levels of discomfort and disapproval, for example those voices associated with Black and working-class masculinities that were repeatedly constructed as noisy and disruptive. Student voices perceived as unruly were connected to constructions of hyper-masculinity and as we discuss in Chapter seven, this is linked to pejorative discourses of 'Other' students associated with classed and racialised misrecognitions. This is illustrated in the following exchange between two White male Business Studies lecturers in a GaP focus group discussion:

Male lecturer 1:   I can hear blokes. Again I can usually hear their chatter let's say more acutely more than I can hear some female chatter simply because of the difference in pitch.

Male lecturer 2:   I really can't tolerate talking. It really drives me nuts and I will stop a lecture and they know. Whereas in the old days I used to just get louder and louder and they got louder and it got out of control. But I think you learn as a lecturer how to control a group.

The neo-liberal reframing of higher education tends to reposition students and teachers in relation to market discourses, challenging the traditional forms of authority of the lecturer. This sometimes raised the question of how students have the potential to exercise their rights as a consumer, and to what extent teachers could or should control students. Such accounts seemed to be connected to an implicit fear of the Other in the classroom; those 'new' groups of students who occupy a different and unfamiliar subject position. This was implicitly tied to classed and racialised forms of masculinity, and to narratives of those Other students who are seen as not fitting in to expectations of how university student should behave. In such instances, as we also explore in Chapters five and seven, the intersections of working class, Black, young masculinities are posed as undermining the authoritative position of the university lecturer. Anxiety about the risk of contamination of the (pure/legitimate) HE cultural context is suggested, raising questions about the complex dynamics of gendered pedagogical relations.

The lecturer that follows implies the personal anxiety connected with students exercising rights as a consumer of higher education. We found that in some disciplinary fields, university teachers expressed their concern over the lack of control they had over Black male student groups who were constructed as having the 'wrong' kinds of attitudes and behaviours (see also Chapter five). The students thus were constructed as not belonging or fitting into the academic environment and as a problem linked to the lowering of standards, as we have explored in Chapter five.

> . . . they are the same group who's actually been making noises – so affecting the students' hearing, and the problem, sometimes, you find it's the same group time and time again. When you warn the first time, come the following week, and exactly the same. So the question we raised as well, before, how far you can go to say OK, enough is enough. . . . I mean I've done it, I think, twice or three times, and one of them is going and complain to the boss, you know. But I mean I have nothing to hide, you know.
>
> (Male lecturer, GaP project)

The above account is grounded in a wider set of assumptions about the teacher's role in regulating, disciplining and containing student behaviour (see also Nicoll and Harrison, 2003; Llamas, 2006). However such accounts tend to ignore deeper pedagogical questions about processes of engaging diverse groups of students in ways that facilitate a sense of belonging and participation in the context of massification, widening participation, changing student populations and pedagogical cultures. It is our perspective that such questions demand deeper engagement of universities about the intersections between teaching, learning, equity and difference. Individual university teachers require institutional resources and support to develop pedagogies that are able to address equity concerns and the complex dynamics of diversity and difference.

The gendering of silence in higher education pedagogies

In discourses about the authority and control of the university lecturer, students who are the quiet and disciplined subject might be seen as easier to control, more obedient and docile and thus less likely to pose a threat to the authority of the lecturer. This might reinforce assumptions that higher education pedagogies privilege feminine dispositions, reinforcing assumptions that higher education is feminised and exclusive of men and masculinities.

Yet silence is also constructed as a signifier of lack in some national contexts such as England. Feminists have argued that girls learn silence through schooling and higher education practices (Luke, 1994). Yet in higher education contexts, silence is often seen as indicative of a student's lack of ability, confidence and engagement. Silence often provokes discomfort for university teachers who then feel compelled to exercise power despite attempting to create opportunities for 'student voice'. The complex negotiations of university teachers in engaging student voice is illustrated in the following data extract. There is reference to ability in relation to participation, but it is unclear if this is about (the teacher's constructed sense of) student ability or about particular power relations. Overall, participation is presented as risky for students.

> But a lot of Business language is around football, male sports, moving the goal post, team player, all this rubbish and I just wonder if you know it's largely written by men, a lot of the Business Management literature and it's very geared towards the systems type learning as well that maybe women, female students are excluded to a certain extent and a sort of silent lecture until the questions at the end. I thought of that word silent, the bit of research I did with students about women's ways of knowing. Basically silence being the lowest level of engagement and you know by doing a lecture, we are imposing that silence but in the next minute, we're saying let's have a discussion about this and let's engage, but we're controlling that as opposed to them really critically engaging. So I think there may be something wrong there in terms of imposing silence on the people. I mean I'm finding it more and more – they're just not able to engage. They don't take the risk and my group this year, there's only about one or two that would participate. Whereas previously it would be a really good dynamic – engaged.
>
> (Male lecturer, GaP project)

The data across the projects showed that teachers are highly reflexive about their approaches and concerned about gendered power relations at play in their classrooms. This of course does not simply translate into inclusive practices not least due to the complexities of pedagogical relations across difference. The teachers demonstrate awareness of such complexities and describe the particular issues and dilemmas they face as higher education teachers. Their accounts support the theoretical assertion that not only are student and teacher identities gendered but so are subject/disciplines and their associated practices, for example the Business Studies lecturer above argues that Business Studies is masculinised.

Passivity, which is seen to be connected to silence, is identified as challenging to teachers. Certain strategies to combat silence are drawn on. One female lecturer introduces the notion of teaching and learning as 'play'. She strongly adopts a maternalistic positioning of (female) teacher. In her account, teaching is constructed as about bringing students out as people, resonant of birthing, nurturing and caring. The teacher's role is presented in the below account as "connecting", which can be achieved through active forms of student participation. Participation is strongly signalled by student voice.

> Because I tell you, if in doubt I start playing. I either go "what's the matter babies, tell me", or I start playing. Because I can't bear silence, lack of engagement, I can't bear it, so . . . it's also partly because there is this shared belief, I think I'm right in saying, underneath, that students need to connect with themselves, and they need to connect with one another, in order to write well . . . So it's essential that we bring them out as people, that's part of our job. We are not just teaching a subject. You have to take part or you are not learning. I think that's what we believe.
>
> (Female lecturer, GaP project)

Femininity as a resource of power is suggested in her account, as she draws on explicitly feminised codes to 'play' the students. Similar perhaps to parenting, teaching is presented as a form of coercion, and the teacher is seen as able to draw on her gendered and generational authority as teacher. Thus, a strong maternalistic position is presented as a form of power in the classroom space. Indeed, our analysis of the students' accounts suggested that they responded well to such approaches. However, it is also important to note that the exploitation of women's emotional labour has been discussed in detail in feminist research and literature (Burke and Jackson, 2007). Therefore, this feminised approach to teaching can be both an important and generative form of inclusive pedagogic practice whilst also problematic in the way it positions women lecturers across gendered divisions.

Interviewer: You said the day everybody was tired you put everybody in a circle and you said you did the maternal thing of OK, what's going on, what's the matter? So do you actively draw on that, to get people engaged?

Lecturer: I'm aware I'm doing that. I think I've just always done it. I think the older I've become the more I do it actually. It was, I actually will explicitly refer to myself as Auntie occasionally. Not in the

initial classes, but as we all get to know each other, I will often . . .
maybe not often, but often enough, kind of coerce people into saying things, or taking part, on the basis of "because Auntie knows so
and so and so and so".

(Female lecturer, GaP project)

However, for many university teachers the connection between maternalistic
positioning and being a lecturer are seen as incompatible and in tension. The
teachers repeatedly articulated their anxieties about inappropriate forms of caring, which might be seen as evidence of the 'dumbing down' and the 'feminisation' of teaching and learning. For example, they made reference to hegemonic
and heterosexist discourses of appropriate (and inappropriate) spaces for exercising caring dispositions, and they articulate their anxiety about the blurring of
teaching with caring.

Part of me thinks it's not my job to look after them. I have a husband and
two children at home that I have to look after, I have to get these students
through, I'm not their mother, I have no intention of being their mother . . .
and sometimes I get really cross that there is an expectation from the university, from my programme convenor and from society, that I am going to mind
these students.

(Female lecturer, GaP project)

I feel because of retention rates and all these systems which are in place when
you first . . . I am expected to be caring, more caring than I actually want
to be.

(Male lecturer, GaP project)

The suggestion seems to be that teachers have to remedy students' deficits
through performing a maternal, nurturing role that is devalued and seen as inappropriate in the context of university. This reinforces certain assumptions that
some pedagogical relations are inappropriate, as we saw in Chapter five, constructing those students associated with difference as immature, and requiring
inappropriate forms of (feminised) support. It has been argued that this places
female staff in a 'double-bind' (Murray, 2006, p. 390) and that women are often
expected to carry out the nurturing role despite this being hidden or devalued
in the academy:

I propose that female faculty members are under the watchful eye of a meta-
phoric audience in the form of gender norms present in campus policies,
practices, and informal cultural definitions of gender, such as the finding that
female faculty members feel obligated to perform in a more motherly fashion
as caring and compassionate teachers.

(Lester, 2011, p. 145)

Due to widening participation, and by implication a perceived 'lowering of standards', many of the lecturer participants in our study expressed concern that they are increasingly expected to play an incongruous nurturing role in order to fix the perceived attitudinal problems of students from non-traditional backgrounds. Importantly, the discourse of the feminisation of HE works powerfully to implicitly denigrate those dispositions associated with femininity precisely at a moment when more women than ever before are gaining access to higher education. The teachers are not only fearful of taking on (perceived) feminised positions seen as at odds with being a higher education lecturer but also of encouraging (perceived) feminised orientations of their students (such as 'passivity'). One teacher explains this passivity or feminised disposition in terms of students' fear of 'taking initiative':

> It's perhaps fear of taking initiative . . . is it fear . . . have we created that perhaps a bit?
>
> (Male lecturer, GaP project)

Anxieties and desires to distance from softness and passivity are connected to the dominant concern to produce active and independent learners. However, to be active and independent has connotations with characteristics historically associated with masculinity, and increasingly with individualisation; including being competitive and foregrounding rational thought over emotional, intuitive and/or personal approaches to meaning-making. Testa and Egan (2014) argue that:

> Pedagogies which emphasise independent scholarship tend to label those who need support. Those who are already enculturated into the expectation of independent learning may learn well independently, but for others, especially women and those from more communitarian cultures, independence must be newly acquired, potentially in negation of their cultural identities.
>
> (p. 232)

Students associated with equity often become characterised by dividing practices that operate to re/classify those students in ways that re/position them as the 'Other'. This is a form of symbolic violence in which the gaze is placed on individual students blamed for lowering standards. Through invoking historically feminised traits, such as 'weakness', 'dependence' and 'passivity' and through dividing the public domain (of masculinity and higher education) from the private domain (of femininity and domesticity), those students associated with feminised traits are subject to misrecognition in ways that is felt in and through the body.

The gendering of confidence

Confidence becomes a signifier of the 'proper' university student and yet is often framed as a neutral, decontextualised and disembodied trait that 'non-traditional' students lack. The wider patriarchal structures and discourses that might work on the feminised student (whether male or female) to recast them as lacking in confidence are hidden while the individual becomes the focus of the need for remedial forms of support. Such forms of support are in turn attached to anxieties about lowering of standards and the assumed feminisation of higher education (Leathwood and Read, 2009). The student constructed as 'non-traditional' often reproduces the narrative of lack of self-confidence and is thus repositioned as the weak, needy, passive and feminised student at the centre of derogatory discourses of widening participation. A vicious cycle of misrecognition is put into place, subtly reasserting the dominance of certain forms of hegemonic masculinity.

Confidence is seen as a signifier of potential and capability. Students constructed as 'lacking confidence' are connected to anxieties about lowering of standards. This is linked to contemporary discourses of teaching that emphasise 'student engagement' as an indication of participation. Yet, speaking out in pedagogical spaces has been identified in the wider literature as a significant source of anxiety for many students associated with equity and difference in higher education (Batchelor, 2006; McLeod, 2011; Sellar and Gale, 2011). Test and Egan (2014) explain that:

> The social structures of race, class, and age remain a feature of the higher education sector to the detriment of all students, especially those from non-traditional backgrounds. Most participants reported that earlier in the course, they have been afraid to speak.
>
> (p. 232)

The data suggest that expressing voice is indeed daunting for many students, particularly those from under-represented backgrounds. For example, the following student talks about her experiences of being forced to read out loud in the classroom, despite her disability. Although, Agda (female, middle-class student with disability) believes that her lecturers are aware that she is dyslexic, she is still forced into this form of participation. This raises particular challenges to assumptions about voice and participation as a form of empowerment and the ethics of voice in the classroom.

Agda: Also I generally don't like speaking in front of class 'cause I get very nervous. And because of my dyslexia I feel – they ask us to read stuff – I find it very difficult to read something loud in front of someone. But they're not really supposed to ask me that but they still do and I just get, I get so nervous and I focus so hard on reading that I don't get the context or contents or anything. I just read it and focus on not stumbling through.

Interviewer: Are they aware of that – you're teachers?

Agda: They should be. I find the person who does this most is actually my Personal Teacher and he's the one who knows most about it.

Agda seems to suggest that formal pedagogical space makes it risky to speak, when she explains that in other contexts she is 'good at speaking to people'. Many of the students express these kinds of anxieties about being seen and heard in case they might be read off as an illegitimate subject of the HE space or (mis) recognised as not belonging at university.

Interviewer: And you've given an account of feeling quite anxious when you're having to read because of your dyslexia. Are there any other times when you remember feeling particularly anxious about your studies?

Agda: Well I basically feel anxious if I have to like, like I don't like, I think it's just because I'm scared of being stupid like I don't like if I want to say something and I know that what I want to say is right and if I don't say it, the teacher points it out. So I should have said it to show how clever I was but I didn't and no-one did. But I'm just too scared to put up my arm or just to say it. And sometimes I even feel nauseous – I like I want to be sick just from having to say a sentence. And it's not because like I sometimes I got good stuff up there as well but it's just scary to say it. And I'm not shy – I'm not a shy person. I get in contact with people quite easily and I'm good at speaking to people I think but I'm just very nervous.

In the Portuguese context, one lecturer explains that the female students often remain silent, deferring to male students to speak in class:

> Having a group that has five girls and one guy, when the time comes for them to give the group response, the girls themselves say (to the guy), "you speak," so it's just the guy in charge. . . . [There is] silence, a high level of silence [of girls].
>
> (Female lecturer, Fulbright project, Portugal)

A lecturer expresses her concerns about female students who are 'silent' and her sense of not having access to pedagogic strategies to overcome this dynamic:

> I'm lacking strategies. But what I've tried to do is have them take responsibility for what is occurring in the classroom. I don't like. . . . I've tried, and I don't think it's gone badly, that we're all responsible for what's occurring. . . . Get away from 'victimization.' They are also silent, allowing this situation, . . . comfortable in blaming the ones that are the leaders. . . . I'm more worried about those who don't speak than those who speak, . . . the ones who always hide.
>
> (Female lecturer, Fulbright project, Spain)

Some students also talked of hiding behind friends since they were too inhibited to discuss in the seminar. Importantly, this anxiety is not in the abstract but is often said to be in relation to peers who are seen as intimidating. Some students expressed the view that: 'it's the students that are scary not the lecturers' and talk of trauma and mistrust. Seminars and related expectations about participation paradoxically create uncomfortable and disempowering spaces for some students. Assumptions that (certain kinds of) voice is the 'proper' form of HE participation makes some students feel 'stupid'. Such forms of participation require displaying the appropriate student dispositions, citing the discourses that generate recognition, embodying legitimated subjectivities and displaying the forms of performatives that position the student as a valid subject of higher education pedagogy. This highlights the complexity of participation for students who are trying to address a number of competing regulatory discourses on a range of contradictory levels and across shifting power relations.

Interviewer: How does it feel in a seminar compared to a lecture?
Diana: Well in a lecture you can sit there and you can listen if they are a good lecturer, if they can engage me. And I quite like that as I write down my own notes and make up my own feelings so people contribute what they want if they want to. Whereas seminars you actually like you are meant to be contributing. So I feel like I look stupid because I'm not saying anything but I'll sound stupid if I do say something so I just don't really like them.
(Diana, female, middle-class, first generation student)

A lecturer explains that attempting to overcome the gendered dynamics through small group work often reproduces gendered relations in the classroom:

When there are guys, I often put . . . one guy in every group and then we always fall back into – there's a person who has to do the report, take notes about the discussion, that has to carry out the role of secretary and . . . later there has to be another person who gives the presentation to the large group [about] what's been discussed. It's true that I'd say in 99% of the groups where there's a guy, or more than one guy, it's normally a guy that does the exposition. . . . The guys usually call the shots.
(Female professor, Fulbright project, Spain)

One lecturer points to the contradictory expectations of WP on the HE teacher. She suggests that on the one hand institutional racism is a pernicious force that operates to reproduce inequalities in higher education. Yet, on the other hand, she suggests that exclusion of 'these people' might be inevitable in maintaining standards and not 'dumbing down', although she recognises that this is problematic as it might be related to the 'tendency to be institutionally racist'. She is trying to grapple with the complexities of challenging structural and historical inequalities as an individual lecturer. She raises the ethical question of who should be held responsible for challenging institutional racism.

> But again a lot of it comes down to the culture, and the culture of expectation. And, you know, the . . . what do we expect and what do they expect, and what is acceptable within a culture, and what is not acceptable within a culture? And part of that is about education, us educating ourselves and us educating them. But in . . . it's impossible to educate, you know, in the sense that we don't have time to sit down and navel gaze about how can we engage these people better in order to do this, that and the other, or do we look right back to our admissions criteria and say OK, well, we only choose the ones who are like us. And, you know, it comes down to what's institutional racism? And I think, I think without question higher education has a tendency to be institutionally racist, but to what extent can I address it and can the university address it, or is it just a societal issue that we have to get over, you know?
>
> (Female lecturer, GaP project)

Competing forms of masculinity in pedagogical spaces

Educational aspiration and higher education are profoundly linked to constellations of subjectivity, formed through gendered intersections with other social identities. However, this does not play out in any predictable way due to the complexity of these intricate formations. This means that questions of men's higher educational access and participation must engage the complexity of social identity formations across a range of differences, structured by hegemonic discourses, including patriarchy, meritocracy and neo-liberalism. The interconnections of such structures themselves have no absolute predictable effects particularly because they are often in contradiction and are operating through complex modes of stratification and differentiation. For example, there are competing forms of hegemonic patriarchal masculinity, which are reshaped by global neo-liberalism and discourses of meritocracy. This is layered in relation to the demands of neo-liberalism, in which the masculinised subject is compelled to produce himself in particular ways to meet the demands of neo-liberal and meritocratic discourses, including through self-disciplining practices (such as involving time management, diligence and demonstrating good organisational and team-working skills). Feminist scholars have shown that some narratives of masculinity run counter to the production of a legitimate subject position as student in both schooling and higher education, including narratives of "laziness" related to discourses of 'laddishness' (Jackson, 2006). This requires a delicate rebalancing between different and competing sets of perfomatives, demonstrated by the following account of a male, working-class White English, first generation student, Andrew. When asked if he ever feels bored during formal pedagogical encounters the student explains that:

> School's always going to be uncool. There is going to be no way of making it more popular than the newest thing in. But my sleeping probably ruins me for that. I always come in tired and that's my own fault. I drift off in my own head as well. Yeah, like it depends on what you are learning. Like you get a good choice of modules and we choose them. But sometimes it's not going to be the most interesting of things that you are learning.
>
> (Andrew)

Although Andrew draws on hegemonic forms of 'laddish' White masculinity in his disposition towards learning and his narrative of his experiences as a student, he also demonstrates the skills of neo-liberalism, which call on the discursive citations of 'flexibility'. However, his narrative of flexibility is arguably formed through discourses of masculinity, as this is not about the juggling of multiple tasks associated with femininity. Rather he draws on discourses of flexibility that require moving across social and pedagogical spaces with ease and confidence, whilst accessing the necessary resources and networks to operate flexibly.

> My main needs are probably social reasons 'cause if I'm comfortable with that and having fun. And I can mix and match work, as long as I'm balancing it out. I'm not the sort of person who could sit and work all day every day. I need to have a social side of it. But on the learning side all the resources are there. So my needs if I did need an academic reason the library is just there. The books are available. The journals are available online so academic wise I'm satisfied. All my needs are met.
>
> (Andrew)

Conclusion

The narrative of a crisis of masculinity presents an over-simplistic analysis of the increasing numbers of women accessing higher education in some parts of the world. It also rests on patriarchal and misogynist assumptions that women's position should always be in a minority (Morley, 2010). In the context of higher education, this has reduced complex gendered inequalities to a presumed battle of the sexes, failing to engage with the intricate ways that formations of gender are produced and performed in different pedagogical spaces and disciplinary contexts, privileging particular kinds of practices, knowledge and identities whilst excluding Others. We have written elsewhere about how the GaP data suggest students tend to reject explanations of structural influences on students' behaviour and outcomes (Francis, Burke and Read, 2014). Drawing on the accounts of students and lecturers, we have shown in this chapter how masculinities and femininities play out in complex ways across pedagogical practices, relations and spaces, both influenced by *and* challenging to hegemonic patriarchal discourses of gender. Detailed attention to formations of masculinity within pedagogical relations reveals the important ways that intersections of gender and masculinity with other, pathologised identities inflame problematic anxieties about 'lowering of standards' and the neo-liberal imperative for higher education to produce disciplined subjects, or in Foucault's terms, 'docile bodies' (Foucault, 1977). Indeed, gender is always embodied, and although masculinities can be taken up by different kinds of bodies and selves, only certain bodies can be positioned as legitimate and authoritative in relation to hegemonic patriarchal discourses of masculinity (which play out differently across different pedagogical contexts). This poses a challenge for the inclusion of men from 'Other' kinds of social backgrounds, as well as those not conforming to hegemonic heterosexual masculinities. Gendered formations are shaped in relation to the often-derisive constructions of working-class and Black masculinities, as well as constructions of LGBTQ realities, which reinforce inequalities in pedagogical spaces and problematic subjective positions of both students and lecturers. Higher education pedagogies thus require reformation to address such complex issues and concerns but in ways that reject the highly problematic claim that masculinity is in crisis due to the feminisation of higher education.

Chapter 7

Pedagogies of difference

'Race', ethnicity and social class in higher education

In spite of the immense demographic changes that have taken place in British universities as a result of WP policies, they remain predominantly White middle-class spaces (HEFCE, 2010, 2013). Some universities of course are more successful at recruiting Black and Minority Ethnic and White working-class students than others (HEFCE, 2003) but this has contributed to a hierarchy of universities and a suggestion of certain universities being easier to access than others. Hierarchies of disciplinary subjects already exist with not only the polarisation of vocational and academic but also interdisciplinary subjects so pejoratively termed 'Mickey Mouse' subjects by amongst others the former Minister of State for Universities and Science, David Willetts as well as the right wing press (Doughty, 2007; Shepherd, 2010). Higher Education is highly competitive: for places, for status and post HE for graduate jobs. This has been heightened by the imposition of £9,000 fees plus living costs and the demand for value for money. Although the students in our research were not yet faced with these excessive expenses they were subjected to the surrounding discourses and were acutely aware of the value and authenticity of their university and their university experience. Most of the students we interviewed talked about how they loved Riverside University, for its location, the support, friendships and the diversity as well as the teaching experience but many also said it had not been their first choice of university and they had gone there because they had failed to get their expected grades: in other words, it was second best. We suggest, therefore, authenticity takes on added meanings and may serve as a lens through which to view and evaluate their university experience and (or) an influence on what will add or detract from that value.

In Chapter five we discussed the importance of friendship (see also Read et al., forthcoming for a further analysis of this) not just as a means of enabling feelings of belonging but also as dimensions of social networking. As we argued, social networking can provide students with useful opportunities to access valuable resources for furthering their studies and gain high-status employment opportunities. Peer relations therefore arguably take on added importance. With this is mind, in this chapter, we discuss aspects of peer relations and specifically White student perceptions and constructions of their fellow BME and working-class students.

Authenticity

Whilst the financial cuts and student fee increases to threaten widening participation in overt ways, the more subtle innuendos regarding authenticity and legitimacy are equally damaging. The potential danger of these discourses on the students and the ways they can undermine the value of the university experience is particularly an issue for the post-1992 universities – the universities which have been the most successful at recruiting working-class and Black and Minority Ethnic students. Since the HE/FE Education Act in 1992 when Polytechnics were awarded university status, there has been an ongoing tussle between what are still in effect the two sectors – the pre- and post-1992 universities as they are called. The raising of student fees together with cuts in the teaching grant has again brought these tensions to the fore. We have on the one hand from the previous Coalition government ministers, notions of 'pointless' degrees and on the other that universities need to equip graduates with work-related skills (Trowler, 1998; Burke, 2012). We have sentiments from the CBI but also the Russell group and 1994 universities' group distancing themselves from post-1992 universities and implying that they are inadequate. Certain universities also have a list of 'unsuitable' qualifications for entry to their college/university. On the Trinity College Cambridge website (www.trin.cam.ac.uk, accessed 1/05/16) for example, it explains that to study at Cambridge, thirteen A-levels are of 'limited suitability' including business studies, film studies, sociology, psychology, law, drama/theatre studies, art and design and archaeology. Twenty-four A-levels that are only suitable as fourth subjects include accounting, citizenship, dance, health and social care, music technology, photography and ICT. It goes on to explain that 'VCE [Vocational Certificate of Education], GNVQs [General National and Vocational Qualifications] and/or BTECs [Business and Technology Education Council] do not prepare applicants sufficiently for Cambridge, so our offers do not include them.' Black and Minority Ethnic (BME) students, and women who now attend university in slightly greater numbers to men, continue to predominate in the less valued subject areas.

For years now there has also been the implication that post-1992 universities were not doing their job properly because of the high attrition rates. There is therefore an implication that certain universities lack authenticity and by implication so do their students and also in some cases their subjects of study. This raises questions about social class, and other marginalised identities, and the stratification of the higher education system. But it also raises questions about what is education for? And who is it for?

The widening participation initiative in Britain has been an important step in challenging the stratification of society in general and in some respects the academic power and hierarchisation of higher education in particular. Interdisciplinary subjects are part of this challenge. Although the structural factors serve to reinforce such stratification there are also psychic implications propounded by stereotypical assumptions, which are embedded in society and pervade attitudes and support mythologies. As Charles Taylor (1992) has argued, whatever socially derived identity one develops, there is the idea of authenticity itself that is central in identity formation (47) – and one might add, in a neo-liberal society in particular, both globally as well as nationally.

The point of the argument here is to put into perspective, alongside other contextual issues already identified, the socio-political conditions that serve as a backdrop to the students' university experience. In this chapter we recount from our data some students' perceptions of their peers. We are not drawing a correlation between these perspectives and the above scenario but we do raise the question that this tenuous and competitive environment gives rise not just to anxieties as we have seen in previous chapters but also to peer antagonisms and potential disharmony. We utilise the context to locate their accounts within the wider socio-political changes in HE, which shape student identities and experiences.

In Chapters four, five and six we discussed issues around 'difference and diversity' in relation to pedagogical experiences from both staff and student perspectives, respectively. In this Chapter we take these recurring themes and explore their nature and meaning for students in relation to their perceptions of what the university and its student body 'should be like' or means to them. In our data we discovered some 'racialised' and classed polarities of perceptions and experiences, which were expressed by White students as antagonisms towards and fear of certain social groups. For all students though there was an element of fear at different levels throughout the university experience. In this chapter we explore those personal relations and associations, which overtly for some and more dysconsciously (King, 1991) for others, impinge on identity and identification and are also imbued with notions of authenticity: the 'authentic student' and the authentic university. In particular, we discuss the objectification of BME and White working-class students by their White middle-class counterparts and their construction and positioning as Other. We contrast this with BME and White working-class students' accounts of their experiences of and relationship to the university.

Out of place

As we argued in Chapter five, fitting in and belonging has been a central theme in studies of widening participation in HE, particularly in the UK. Most often it has been discussed with respect to social class and accessing the necessary capitals in order to get to university and progress when there (Archer, Hutchings and Ross, 2003; Read, Archer and Leathwood, 2003; Lehman, 2009). Crozier, Reay, Clayton and Colliander (2008) found that 'fitting-in' for working-class students had different manifestations within the social field and the academic field depending on their educational histories and learning resources and the different social and academic milieu they found themselves in. Research has shown that for Black and Minority Ethnic (BME) students in a White-dominated setting there are additional issues. Bhopal (2010) for example has demonstrated that many of the Asian women in her research sought friendship with other Asian women as a means of mutual identity, shared understanding of their life and cultural experiences, and a sense of security. In their work on university choice, Reay, David and Ball (2005) clearly demonstrated that BME applicants chose universities where they felt they identified; they chose institutions where there were people 'like me' and where they felt comfortable. Also in Crozier, Reay & Clayton's study (2010) for example, a British South Asian heritage student, Nasir, explained his reasons for going to a city (although not necessarily his university) where there were other British Asians because of fear of racism which he had experienced at school and in his city of origin, in order to try to avoid this. When he got to university he gravitated towards the other Asian students, which as he ultimately reflected had the effect of cutting him off from a range of new life experiences. In this sense we can see how BME students are in effect separated into certain spaces (see also Archer, Hutchings and Ross, 2003).

Few of the BME students in the GaP project (23% of our respondents) spoke explicitly about this; however, Greg, a third-year student described a range of divisions across the university which served to separate or as he said 'segregate' students. In the extract below Greg talks about the social organisation of the College system, which was in the process of being modified, and he identifies how it has this exclusionary effect:

> I think it's kind of going now 'cause they got rid of [the Luxembourg] bar and [Tower] bar. Everything's sort of neutral where we've got the student union. Before there was a lot more banter between colleges like [Parks, Luxembourg, Pankhurst]. I think they needed to bring the university together though because other unis don't do that. It was really unique to Riverside, which is good in one way but then that meant that you would sort of just be with your [Luxembourg] people or with your [Parks] people. Now I know a lot of people from [Parks] that I wouldn't have known if we had sort of segregation . . . in the bar. Whereas before we would just be in [Luxembourg] bar and they don't really come there, so.
>   (Greg, Black Caribbean, working-class, male student)

This is interesting since as we will show, BME students tend to occupy Luxembourg College because of their subject of study. What we appear to hear from the BME students in our data is a desire for an integrated and collective community. Only one BME student talked explicitly about racialised cliques at her school when she was specifically asked but she denies these existing at university:

> No, the cliquey thing no way. . . . in primary school yeah we had our little cliques and the cliques were usually in areas – the families that live around the school you would be close with. And you would be with kids with similar backgrounds. Like my Mum is Jamaican [and so:] [they say: "oh] your Mum is Jamaican" . . . . And in secondary school it was more or less the same thing

but the cliques were not as strong. You had different people coming from different areas. But usually you would have a common interest like how us girls thought. You would have the bad girls; the geeky girls; or the ordinary girls that just didn't fit into any cliché but were just friends.

Whereas here now I have Asian friends. I have an African friend. I have friends from different religions. And it's like there is nothing social that links us together it's just we are at university and we are doing our work. Literally there are no other background links between us. We are all different religions, different colours.

(Simone, Black British, working-class, female student)

Here she replicates the experience of 'sticking together' but implies that it was more associated with ethnic and teenage interests than racial discrimination. She compares her experience at Riverside as very diverse and yet interestingly in her group of friends and associates she only identifies other BME students. Greg adds to this interpretation when he talked about the subsequently disbanded African Caribbean Society (ACS). Asked if he had been involved in the ACS he replied:

I went in my first year to a couple of the meetings but I thought I didn't want to go to it 'cause I felt like I was segregating myself and I don't like that. I like to be with everyone. I feel like it might be a bit controversial saying it but I don't think there should be any society in terms of your race; like I don't' think there should be an Asian Society, a Black Society. I think everyone should just be neutral 'cause then people will get to know each other much more.

We are not suggesting that either of these BME students were seeking to assimilate or deny their BME identities but we cite these extracts as a contrast to the perspectives of the White students that follow. The perception by some White students of BME students is markedly different. BME students were often seen as forming cliques which were interpreted as standoffish and as will be seen, at times threatening. These perceptions echo similar accusations of BME school students as 'not mixing' and forming gangs that others have written about (e.g. Crozier and Davies, 2008). Indeed any grouping of BME young people seems to denote a gang formation and with that its aggressive connotation (see for example Alexander, 2000; Shain, 2011). This accusation of not mixing, rather than the White students separating themselves off, is echoed by many of the White students at Riverside University. For them, concerns about cliques amongst students are an ongoing theme and typically White students allege that these are based on ethnicity, together with an accusation that 'Black people stick together'.

There are those sort of cliques that people still sort of stick in that's like school a bit which I didn't really expect at university . . . ethnicity would be the main group. I'm not, I don't know how to say this without sounding racist. . . . all I will say is groups are very much dominated by ethnicity and not so much gender . . . definitely ethnicity . . . ethnicity would be the biggest factor.

(Gerald, White, male, middle-class student)

Ethnicity I think is definitely a big influence. There are a lot of Black people that tend to stick together.

(Christopher, White, middle-class, male student)

Racialised and gendered groupings are manifest nationally in geographic as well as social and academic spaces such as types of university and particular subjects of study. At Riverside the visibility of BME students is dependent on time of day and College location related to subject of study. The BME students come into the University in the day for their lectures, as we have said, most living off campus and at home (only one of our BME respondents out of 14 lived on campus at the time of interview). Nevertheless, or perhaps because of this, as indicated in Chapter four, Black and especially male students seemingly draw attention to themselves; Nirmal Puwar (2004) refers to this as 'Black bodies out of place'. In her thesis she discusses colonial power as an illustration of White domination in perhaps its starkest form. As part of the power relationship and efforts to maintain White control, assimilation was (and arguably remains) a key device. However, this is not without its problems for the ruling group; as Puwar puts it: 'White superiority is called into question by this colonial encounter' (p. 115). She utilises Bhabha's (1994) concept of 'mimicry' to explain that too much assimilation can be threatening and disrupting or as she says: 'the right words coming out of the wrong mouths' (p. 115).

Whilst we have shown that many White students found Black students to be highly visible at times, in fact Black students were completely absent in certain spheres. As well as not living on campus, they also said they only came in to the University for, on average, three days per week and just for lectures and seminars, and as we have discussed, BME students tended to take Business and Sports Studies; thus frequenting only those or certain areas of those two colleges: Luxembourg and Park. In addition, there was little reflection of diversity in the general social provision for students. Whilst we are not advocating tokenistic gestures, such manifestations are important signifiers of diversity, recognition and value. Therefore, when, for example, the African Caribbean Society, which was an important source of 'Black representation', was disbanded, it conveyed, we suggest, a negative message of rejection. Also the few African Caribbean heritage students whom we interviewed talked of the lack of appeal of Student Union events for them and other BME students. Likewise, even basic catering provision gave no recognition to the requirement for halal meat for instance.

I think there's a lot of especially some of the Black people that go to university, they feel that the music isn't catered for them so they don't really come out as much. If you came out [at night] you'd see that it's less Black people and more White people.

(Simone, female, Black British, working-class student)

When they do Freshers'[1] week. They do a lot of concerts or disco or whatever. It ends up being . . . for people who like music like rock or pop or things like that. Whereas I am more of an urban Black. We like R&B, reggae and we usually we look towards African Caribbean Society to put on events for us to go to. It's like the university especially the student union isolate not intentionally – the activities that they provide. People from different other ethnic backgrounds are not going to go to it. It does not entice you to go. So I remember like in Freshers' Week this year, everyone was like "are you going?" And a lot of people were saying "no – I'm not going; I'm not going. I'm not going."

(Simone, female, Black British student)

Nevertheless, BME but also White working-class students, at Riverside, not traditionally university students at all, have been 'too' visible. Given these sentiments it is not surprising that Greg and Simone played down any racialised separation although we emphasise that they did not make any such references themselves nor indeed did the other twelve respondents. In fact there was little mention at all of race from any of the BME students. This echoes Francis, Burke and Read's (2014) (writing about the GaP project) analysis of the students' denial of 'structural distinction'. Whilst as Francis et al. say the impression from the students is 'one of no problem here (Gaine, 1995)' (p. 6) with regard to the BME students we suggest that there is a fear of drawing attention to themselves (ironically in the light of our analysis); as Greg said he wanted to 'remain neutral'.

Riverside is unreal: 'like how the other half live'

Throughout the GaP data there is a sense that many of our respondents found the classed and ethnic diversity of the university a surprising and unsettling experience. Several students talked about coming from private schools where the majority were very similar in their backgrounds (White and middle class) and their identities were taken for granted as the norm. Some White students said how much they had learnt in this diverse environment of Riverside but at the same time there was an objectification of this as strange and exotic. There are recurring references made by White middle-class students to the Other, (racialised, classed and gendered) as separate, as difficult, as disruptive and/or threatening. These identifications are often implicit rather than explicit, identified by default or association. Social class and ethnicity are made visible only when contrasted to the White middle-class norm as explained by this White middle-class student:

> If you are living in [Luxembourg College] you are around people, you know, people [who] greet each other by saying – "wa gwan, blud". It's different to what they [the White middle class students] are going to be used to. . . .
> (Stephen, White, male, middle-class student)

Although this student went on to say how he loved being in this ethnically diverse setting he also, albeit, 'dysconsciously', mocked and exoticised some of his fellow students:

> Different cultural backgrounds, they come together, you get different lingo, different culture. I just found it all hilarious and fascinating, I loved it all. I would entertain certain friends, you know, [about people] who speak like that, by me doing it, you've got this guy coming from [Home Counties, suburbs], saying this language, they found it hilarious, you know. I found them just all lapping it up and not taking it too seriously, not being prejudiced.
> (Stephen, White, middle-class, male student)

In this instance he asserts that his friends are not being prejudiced in enjoying this 'diversity' which demonstrates the ways that constructions of 'diversity' are often steeped in colonialist histories of racialised inequalities and yet are seen to be inclusive and non-discriminatory. Historically the White view of Black people is as fascinatingly strange and entertaining (Said, 2003). In this way Black people are seen as less threatening and can be kept in their place. The Other is both ridiculed ('I just found it all hilarious and fascinating, I loved it all') and exoticised as entertainment, ('I would entertain certain friends, by me doing it [that is mimicking the accent]. They found it hilarious . . . so damn great'). Holt and Griffin (2005) discuss how the dialectic between fascination and disgust informs the relationship with the Other, aiming to ensure that they are kept at a distance. A stark example of that distancing is in some White middle-class students' description of being at Riverside as an 'unreal' experience, as described by this student who likened the experience to being in the television programme, East Enders and describing BME students and White working-class students, again, in terms of 'gangs':

> I'm kind of middle class, we're quite well off. It's just interesting to see people who aren't so well off and live in really crowded places. They are all gangs. It's like the kind of thing you see in East Enders [a soap opera] . . .It's kind of like the programme How the Other Half Live.
> (Daniel, White, male, middle-class student)

There are undertones of anxiety and a construction and fear of the 'Other'. They are alien and threatening: 'they are all gangs'. There's almost a sense that this experience is surreal and it raises the question of being out of place here. Black and Minority Ethnic students and White working-class people at university is unsettling for some White middle-class students, particularly in the highly competitive space that HE represents: the presence of Others is seen to devalue the experience (or the potential capital that can be derived from the experience); hence the need to assert some differentiation, and create some distance. As we saw in Chapter five there is no recognition of these views amongst students and no apparent pedagogic strategies to address, critique or disrupt these issues and constructions within what is proudly referred to as a diverse HE community.

It is this terrain of difference which marks the, albeit, implicit tensions and struggles which in our interviews are articulated in terms of stereotypical perceptions and also territoriality. Drawing on wider dominant/public pathologising discourses and fears around Black masculinity (e.g. Westwood, 1990; Majors and Billson, 1992; Sewell, 1997; Neal, 2013; Noguera, 2014) Black male students are often demonised as gangsters, bad boys, 'tearabouts', threatening and troublesome. As one student explains 'most of the boys' in Luxembourg are Black and are 'a bit like gangsters'.

> I've noticed that like – this is not to be racist or like horrible or anything like that – but most of the boys, like most of the people that go to [Luxembourg College] are boys and a lot of them are like Black boys, more a bit like gangsters and the people who have come to [one of the other Colleges] are a bit more like quieter. . . .
>
> (Josephine, White British/East Asian,
> middle-class, female student)

And another student refers to Luxembourg College as 'the ghetto':

> Um . . . there's a . . . I don't think there's any racism at [Riverside], it's so mixed, although, I say there's no racism, but there are jokes like about [Luxembourg College] because most of . . . it seems that on [Eliot] there's no Black residents, on [Parks] you never really see Black residents, and then on [Luxembourg] it's all Black residents. And I've got friends on [Luxembourg] who are Black, and it's a joke. It's called the ghetto . . . and we have banter about it, I say you don't fit in on [Luxembourg] unless you've got two Blackberries, because everyone's always typing on their Blackberries, it's ridiculous.
>
> (Rebekka, White, female, middle-class student)

> [Luxembourg College] people will generally be recognised as being, I suppose, I don't know, sort of bad boys on campus, because [Riverside]

University is approximately seventy five per cent female, but in [Luxembourg] you've got pretty much an even gender balance, because [Luxembourg] is primarily a Business school and a lot of Business students are guys. . . . So, yeah, there's something about the Business course that seems to attract a certain, certain, you know, mentality, kind of range of guys, and you end up with lots of, you know, [Luxembourg] is madness, you know, after nights out. . . .

(Stephen, White middle-class, male student)

The sense of disruption and challenge to normality is palpable:

[Luxembourg College] is more urban sort of 'cause you've got lots of people doing Business. . . . So I'd say [Luxembourg] College is more urban sort of thing.

Interviewer: What do you mean by urban?

They're sort of more London. I dunno, they're a London sort of type. More working class sort of people. Um yeah, people from a more working class sort of background. None the less very nice people I've met there. And then you've also got people, I dunno, tearabouts maybe as well, at [Luxembourg College]. I've heard it's quite hairy, not hairy but.

Interviewer: What does tearabout mean?

Um people who were maybe a bit rebellious when they were younger.

. . . Tearabouts yeah. [Luxembourg] College is quite hard. That's what I'd kind of say. People who were rebellious or like from a working class background. . . .

(Bradley, White, male, middle-class student)

There is an accusation that BME and by implication working class students, don't belong at university and/or are out of control. These descriptions both construct BME and White working-class students as illegitimate subjects of and in higher education and reinforce their illegitimacy as students. Not only are they constructed as interlopers in the university but they are also positioned as alien, 'rebellious' and potentially threatening to HE and society in general. As Skeggs (2004) suggests excess and vulgarity are projected onto the working class in order that the middle class can preserve their 'respectability, reflexivity and responsibility' (p. 119); the same argument can also be transposed to constructions of Black masculinities (BME students are most often regarded as working class even when they are not). In previous chapters we have discussed the criticisms by students of their peers for apparent 'disruptive' behaviour and behaving, in their view, inappropriately. The White middle-class students described 'the Other' as 'idiots', 'people who would come to university not really knowing what they were doing'; 'people who are just not interested in anything'. Positioning working class and in this case also BME people, as inferior, violent, out of control and marginal, helps to justify the separation of classed and racialised groups to prevent contamination. In turn the White middle-class (and masculine) identity is asserted as superior (Holt and Griffin, 2005).

Irrespective of race, class or gender, however, in this highly competitive environment, the pressure to comply, and more importantly perform, appropriately often engendered fear and anxiety about losing face or being ridiculed amongst some students, or worse still, failing to achieve the grades. Many of the White students express these kinds of anxieties about being seen as inadequate; they fear appearing as stupid or lacking in some way (Burke and Crozier, 2014). Thus the spectre of inauthenticity haunts many students which we suggest is likely to heighten the urgency of distancing from those more identifiable as 'out of place'. As we showed in Chapter six some of this distancing is conveyed in the criticisms of fellow students' learning behaviours and (non) participation in the learning/ teaching situation, made by White middle-class students. The following extract however shows this student taking these criticisms further:

> I think the government has set this unrealistic goal of having fifty per cent of the population go through university. Now that inevitably means a massive proportion of people at university today probably shouldn't be here, and from my experience I can think of several people who obviously shouldn't be at university, and call me very, you can say I'm being very harsh there, I probably am, but the simple fact is I don't think they should be here, I don't think they are bright enough.
>
> (Damien, White, male, middle-class student)

He asserts that there are certain students who are not entitled to be university students, ignoring their legitimacy of getting their entry grades.

There is clearly a clash of experiences and perceptions expressed here. Similar views of frustration and disquiet at this reluctance or refusal to conform is also expressed by many of the lecturers in these particular subject areas. The evidence suggests that these White students are condemnatory of and seek to disassociate themselves from, these recalcitrant behaviours and attitudes. In so doing they are implicitly defining *themselves* as entitled and 'good' students in relation to the Other's 'idiocy' and waywardness. As Holt and Griffin argue (2005):

> Othering enables the middle classes to focus on aspects of their identities which they wish to hold up as defining their group's characteristics (for example middle class taste, intelligence, refinement) while denying these characteristics for the working class [and we would add BME] Other.
>
> (p. 248)

Conclusion

In this chapter we have shown that in spite of the successes of WP policies and practices, BME and White working-class students are still positioned as 'out of place' in the university setting. Through the analysis of student data we have shown how the White middle-class students' gaze is focused on the Black presence dialectically as something both entertaining (exotic) and disconcerting/dangerous. BME students continue to be 'misrecognised' and constructed as 'folk devils' around which there have been and are moral panics (Sibley, 1995; Crozier and Davies, 2008), not least from their fellow, White middle-class students. Historically folk devils, as Sibley (1995) suggests, represent oppositional forces and a threat to the status quo and concomitantly the 'moral panic' urges the need 'to define the contours of normality and to eliminate difference.' (p. 40).

Patricia Hill Collins (1998) provided insights into the implications of what is behind BME marginalisation. She pointed to the surveillance employed in monitoring Black people 'when they enter White spaces of the public and private spheres'. Ways of achieving this surveillance centre around assimilationist strategies: through maintaining 'White norms' – behaviours, language, accents and cultural artefacts; to adapt, take on White middle-class values and ways of being in order to get on and be accepted. With reference to the USA, Collins reflects on the shift in historical imperatives and argues that the necessity to maintain control of the Other remains:

> Whereas racial segregation was designed to keep Blacks as a group or class outside centers of power, surveillance now aims to control Black individuals inside centers of power when they enter the White spaces of the public and private spheres.
>
> (p. 921)

Again in his discussion of moral panics, Sibley (1995, p. 39) argues that 'boundary consciousness' is sharpened in order to exclude and ensure that the 'Other' is eliminated or prevented from appropriating such spaces for themselves. The 'space' referred to here is both physical and 'cultural' space within the university. The struggle for 'cultural space' represents a power struggle. The metaphorical struggle that takes place in the university is to ensure that the 'dominant culture' endures. In our data there is evidence of such 'cultural' boundaries, both institutional but as we have shown, also interpersonal, through the discourse and behaviours of White middle-class students which marginalise and exclude the BME and White working-class students and render them invisible or marginalised in various ways. And yet as we have argued the novelty of their presence for many White middle-class students means they are constantly under the spotlight of surveillance (Puwar, 2004, p. 117).

As we discussed in Chapter four, some of the lecturers also expressed concern and disquiet about students' non-conforming behaviour. In this way, diversity might sometimes be seen by White staff and students as a form of contamination of HE culture, particularly when tied to polarising discourses of the 'Other' kind of student, implicitly connected to widening participation agendas (Williams, 1997; Burke, 2012). The WP subject is constructed as not knowing what is acceptable or understanding the (unspoken) rules of the game. The student associated with WP is constructed in such instances as a threat to HE standards and more personally White middle class students are concerned that he/she threatens the symbolic and exchange value of their HE capital. This as we have argued is exacerbated by the neo-liberal market conditions and the discourse of university authenticity together with the intensification of competition for graduate jobs.

As we suggested earlier, getting value for money and a 'valuable' degree is important for all students, irrespective of ethnicity or social class although the expression of this may differ accordingly. However, the climate of racialised, classed and frequently gendered antagonisms for BME and White working-class students cannot be underestimated. In 2014 the National Union of Students (NUS) carried out a 'Race' Equality Survey of university staff and students, which resulted in a report of overwhelming evidence of racism in the university sector (in England). We suggest that in our study, the White middle-class student attitudes and perceptions, contribute to a particular ethos and environment, which is unlikely to be wholly conducive to a positive social or critically engaging learning experience. Further, the prevalence of racial and class antagonisms, the disquiet over cliques and the apparent 'fear' expressed by some of the White middle-class students, creates a 'background noise' which is potentially destabilising for BME and White working-class students, with implications as well for the reproduction of race, gender and class inequalities.

Note

1 Freshers' Week in the UK is the first week of the University term for first year undergraduate students – those just commencing their degree programmes. It is intended to be an opportunity to introduce the students to how the university and their programmes are organised; to meet the programme convenors, the head of department, as well as their teachers. It is also an opportunity to meet fellow students and potentially make friends. The Students' Union usually organises special events for new students. Traditionally these have been focused on a drinking culture which is not appropriate for many students, especially those who have particular religious principles. Also the events are often masculinised according to anecdotal evidence, and as the student quoted here says, the music events are ethnocentric.

Chapter 8

Theorising the early career experience

Towards collective engaged pedagogies

This chapter argues that precariousness in higher education disrupts higher education teachers' identity formation and pedagogies, leading to misrecognition and inequality. Precariousness is often a term connected to the newness of early career academics. As Gill (2010, p. 232) notes, 'precariousness is one of the defining experiences of contemporary academic life – particularly, but not exclusively, for younger or 'career early' staff (a designation that can now extend for one's entire 'career', given the few opportunities for development or secure employment)'. She goes on to note that this precariousness for PhD students, new postdocs and teaching fellows, among other positions, is related to issues such as short-term contracts, tasks of delivering mass undergraduate programmes 'with little training, inadequate support, and rates of pay that – when preparation and marking are taken into account – frequently fall (de facto) below the minimum wage' (Gill, 2010). Gill also notes that lack of benefits and summer pay are also issues of precariousness. Non/visibility of ECTs within their working environment (departments, faculties, universities) contributes to the development of this trajectory. Drawing on Burke (2012), we argue that the way academics experience their 'early-careerness' contributes to their 'mis/recognition as il/legitimate subjects in higher education'. We build on this work to explore ECTs' experiences, considering how mis/recognition (as theorised in Chapter two) illuminates:

> A way of talking about forms of respect and disrespect that drop out of the standard models of distributive justice which focus on who gets what. . . . Recognition has to do with respect, esteem, prestige: the way society values different traits, different activities. It has to do with what I would call "patterns" of cultural value.
>
> (Fraser, 2011)

Precariousness, and the interconnected politics of misrecognition that play out in precarious relations and contexts, can be connected to bell hooks' conceptualisation of engaged pedagogy, a concept which builds on critical and feminist pedagogies and emphasises a commitment to a process of self-actualization that promotes well-being and wholeness (hooks, 1994, pp. 15–16). 'Wholeness' is a concept developed by Thich Nhat Hanh, referring to 'a union of mind body and spirit' (hooks, 1994, pp. 14–15). Importantly, from a post-structural sense, however, the notion of 'self-actualization' as an individualising discourse and that there is an 'essential self' that can be unified to be made 'whole', are problematic. Yet neither do we wish to throw the proverbial baby out with the bath water. Indeed, as we stated in Chapter one, pedagogical experiences are entangled with identity formations and processes of becoming and are necessarily emotional. In Chapter two, we further explored emotion, noting that 'fear *of* emotion' (Hey and Leathwood, 2009) is deeply connected to those 'dividing practices' that operate to recover the hegemony of rationality and the exclusion of emotion from higher education pedagogical spaces.

While we recognise that precariousness is an issue for all higher education teachers in general, in this chapter and as an example of how precariousness plays out in different ways, we explore early career teachers' (ECT) experiences in higher education, impacted in particular ways due to their 'new' professional positionalities. The idea of 'early career' highlights a specific perspective on the experience of being academic staff, an experience which we explored in Chapter four. This experience is tied to a sense of 'newness'. Yet this newness must be problematised, since long before embarking on a journey to become a HE teacher, the person may already have played a role in an academic community, for example, as a researcher. Depending on the country context and discipline, possessing academic and/or other professional experience may be a requisite for entering the PhD in the first place. Thus, 'early career' tells very little about the person's previous experiences and large variances exist among the so-called early-career teachers. For instance, the age at which the person enters and at which she/he completes the PhD is tied to these variances – a 'traditional' early career versus 'mature' early career (i.e. the ECT is not necessarily young). Social class, 'race' and ethnicity, and gender are important interwoven differences and inequalities that shape the ECT's experience (Misiaszek, 2015, p. 5).

Bearing this in mind, in this chapter we argue for the need to explore ECTs' identity formations and processes of becoming and for the recognition of the emotion of the experience and how this emotion necessarily entails mind-body-spirit reflection. To address these issues, we argue for the need to adapt hooks' concept of engaged pedagogy, to draw out its important emphasis on well-being and on reflection on the body, mind and spirit. We define 'spirit'/'spirituality' not as something 'understood within a particular religious framework', but instead concerned with 'awareness' (Glazer in hooks, 2003, p. 180) of 'the qualities of the human spirit – such as love and compassion, patience, tolerance, forgiveness, contentment, a sense of responsibility, [and] a sense of harmony' (His Holiness the Dalai Lama in hooks, 2003, p. 178). Spirituality is affirmed by an 'inner life' (hooks, 2010, p. 149) that shapes our 'practice, how we live in the world and how we relate to self and others' (hooks, 2010, p. 149).

We will use the concept of 'collective engaged pedagogy' to describe this adaption. Collective engaged pedagogy promotes well-being and spaces for reflexivity beginning at a personal level but beyond that to the collective sense, which we argue ultimately promotes social justice.

We contend that precariousness significantly constrains opportunities and possibilities for ECTs' to be engaged with their colleagues, their students, and perhaps more significantly, with themselves. What higher education spaces do ECTs have in order to cultivate engagement? We argue that these spaces for engagement are increasingly restricted, and without these spaces, the potential for knowledge creation by ECTs, as well as the trajectories they can forge, are also constrained. This in turn perpetuates patterns of inequality and misrecognition that are in danger of persisting in middle and later career.

In the two sections that follow, we first present a conceptual exploration of temporality as it relates to the ECT experience, further exploring 'newness', a concept interwoven with precariousness. This grounds our second section, a conceptual and empirical exploration of precariousness as it relates to ECTs' identity formations and pedagogical experiences, drawing on the Fulbright project (we have included the ages of ECTs in the text as we believe this is relevant to the discussion). We conclude with a reflection on how collective engaged pedagogies can offer ways forward for work by and with ECTs.

Temporalities and the ECT experience

Returning to the idea of 'newness' as a characteristic of ETAs led us to consider how 'newness' is tied into the concept of temporality, a concept we highlighted in Chapter two in our discussion of 'space' where we argue that spaces are also deeply tied in with temporalities and the ways that time is structured within and across those spaces as well as within our different relationalities to time across structural and symbolic inequalities. Indeed, an ECT being 'new' in the 'space' of higher education is a temporal experience. In considering how ECTs engage in processes of critical reflexivity surrounding their newness, McNay's analysis of temporality is particularly useful:

> Following Husserl, Bourdieu invokes a more praxeological notion of temporality as protention – time as involving a 'practical reference to the future' – and thereby opens up the act of reproduction to indeterminacy and the potential for change (1992, p. 129). For example, the idea of a detraditionalization of gender norms cannot be accounted for in Butler's static model of domination because it does not allow a notion of decomposition from within. A more active notion of praxis is required where social being is regarded not just as repetition but as a creative anticipation of future uncertainty on the part of social actors.
>
> (McNay, 1999, p. 102)

This notion of praxis in which a social being is regarded as a 'creative anticipation of future uncertainty' brings to mind the *inédito viável* (untested feasibility)

(Freire, 1970), a concept associated with 'incompleteness, inconclusiveness, and unfinishedness' (Romão, 2007; Torres, 2007). If ECTs' engagement is rooted in this understanding of time and the potentialities associated with it, this will arguably contribute to ECTs' ability to see their own identities and pedagogies in more transformative ways. This counters deficit thinking about ECTs' agency: perhaps, because they have no sense of 'loss' from changes in higher education, with their 'newness' (and without the temporal experiences of the past), they may be able to creatively embrace challenges that come from, to employ McNay's term above, 'future uncertainty.'

Temporality is connected to the notion of presence, and we argue that hooks' analysis of presence has important implications for ECTs. In a later work, hooks describes how these pressures affect our ability to be in the present:

> As teachers we join them [students] in this fixation on the future when we work for promotion, tenure, good evaluations. Academically, intellectually, much of the work we do invites us to engage in constant analytical process-ing. More often than not our thinking is aimed in the direction of the past or the future (especially as we work with ideas trying to discover original thoughts that will set us apart from our peers and advance our careers). This mode of thinking can be incredibly fruitful, but unless we can combine it with more passive forms, what Richard Carson and Joseph Bailey call "the free flowing mode," it can *deaden our capacity to be in touch with the present*.
> (hooks, 2003, p. 167, our emphasis)

She goes on to note that during her graduate school years, the courses in which she 'truly learned' combined the analytical thinking most valued in conventional pedagogy and free thinking ('which moves naturally, constantly bringing you fresh, harmonious, thoughts'): 'yet today's frantic need to push toward dead-lines, covering set amounts of material, allows very little room, if any, for silence, for free-flowing work. *Most of us teach and are taught that it is only the future that matters*' (hooks, 2003, p. 167, our emphasis).

We argue that in thinking about classroom pedagogy and complex identity formations while working with future-oriented auditing practices and publishing pressures, ECTs are facing a severe risk of 'deaden[ing] [their] capacity to be in touch with the present'. ECTs relation to time in the contemporary higher edu-cation landscape, as set out in Chapter one, may look very different than what it looked like for later career teachers, pointing to interesting ontological and epistemological differences about notions of and relations to 'time' as it dis/con-nects with professional trajectories, and, to draw on Sellar (2013), performativity, regulation and datafication.

These temporal differences also emerge in hooks' work. She reflects that:

> I am among the baby boomer generation of professors who initially entered an academic climate where we expected to work hard and be poorly paid for

a lifetime. For many of us the trade off is that we would have time. We would have long vacations and summers off to think, to write, to dream.

(hooks, 2003, p. 168)

She goes on to discuss how her later-achieved six-figure salary was not enough to keep her in an academic position in which she felt unsatisfied. While this experience does not resonate universally, we would argue that prioritising the present 'thinking, writing, and dreaming' in higher education is not a radical, naïve dream but a needed reality in order to support the creation of institutions in which collectively engaged professors and students can emerge.

hooks offers a conceptualisation of the practice and the potential benefits of 'being present' in the classroom:

> Teaching students to be fully present, enjoying the moment, the Now in the classroom without fearing that this places the future in jeopardy: that is essential mindfulness practice for a true teacher. . . . It sharpens our awareness; we are better able to respond to one another and to our subject matter.
>
> (2003, p. 173)

Otherwise, as she goes on to note:

> In every classroom there are times when teacher and students are "caught" up, are somewhere else. *It is as though we are collectively in a trance.* . . . Within a utopian world we would be able to dismiss class on such days because educating anyone where they are not present is impossible. Since we cannot leave we try to work with a reality that we have to produce the conditions for learning. *We work with our absence to become present.*
>
> (hooks, 2003, p. 173, our emphasis)

This idea of a 'trance,' which is a temporal experience, leads us into a discussion of identity formations and pedagogy, with reference to the Fulbright project.

Precariousness, identity formations and pedagogy

We argue that a product of this trance, a temporal experience, is what Fulbright participant Federico (Spanish professor, male) called a 'social schizophrenia', which leads us into a discussion of ECTs' identity formations and pedagogy:

> What happens? It's one thing what we say and it's another thing what we do. Not everyone, but there are a lot of people that give medals to themselves [because they think they're] doing *participatory processes* in the classrooms; it's an image they've created that doesn't exist . . . I've started calling it a "social schizophrenia." There isn't full participation. It creates distrust. And

when you're somewhere that you don't trust . . . participation can't emerge; it can't "be born".

(our emphasis)

In thinking about this concept of social schizophrenia, it is useful to bring in McNay (1999, p. 103), who offers that

> A weakness of alternative theories of reflexive transformation is that the emphasis on strategic and conscious processes of self-monitoring overlook certain more enduring, reactive aspects of identity. Other theories of reflexive transformation place much weight on "biographically significant life choices" while ignoring the "unconsidered and automatic, habitual routine of conduct" (Campbell, 1996, p. 163). As Bourdieu points out, "determinisms operate to their full only by the help of unconsciousness" (1992, p. 136).

We argue that this 'social schizophrenia' is a result of the phenomena of 'enduring, reactive aspects of identity,' 'unconsidered and automatic, habitual routine' and the 'unconsciousness.' Spaces for ECTs to deconstruct what 'participatory processes' actually mean, and which draw on elements of engaged pedagogy, seem to offer a way out of this 'trance,' a trance which is sustained by the phenomena described by Campbell and Bourdieu in the quote above.

We argue that this trance, and this provocative idea of 'social schizophrenia (in the sense of the dictionary definition of 'contradictory or antagonistic qualities or attitudes,' not of the medical disorder) could be seen as both a product of and a cause of teachers' isolation at all points of the trajectory. When asked about her autonomy, Paola (Spanish professor, female) reflected, 'my autonomy . . . is sometimes so absolute that it's isolating. . . . My classes aren't evaluated [from the outside]. . . . We have a lot of didactic liberty. . . . I wouldn't call it autonomy – I'd call it isolation.' Although her experience was shared by other participants, others noted that these spaces for collaboration did exist – and collaboration that coexisted with autonomy:

> My discipline is relatively small. . . . And there are many classes that two professors give together. So there's lots of dialogue between colleagues so they can reach an agreement about what material they're going to use, how they're going to do it, the division of work, who's doing what, with whom, so, in my discipline, there's quite a bit of dialogue. There's a lot of autonomy, as well.

(Tómas, Spanish visiting assistant
professor, male, thirty-five)

This is particularly heartening given the potential precariousness of Tómas who had 'visiting assistant professor' status. Tiago (Spanish Educational Director, male) raises a different understanding of autonomy, which breaks from a binary notion of having/not having autonomy:

> It's not really "auto-nomous." It's another thing. I think it's autonomy in the sense that "We, the men and women, are the ones that [do] X] in relationship [with each other], in cooperation [with each other] . . . that decide what we want to do." So, we're talking about an autonomy that is auto-independence – making decisions together.

We argue that here, Tiago presented an interesting alternative to isolation – that of 'auto-independence.'

Discourses of mis/recognition (Fraser, 2003; Burke, 2012) also emerged for the participants in discussions of identity formations. As Tiago notes, faculty must realise that:

> We are not very different from the students (laughter – group agrees). If we don't start there, it's hard to get anywhere. Because we'd be falsifying or mystifying the process of education . . . it's hard for us to participate. It's hard for us to "recognise" each other. . . . Once we recognize this, from that moment on, the processes that we can start, let's say, are more creative, more critical. Because we each situate ourselves, let's say, in a starting point that is real. *It's not hypothetical.* . . .
>
> (our emphasis)

Acknowledging these discourses of recognition, Tiago tied this into a contrast between what is 'real' and what is 'hypothetical.' This brings to mind the idea of a 'hypothetical' holding pattern in the psyches of ECTs. If ECTs are immersed in institutions that do not promote that faculty are 'not very different from the students,' arguably these institutions are creating another generation of teachers whose identities and related pedagogical experiences are being falsified and mystified. Buying into a 'fake it until you make it' mentality could result in ECTs developing faux authoritarian personae. A result of this is that as these identities and pedagogical experiences end up caught in this hypothetical holding pattern, individuals and the institutions further away from the purposes of education for social justice.

In addition, identity formation is often complicated by the fact that, as Lupe (Spanish pre-doctoral researcher, female, twenty-nine) noted, 'I've gone from sitting [in class] as a student to now standing [in class] as a professor but with nothing more than a little pat on the back, "Good luck! Do well!"' The *abruptness in the transition process from student to professor* punctuated Lupe's experience. This transition is characterised by a lack of intellectual agency, as expressed through her comment that 'they give you the topics'- she has no capacity to act independently, which subsequently affects the development of her own identity formation as a teacher (if Lupe was able to present her own work, then this abrupt transition could be interpreted differently). Lupe went on to connect an inherent lack of support – 'deal with it! deal with it!' – with a need for more pedagogical strategies. She notably returned at the end of her comment to this lack of support – 'nothing more than a little pat on the back', which is greeted by knowing laughter from the rest of the group, composed of other ECTs.

Diego (Spanish lecturer, male, twenty-nine) echoed these issues of complex identity formations/transitions:

> The first phase would be a [that of] . . . grantee, [two years] during which you can't give classes. And the other two years, you're not obligated to, but you can. . . . How does this work? *We finish being a grantee and begin to be a professor without stopping being a researcher at the same time.* It's a double identity – investigator and teacher – at the same time. . . . You're faced with a group of students, many of whom are [just] ten years younger than you; they see you as really young compared to the rest of the professors. This makes for a different [sort of] relationship. The students, in some ways, *recognise you as a part of them.* You're not exactly the same because obviously you're the one giving the grades, but *something built* [between you and them]. Something is different and you notice it . . . the way they talk to you. . . .
>
> (our emphases)

In this quote, Diego grappled with the complexities of being a grantee that continues as a researcher as he becomes a professor. Being early career, which in his case implies being close in age to the students, can be parleyed into 'something built' between the lecturer and the students – the students 'recognise you as a part of them.' Yet we would argue that trying to figure out pedagogically how to take advantage (in a positive sense) of that 'something built' (departing from this notion, to return to Tiago's words, that 'we are not very different from the students') – while simultaneously dealing with the pressures that come from being a subject within an institutional system – contributes to ECTs' conflicted experiences in the classroom. In other words, the possibilities are there but so are the pressures. And it is these pressures that affect the well-being needed to teach, to do research, and to publish.

A reflection on well-being is offered by Ana (Portuguese pre-PhD researcher, female, thirty-six), who, to describe the pressures from the European Bologna process, the 'tightening of [increased regulation within] the university', and her workload, said, 'you're not able to breathe' (Misiaszek, 2015, p. 10). This phrase highlights how subjects embody the impacts of these pressures. This embodiment is tied to the notion of breath. Breathing is considered in many traditions to be a mind-body-spirit link that goes with humans everywhere, which would include into the classroom. (Re)actions are manifested in breath and, thus, it plays a subtle, unconscious role in identity formations (we will return to the role of this idea of the unconscious in a moment). Ana's description of her embodiment of these pressures is a metaphor for both feeling pressure from and feeling out of control of her situation.

Conclusion: towards a collective engaged pedagogy

In this chapter we have considered how temporalities connect to the ECT experience, and how these ideas connect to precariousness, identity formation and pedagogy. In response to the issues that we have raised, we argue that a collective engaged pedagogy offers new ways forward in work by and with ECTs. The need for and the challenge to develop collective engaged pedagogies are intensified by increasing audit pressures and less staff/higher teaching loads, two issues which emerged in both projects. This 'perverse reality', as hooks points out, is that 'part of the luxury and privilege of the role of teacher/professor today is the absence of any requirement to be self-actualised' (hooks, 1994, p. 17). hooks reflects on discussions with soon-to-be teachers by

> Listen[ing] to students express the concern that they will not succeed in academic professions if they want to be well, if they eschew dysfunctional behavior or participation in coercive hierarchies. These students are often fearful, as I was, that there are no spaces in the academy where the will to be self-actualised can be affirmed.
>
> (hooks, 1994, p. 18)

While recognising the challenges of co-mentoring in highly competitive, surveilled university systems, to counter this 'perverse reality', we argue for a new understanding of 'co-mentoring' rooted in collective engaged pedagogy. We envision collective engaged co-mentoring as a reciprocal rather than a top-down process, one that acknowledges the risks of positioning either of the partners as having a 'deficit' in order to disrupt traditional notions of what a 'senior' or 'junior' faculty member may act like in such a role, or even if a 'senior' or 'junior' need to play these roles – this points to the possibilities of collective engaged peer mentoring. In addition, there are unique possibilities for partnerships at both ends of the trajectory which may experience precariousness and misrecognition as 'not good enough yet' or 'not good enough anymore.' To counter reactions to this 'not good enough'-ness, co-mentoring can be an opportunity to surrender holds on perpetuating patterns of always appearing 'on' or 'in control,' not just in collegial relationships but also in the classroom.

And, although we do not intend to engage in a psychosocial analysis of higher education teachers here, we believe it is worth noting that 'healing' is one important tenant of hooksian engaged pedagogy. As we have explored in Chapter two, McNay's understanding 'misrecognition and misrepresentation . . . are felt in and through the body as forms of symbolic violence and injury on the self' (McNay, 2008, p. 150). This often leads to feelings of shame and fear' (Ahmed, 2004).

This leads us to ask, how can an ECT (beyond discourses of developing resilience) heal from, for example, an audit result that puts her in an even more precarious situation with her post while she must simultaneously focus on the well-being of her students? Collective engaged co-mentoring has the potential to contribute to a healing process necessary in spaces in which ECTs face precariousness, misrecognition, and misrepresentation.

In addition to co-mentoring, cultivating spaces such as PhD courses in higher education pedagogy, not from a position that the ECTs have a deficit which needed to be 'fixed', but which employ collective engaged pedagogy to confront precariousness and misrecognition, will lead to greater recognition, representation and equality for ECTs. This engaged pedagogy must embrace the fluidities and the possibilities emerging from the *inéditos viáveis* of the ECT experience, a potentially unintended positive consequence of precariousness. Hale (2014, p. 160), in a reflection on a special edition devoted to her ongoing life's work, asked, 'Will the fluid, contingent, irregular, open, unpredictable, and uncertain path lead me to greater creativity?' Collective engaged pedagogy may offer a way towards greater creativity for ECTs, which is not a naïve fantasy but in fact a necessary ongoing adaptation both in professional identity formation and in pedagogy, one which may ultimately make teachers better able to respond to the increased pressures that they are facing at all stages of their teacher trajectory.

Conclusion

Changing pedagogical spaces: reclaiming transformation

This final chapter summarises the key arguments made in the book. It draws out the significance of critical theoretical insights for challenging hegemonic practices and discourses and creating transformative pedagogical spaces in higher education. The chapter will reiterate the argument that hegemonic pedagogies work to silence and make difference and inequality invisible, ironically often through references to social inclusion, widening participation and diversity. Difference tends to be reduced to the marketing images of happy university students from 'Other' kinds of backgrounds. Diversity is often constructed as unproblematic and desirable, whilst difference is controlled through the disciplining technologies of surveillance, regulation, measurement and standardisation. The anxiety about the closeness of the 'Other' to those deemed to be legitimate university participants is often expressed through narratives about the 'dumbing down' of HE pedagogies and the lack of discipline, passion for learning and aspiration implied in and through pathologising and derogatory constructions of students from 'Other' backgrounds. Connected to such anxieties, social inclusion compels those deemed to be 'different' in practices of self-correction. Ultimately, those who have gained access to higher education must conform to and master the normalising and disciplining practices of HE pedagogies. Underpinning such technologies and discourses is the fear of difference in relation to discourses of deficit and lowering of standards. The residual and potential shame of being constructed as different and 'Other' (for both teachers and students) also plays out in asserting legitimacy in the spaces of university.

The research projects expose that mainstream teaching and learning practices in higher education do little to challenge exclusionary classist and racist imaginaries. Indeed, the research demonstrates that HE pedagogies are deeply implicated in the perpetuation of a politics of misrecognition. In times of austerity and crisis, increasing student fees and profound moves towards the marketisation of higher education, students and academics are prone towards risk-averse practices in the pedagogies and identities they engage, unwittingly reinforcing conservative tendencies towards the exclusion and fear of difference. As we have shown some teachers reproduce racist sentiments seemingly unconsciously which suggests that there has been no or little effort on the part of the university to ensure anti-racist practices are implemented.

This is exacerbated by the lack of resources, both material and conceptual, available to support the development of pedagogies that embrace and engage difference, at both the ontological and epistemological levels. We argue that reworking critical and feminist pedagogies and methodologies, by drawing on counter-hegemonic and post/structuralist perspectives and insights, has the potential to open up interventionist spaces, working towards transforming pedagogical spaces for redistribution, recognition and representation. This requires reflexive attention to the affective, cultural, subjective, embodied and symbolic dimensions of pedagogical experiences, subjectivities and meaning-making.

This book has argued that higher education pedagogies are gendered, classed and racialised, reproducing inequalities through taken-for-granted practices and assumptions. We have drawn on research data to explore the ways that pedagogical spaces are experienced across and through complex formations of difference and emotion, entangled in processes of becoming and subjective construction. This is tied in with struggles over the right to higher education and deeper questions about what and who higher education is for. However, we have shown how such questions are buried in the hegemonic discourses of globalisation, neoconservatism and neo-liberalisms, which have reconfigured higher education and pedagogical practices in terms of market-oriented and economic imperatives. This has profound effects on teachers and students and the possibilities for social and cultural change and transformation beyond the hegemonic, corporatised imperatives posed by contemporary and intersecting political forces.

Our position is that pedagogical spaces must be reshaped in relation to broader social justice imperatives, that foreground higher education as an institution that bears social responsibility, including but not exclusive to business and industry. This includes questions of social well-being that involve challenging growing and multiple social and cultural inequalities and injustices. Our research reveals the restrictive and limiting ways that higher education pedagogies are currently being experienced. Drawing on critical voices in the field, we argue that it is vital to pay detailed attention to the forces that are increasingly influencing higher educational policy and as a result the kinds of practices, spaces and identities available to teachers and students in universities. However, we want to intervene in narratives of 'there is no alternative' or that we must prepare students for the 'real world as it exists'. Our position is that spaces of resistance and refusal might become available through reframing higher education pedagogies and teachers' and students' relationalities within them.

Revisiting key themes and debates

In the book we have argued that neo-liberalism is a key force in relation to the politics of higher education reform in the contemporary landscape. New public management is a feature of neo-liberalism and the 'age of performativity'

(Ball, 2003). This has led to a dramatic proliferation of new data infrastructures and new accountabilities in the governance of education systems (Sellar, 2013), including of higher education. However, we also argue that neo-liberalism is not the only force at play in understanding the landscape of higher education, and complex pedagogical relations within it. We must understand neo-liberalism as an intersecting political force with other powerful dynamics. The move towards a global market of higher education is itself intimately bound up with complex social inequalities, injustices and oppressions.

The discourses of 'excellence' have increasingly gained traction and are under-pinned by new public management. This has led to increasing attention to exter-nal accountability, organisation of quality, and efficiency of resource use in higher education. The focus on excellence at a global level has reshaped higher edu-cation systems internationally. Discourses of excellence associated with univer-sity prestige compel institutions to participate in performative and competitive practices in the race to be ranked as 'world-class'. Indeed, Nixon (2013) traces the ways that the drive for 'excellence' often undermines widening participation policy regimes. He warns that competition for funds and for students has led to institutional stratification and the self-protective groupings of institutions, which lobbied intensively for their market niche.

> What we see are levels of institutional sedimentation that provide the bases for structural inequalities that define, restrict and control the horizons of expectation and possibility. "Competition between and within universities", as Stromquist (2012) points out, "does not foster equity but instead creates 'winners' and 'losers.'".
>
> (Nixon, 2013, p. 178 cited in Burke and Kuo, 2015, pp. 551–552)

Nixon argues that in the UK context, 'institutional prestige has itself become a marketable commodity' (Nixon, 2013, p. 178). This has reinforced institutional stratification, across the broad spectrum of differently positioned institutions. Those institutions that have gained university status more recently almost entirely occupy the bottom league, according to world league tables. Many of these insti-tutions have played a crucial role in widening participation and in valuing teach-ing. As Burke and Kuo (2015) have argued:

> the current practices related to WP policy regimes in China, England and the United States have perpetuated a vicious cycle of structural inequalities and discourses of excellence and meritocracy often play a significant part in reproducing this cycle.
>
> (Burke and Kuo, 2015, p. 563)

Building on the work of Reay, Ball and David (2005), we have argued that dis-courses of 'choice' work to conceal the stratification of higher education and its relationship to teaching and widening participation, what Stevenson, Burke and Whelan (2014) conceptualise as 'pedagogic stratification':

> Performative modes of assessing teaching excellence potentially preclude deeper consideration of pedagogical issues, while the absence of meaningful engagement with issues of pedagogy in institutional documentation sidelines core issues of teaching, and detaches pedagogy from issues of equity and inclusion.
>
> (Stevenson, Burke and Whelan, 2014, p. 5)

Notions of choice are tied in to the discourses of marketisation, meritocracy and individualism. The right to higher education tends to be understood in terms of individual ability, efficacy, potential and hard work, rather than as shaped by structural, cultural and institutional inequalities and misrecognitions. Students are being reconstructed as consumers of a market of higher education. Through such processes, modes of performativity are intensified, and education, as well as pedagogical participation, becomes subjected to modes of measurement. Increasingly, if it can't be measured it does not count, so that the affective experiences of inequalities become more and more insidious and impossible to articulate or capture through hegemonic modes of measurement and data collection. Yet, at the same time, the affective dimensions are being pulled into a broader reconceptualisation of human capital, so that 'all that we are' is being subject to forms of measurement and evaluation (Sellar, 2013). We have argued that pedagogical participants are being pulled into a narrow framework that aims to produce human capital. A person's worth is not only measured in terms of skills and competencies but also through judgments about the person's affective value as an aspirational, employable, motivational and future-oriented individual. Ironically, this contradicts the (neo-liberal) notion that workers must be flexible and always changing to be able to respond to the market.

Our conceptual framework has drawn on a range of intellectual sources, including Foucault, Bourdieu, Bernstein, Butler, Fraser, Freire and hooks. We have challenged conceptualisations of equity and equality that rest on over-simplified notions of treating everyone the same and have foregrounded difference as a central theme to illuminate the heterogeneity of experiences of inequalities in and through pedagogical spaces. *Transforming pedagogies for social justice relies on equitable distributive, recognition and representation processes that work with and through difference.* Although we argue that structural inequalities are key to understanding questions of inclusion and equity in higher education, we work with the concept of intersectionality to argue for institutional mechanisms of representation *across* different groups and communities, whilst recognising differences *within* those groups and communities.

In relation to the above, we theorise pedagogies as relational, and as always tied to complex formations of power that circulate fluidly across and between pedagogical spaces. However, we also take the 'non-relativist' view that structural and material inequalities matter and continue to characterise pedagogical spaces, which are structured by gendered, classed and racialised formations and inequalities. The concept of 'pedagogies' pushes our thinking beyond the hegemonic notions of teaching as 'delivery' of educational programmes, to capture the ways that subjectivities and meanings are formed through pedagogical participation.

We have drawn on 'space' as a broader conceptual framework with which to reimagine teaching and learning in higher education. The physical spaces available in higher education institutions generate complex pedagogical relations that are linked to formations of difference and power in and across time and space. We have analysed the ways that participants take up, embody and move through the different spaces in higher education and how this produces marginalising and/or inclusive pedagogical relations. The book pays attention to the relationship between spatial dynamics and personal connections to learning and inclusive pedagogies. It considers that the spaces available might be experienced as both reproductive of privilege and inequality as well as enabling, transformative and potentially counter-hegemonic. We have highlighted the importance of creating spaces of reflexivity and praxis through pedagogical methodologies aiming to unearth the ways that inequalities are subtly re/formed through pedagogical relations and spaces.

The book draws on two projects that attempted to provide such critical spaces to create spaces that otherwise do not exist in higher education in order to develop critical reflexive praxis in relation to pedagogical experiences, identities and transformations. We have developed a framework of 'pedagogical methodology' to create spaces of transformation and to consider how research and theory might make a difference in terms of the recognition and representation of different teachers and students. The pedagogical methodological (PM) framework aims to create and open up collaborative, collective, dialogical and participatory spaces that, through the research processes, engage participants in pedagogical relations. PM provides opportunities to talk about pedagogical experiences and expectations, pedagogical frustrations, and identities that would never happen in formal and bureaucratic committee meetings that are driven by performative and regulatory governance frameworks. PM frameworks allow for meaning-making to be collaboratively refined through participatory practices, creating spaces of praxis both through and *beyond the research*. These are counter-hegemonic spaces of refusal, resistance, and of doing things differently.

The participatory spaces created through the PM framework enabled the participant teachers to work with us to consider multiple pedagogical challenges and contradictions at play across the 'excellence' and 'equity' policy discourses. The individual academic is often caught up in the complex sets of competing demands and expectations of the specific disciplinary context, the overarching and standardising frameworks of research excellence and quality assurance and the ethos, missions and strategic plans of the institution. This affects all academics but in different ways in a highly stratified and competitive sector. The institutional focus on retention, student satisfaction and maintaining student numbers for example, led some academic staff to feel that identity as an academic, intellectual leader or disciplinary expert is valued less.

The participants welcomed the opportunity afforded through the research to explore complex pedagogical questions, issues and concerns in relation to equity, diversity and difference. It emerged that there is limited space for such exchange and reflexivity in higher education and this impacts staff differently across formations of difference. Indeed our book has shown that concerns to develop 'inclusive pedagogies' must extend to considerations of the experiences of inequalities and misrecognitions of teachers as well as students in higher education.

Throughout the book we have intentionally used the term 'teacher' to emphasise the centrality of teaching in higher education and in shaping academic and professional identities. However, this is a contested space and not all our participants would identify with the descriptor of 'teacher'. We have drawn on other descriptors as well, such as 'teacher' and 'lecturer' but all of these carry different connotations, subjectivities, and national and historical meanings. As co-authors we debated this ourselves, and so we acknowledge the problematic nature of naming the pedagogic subjectivities in higher education that are so entangled with hierarchies, stratification, disciplinary identities and tensions between teaching, research and other forms of professional identities. The politics of naming who we are in higher education is deeply entwined with personal histories, (dis) connections and access to and through academic spaces, which are hierarchical, stratified and entwined with discourses of esteem, status and prestige. The increasing levels of precariousness experienced by university teachers in relation to career stage, casualisation, tenure, promotion and the overall status of teaching in (different) higher education (institutions) is deeply entangled with structures of inequality as well as complex formations of difference. However, what we found across all of the pedagogical and national contexts we researched was that all of the teachers experienced increasing levels of surveillance, performativity and regulation as challenging, unsettling and often destabilising. As we have shown through our analysis of the data, emotion runs through this in ways that reinforce the gendering and racialisation of pedagogical spaces and teacher/academic subjectivities in higher education. This plays out differently across different disciplines, subjects and institutions and requires methodological attention to capture such nuances in shaping and reshaping pedagogical subjectivities, practices and possibilities.

We also paid particular attention to the experiences of early career teachers (ECTs) and pointed to the importance of building frameworks for co-mentoring rooted in collective engaged pedagogy. Such an approach to mentoring emphasises the value of reciprocity, working across different experiences and understanding to develop pedagogical spaces for greater creativity and for developing strategies to work together in times of increased pressure and precariousness.

This is a way of undermining the rampant levels of individualism that encourage teachers to position themselves in competition with their peers rather than to collaborate to change pedagogical spaces in higher education as a collective process to make a difference, whilst recognising, valuing and representing our differences. This might contribute to disrupting the damaging and toxic discourses that lead to feelings of shame and fear, which are embedded in the individualising frameworks in which teachers are experiencing greater levels of pressure and regulation through the often dehumanising practices of measurement, assessment and performativity. Cross-institutional mentoring partnerships are another possibility and an important way to uproot traditional notions of competition between institutions. While these partnerships do exist within professional organisations (to differing extents and degrees of success), we would argue that this model could be a particularly useful element to strengthen when universities write joint Memoranda of Understanding with other universities from different regions of the world. The strength of cross-institutional (as well as cross-regional) mentoring is that, when facilitated with sensitivity, it may remove some of the pressure from faculty to always appear 'on' or 'in control' that faculty may feel with their immediate colleagues.

We have also paid close attention to formations of gender within pedagogical relations to analyse the ways that intersections of gender with other, pathologised identities inflame problematic anxieties about 'lowering of standards'. Drawing on feminist perspectives, we have examined the multiple layers of injustices that operate around formations of difference, in relation to embodied intersections and the ways that emotion works on and marks difference on and through the body. This has helped to illuminate the subtle forms of inequality that work through the politics of misrecognition in which the Other is excluded, marginalised and often subjected to ridicule, derision, shame or symbolic violence. We have paid close attention to the affective dimensions of experiences of misrecognition, which have often been ignored or under-theorised in relation to higher education participation. Pedagogies require reformation to address such complex issues and concerns. This includes the problematic discourse of the 'feminisation of higher education', which has unhelpfully recast an over-simplified battle of the sexes, without consideration of the intersection of gender with other formations of difference and how formations of masculinities and femininities are reformed through pedagogical participation in ways that reinforce rather than challenge inequalities and misrecognitions.

We have examined the often-derisive constructions of working-class and Black masculinities, as well as recognising constructions of LGBTQ realities, which reinforce inequalities in pedagogical spaces and problematic subjective positions of both students and lecturers. Higher education pedagogies thus require reformation to address such complex issues and concerns but in ways that are deeply sensitive to complex relations of power. This includes attention to the discomfort and anxiety expressed by some of the teacher participants about difference and how to negotiate power in the formal pedagogical space.

Towards a pedagogy of difference

In this book we have argued that diversity has been increasingly drawn into the discourses of marketisation. Neo-liberal representations of diversity fail to engage the subtle and insidious lived and embodied experiences of marginalisation, misrecognition and inequality. Reducing diversity to fulfil institutional marketplace agendas and market perceptions undermines the social justice imperative for critical recognition of the constellations of difference that re/form complex inequalities and exclusions. Fraser (1997, 2003) illuminates that a limited focus only on redistribution does not address the complexity of inequalities. It is necessary to simultaneously recognise difference and the ways that pedagogical participants are differently positioned. This involves attention to the ways that different histories and experiences are differently valued and are subjectively produced as 'legitimate'. Being recognised as having the right to higher education (or not) is influenced by formations of difference that are deeply enmeshed in a range of social, symbolic, cultural and material inequalities. In relation to these insights emerging from Fraser's social justice framework (1997, 2003), we have argued for the need to emphasise questions of representation through pedagogical spaces. It is important, for example, to consider how difference and different personhoods and experiences are (mis)represented in and through higher education. It is also crucial to pay attention to wider ontological and epistemological questions about whose knowledge is valued and constructed as 'powerful' and who participates in the production of knowledge and meaning-making.

In order to address such troubling and troublesome dynamics of inequality and the (re)production of exclusions, marginalisations and the (re)privileging of (neo-liberal and other hegemonic) subjecthoods, we have argued for *pedagogies of difference*. The approach strongly critiques conventional technologies that work towards the regulation, control and surveillance of difference in and through higher education pedagogies. Instead, pedagogies of difference draw on difference *as a resource* for counter-hegemonic practices towards social justice transformative aspirations. Pedagogies are therefore not simply teaching and learning styles or methods, they are *ways of being and doing* that are shaped and reformed through gendered, classed and racialised practices. Such practices are interconnected with the processes by which certain (disciplinary/professional/vocational) subjectivities and knowledges become constructed as legitimate and 'proper' through higher education as a powerful institution.

Higher education is being profoundly reconfigured by multiple political forces that are also undermining (some) disciplinary and academic forms of knowledge and knowing. For example, those disciplinary fields associated with liberal arts are increasingly undermined by the focus of transnational corporate forces on economic-oriented skills and competencies, as well as other affective dimensions that are seen to form human capital. For students facing financial vulnerabilities, the deepening of competition to gain graduate jobs further exacerbates this. Students are increasingly being reframed by marketised imperatives, as consumers of the education market who freely make choices on the basis of rankings, evaluation and the level of prestige and reputation of different institutions. Those institutions that are most successful at widening participation are often disadvantaged by their unequal position in the market in terms of research prestige, resources and infrastructure. This reproduces stratification of institutions in a global market of higher education, in which institutions, academics, research and teaching and students are all differently, and unequally, located. This also plays into the reproduction of inequalities beyond higher education.

Teachers are confronted with the tensions between these political forces and demands and are often overwhelmed as they are pulled in different directions. Do they respond to the agenda for excellence or equity? Do they focus on research or teaching? How do they juggle these with increasing administrative demands? Where are the opportunities and mechanisms for teachers to develop richer pedagogical understanding and expertise needed to address diversity and difference as well as the multiple and contradictory expectations and demands being imposed? How might they then develop pedagogical strategies that are appropriate to teaching students from a wide range of backgrounds and experiences who are unfamiliar with higher education and have few resources and networks to mobilise for their educational and future advantage and benefit?

Students are also negotiating a confusing set of discourses, expectations and demands and this is exacerbated by an increasing gap between social privilege and social disadvantage. There seems to be a myth that such complexities confront students only before they access higher education and during the admissions processes, with very little attention to such complexities in their interaction with higher education pedagogies. Our research has revealed the ongoing challenges that students face as pedagogical participants, emphasising the imperative for questions of difference and inequalities to be addressed *through teaching as a central aspect of widening participation*.

Pedagogies of difference and inclusion place emphasis on the need for teachers and students to examine reflexively, complex power relations that often unwittingly reproduce inequalities. This collaborative work facilitates a process that: unsettles taken-for-granted enactments of structural inequalities (that work in relation to formations of difference, including but not only gender, class and race); draws on difference as a resource for reciprocal and collaborative processes of teaching, learning and meaning-making; enables epistemic access through foregrounding the construction of knowledge, focusing on deconstructing and understanding disciplinary/subject and academic/professional knowledge; and provides relational spaces to make sense of those knowledges through the experiences and understanding that different students and teachers bring to pedagogical spaces.

Implications for policy and practice

A key implication of this research is that as higher education becomes increasingly diverse, higher education teachers require continuing professional development opportunities (CPD) to develop pedagogical expertise in relation to challenging social inequalities and misrecognitions in and through higher education. Through our pedagogical methodology, our research projects provided a unique space for critical reflexivity for participants to deepen their understanding of gendered identities, inequalities and pedagogies and to feed in to the process of developing inclusive practice. According to their accounts and responses, (both formal and informal) this benefitted both students and teachers. The research projects highlight the profound need for such spaces of critical reflexivity to be provided in higher education, not only in terms of enriching approaches to widening participation but also in valuing teaching and learning and the teachers' and students' experiences, perspectives and insights. Many of the teachers expressed a deep sense of disempowerment in terms of increasing workloads, high levels of institutional expectation not least connected to the marketisation of HE and the rapid pace of change in higher education policy. Policies of widening participation and equity have presented rich pedagogical opportunities but also complex challenges. Institutions and policy-makers at the national level must acknowledge these challenges by providing opportunities for pedagogical development in relation to questions of equity and widening participation.

Inspired by our concern to provide CPD opportunities for university teachers, we produced *Teaching Inclusively: Changing Pedagogical Spaces* (Burke and Crozier, 2013)[1] a set of teaching resources framed by the concept of praxis. *Teaching Inclusively* provides a set of conceptual think pieces designed as resources for teachers to draw on as they work through the reflexive exercises we designed to support them in addressing complex formations of difference in their classrooms.

Our analysis suggests that there is a common assumption amongst both students and teachers that gender is no longer an important issue in terms of widening participation in higher education (see Francis, Burke and Read, 2014). However, the accounts of both the students and teachers reveal that a deeper level of discussion and consideration generates profound issues in relation to gender and how gender intersects with other social inequalities of class and race. It is therefore paramount for widening participation and for social equality and justice that critical awareness is raised around these issues. This requires serious levels of attention to the relationship between higher education pedagogies and the reproduction of social inequalities. This is because, as the findings have shown, gender is not only tied to *individual* identity formations but also shapes pedagogic and disciplinary practices, epistemologies and assumptions. Thus the complexity of the issues at stake point to sophisticated strategies in higher education to address them, including research framed by pedagogical methodologies, providing opportunities for discussion, critical reflexivity and continuing professional development.

Through our research and analysis, we make the following policy and practice recommendations:

1   It is imperative, particularly in terms of widening participation and equity in higher education, for *institutions to provide support and resources for university teachers* to build their understanding of the ways teaching and learning is profoundly shaped by complex formations of difference. This might be in the form of continuing professional development (CPD) resources and programmes (across all stages of early-, mid-, and senior-teachers), participatory research opportunities and the provision of forums or meeting spaces to discuss the significant challenges around developing inclusive pedagogies.

2   It is valuable to develop *critical Communities of Practice, embedded in a framework of praxis*, in order to create the spaces and opportunities whereby university teachers can collaboratively develop inclusive pedagogies, contributing to a form of *awareness-raising about the intricacies of the impact and implications of social inequalities.*

3   Policy-makers and senior leaders in higher education must take seriously the responsibility to provide a *structured framework to tackle issues of pedagogical exclusions and inequalities.* The individualist approach, which only focuses on the performance of individual teachers and students, must be challenged as it is unable to address the complexity of social inequalities and identities in relation to pedagogical practices and relations.

4   It is important to embed in the HE curriculum detailed and critical attention to the implications of gender, class and race in order to develop understandings of the formation of identities, the need to challenge inequalities and the complex ways that exclusions and marginalisation takes place. This provides the opportunity for *staff and students to deconstruct White and classed hegemonic values, and masculinised and feminised forms of identity and practice, which often have oppressive effects.*

6   Enabling teachers and students to *reflect critically on and interrogate their own perspectives of and relationships to cultural, social and political forms of marginalisation and exclusion* is a key aspect of challenging deeply embedded inequalities.

7   There is a need to pay much *closer attention to the kinds of spaces available, including physical and virtual spaces*, which constrain and shape pedagogical relations and practices and create or impede a sense of 'belonging'.

We recognise that higher education cannot eradicate social inequalities but we do strongly argue that higher education has a key role to play. This necessarily involves *interrogating neo-liberal and other intersecting political forces that are seeped in the perpetuation and widening of inequalities.* Higher education must be reframed to acknowledge this role and to pay close attention to its contribution to social, cultural, material and symbolic (in)justices, including in and through pedagogies.

It is our position that frameworks of praxis and reflexivity are crucial to changing pedagogical spaces for greater equity and social justice. Such frameworks bring together pedagogical methodologies and practices in ongoing and sustained dialogue, for more equitable and inclusive higher education structures, cultures and practices. This includes *attention to the politics of knowledge, representation and meaning-making to address complex questions of epistemic access* and to facilitate such access through *inclusive pedagogies and curriculum that recognise the experiences, histories and knowledges of those communities that have been historically marginalised in and excluded* from higher education. This does not mean however providing sub-standard programmes and courses for students constructed as 'Other' and/or different. It requires pedagogical strategies that enable access to those subject/disciplinary knowledges that hold high levels of social esteem, whilst simultaneously acknowledging Other forms of knowledge. It requires cyclical and iterative processes of (re)making meaning through participatory practices.

Building equitable higher education is imperative to all of our futures – growing inequalities across the globe pose a threat to all of us on multiple levels. Higher education has a key role to play in ensuring more socially just and thus peaceful and stable societies into the future. The power of higher education is immeasurable and profound but this power is often *reproductive* of, rather than *disruptive* to, social injustices and inequalities. The project of changing pedagogical spaces in higher education is necessarily long-term and challenging because it is about eradicating deeply entrenched, historical inequalities and misrecognitions. This requires *enduring and sustained levels of commitment and attention to the insidious and subtle ways that inequalities and misrecognitions play out in and through pedagogical spaces.* Individual teachers and students must be part of such enduring and sustained levels of commitment but must also be fully supported by wider policy frameworks and their institutions to develop the theoretical, conceptual, structural and material resources necessary to effect change.

Note

1 Teaching Inclusively is available online: https://www.heacademy.ac.uk/sites/default/files/projects/teaching_inclusively_resource_pack_final_version_opt.pdf

Appendix one

Formations of gender and higher education pedagogies (GaP)

Key research questions

- How (if at all) do current HE pedagogical practices address issues of diversity, difference and power raised by the WP agenda?
- How do students and teachers engage with, resist and experience the different pedagogical practices being used on their courses? How is this different across different disciplinary fields? In what ways do gender and other aspects of identity (age, class, ethnicity and race) shape and/or constrain pedagogical relations, experiences and practices?
- How do students understand and articulate their needs, experiences and expectations of HE pedagogies and in what ways is this specifically shaped by formations of gender?
- How do HE teachers understand and articulate their students' needs and learning in relation to gender and in the wider context of diversity? What are the assumptions and aims that they bring to their teaching practices in relation to addressing the needs of male and female students? How might this differ across different disciplinary fields?

Implementation

This project was led by Professor Penny Jane Burke with the support of the Project Administrator, Carolyn Gallop. The Project Team met regularly, both for formal meetings and for informal meetings, which focused on developing the research instruments, developing the analytical framework including identifying NVivo nodes and planning outputs and dissemination events, including the CPD resource pack. Professor Louise Archer took forward the creation and organisation of the GaP workshops, held for HE teachers and students across the country at King's College London. The workshop discussions were audio recorded and transcribed and served to support the core data collection and analysis as a form of triangulation, to 'check out' our interpretations and findings.

Four Steering Group meetings were held throughout the course of the project. The Steering Group members played a key advisory role in the project development providing insightful and timely guidance.

Pedagogical methodology

This two-year qualitative project involved student cohorts, across six disciplinary programmes of study, at one case study institution, with a second partner institution selected to increase the opportunities for student and teacher engagement in a different university context. In addition, students who were active as Programme Representatives in the case study institution were invited to participate. The case study approach has been specifically selected to: (1) support the aim to work intensively with the students and teachers participating in the project to ensure there is direct benefit to their pedagogical experiences and understanding, (2) facilitate access to participants and (3) improve the chances of sustaining participant commitment throughout the life of the project. The selected programmes involved vocational (Business and Management, Sports Science, English and Creative Writing, Dance) and academic (Philosophy, Classics and History) subjects with diverse, but not equal, representation of male and female students from different social, economic and ethnic backgrounds, including: Classics and History, Business Studies and Management, Creative Writing, Dance, Sports Science and Philosophy. These different disciplines have been selected to represent diversity in their nature, epistemology, and pedagogical and assessment practices; as well as student constituency.

Riverside University (pseudonym) has a college system comprising four colleges – (pseudonyms) Eliot, Pankhurst, Luxembourg and Parks. They are situated across four distinct and bounded areas of the campus. Each college hosts specific subject areas: Luxembourg: Business and Social Sciences; Pankhurst: Life Sciences and Sports Studies and Psychology/Psychotherapy; Parks: the Humanities; Eliot: Education, Dance, and Drama. Recruitment of students from 'low socio-economic classes' at Riverside was above the national average in 2010 with 35% compared to 30.7% nationally; but regarding 'Low Participation Neighbourhoods', whilst Riverside's average was 6.8% the national average was 10.7%.

Seventy-five per cent of students are female although subjects still tend to be gendered, for example women dominate Dance and Education; men dominate certain aspects of Sports Science such as Coaching (100% men), and women (89%) dominate Nutrition; in the Business School there is a similar pattern of more male students although some subjects are more evenly gender mixed whereas Computing (Single honours) is 75% male and Computing (Combined honours) is 100% female. Ethnicity varies across subjects and programmes; White students are in the majority overall and in most subjects with the exception of aspects of Business most notably Business Computing where 100% are Black students, and Human Bio Science and Bio Medical Science where 12.9% and 12% are White respectively.

Access, consent and recruitment

The project followed the ethical guidelines of the British Educational Research Association. After gaining the ethical approval granted by University of Roehampton, the Programme Convener of each of these programme areas was contacted and a meeting was requested between the Programme team and a member of the research team. During the meeting, the research was introduced to the programme team, giving opportunity for questions to be raised and discussion about the importance of the study to be explored. During the meeting, ethical guidelines were discussed and information sheets about the nature of the project were provided, including a consent form. Each individual member of the programme team who wished to take part in the study signed the consent form. A convenient date was identified for a member of the research team to attend a programme session in order for the research to be similarly introduced and explained to second and third year students undertaking the programme. A similar process was followed when meeting with the students; information sheets were provided following discussion about the research and its aims, and consent forms were offered to all students who wished to participate.

Following the collection of the consent forms, the GaP Research Project Administrator, Carolyn Gallop, contacted individual students to arrange a convenient time for individual interviews to take place. There were some difficulties in recruiting the number of students we planned to interview and after some discussion amongst the research team and the Steering Group committee, as mentioned in the previous section, we decided to also include students who acted as Programe Representatives in the case study institution. These students were particularly enthusiastic about participating in the study, and through their experiences as programme representatives had valuable experience to bring to the interview accounts about pedagogical issues on their programmes and were in a stronger position to actively feedback key issues emerging from the research through their role as Programme representative. Out of the 64 students interviewed, 16 were programme representatives.

The constitution of staff participants is as follows: Classics and History (3 women, 2 men), Sports Science (1 woman, 2 men), Philosophy (3 women, 1 man), Business Studies and Management (2 women, 3 men), English and Creative Writing (3 women, 1 man), Dance (2 women).

Student participants comprised: 64; 42 women and 22 men; 14 Black and Minority Ethnic self-identified students (10 female and 4 male) and 22 self-identified as working class (two said they 'did not have a view on their class identity). In addition to asking the students to state how they defined their social class we also collected data on whether their parents had attended a higher education institution, their parents' occupation and also whether they were in receipt of a bursary. We analysed the occupational data utilising Rose and O'Neil's categories. However, as the data were not sufficiently detailed this analysis was very patchy and we therefore decided to use the students' own definitions. Whilst this

Table A1.1 Summary of staff participants

Programme	Total number of staff participants	Women	Men
Classics & History	5	3	2
Sports Science	3	1	2
Philosophy	4	3	1
Business Studies & Management	5	2	3
English & Creative Writing	4	3	1
Dance	2	2	
TOTAL	**23**	**14**	**9**

may not be entirely accurate we believe it is a good reflection of their perceptions of their own backgrounds.

Methods of data collection: individual and group interviews with students

We carried out two sets of interviews with students in their second and third year of undergraduate study at the case study university. In total 64 students participated in qualitative interviews and then these were followed up by 4 focus groups interviews with 14 students.

The initial individual interviews were on average 45 minutes in length, although some were shorter and some were significantly longer, with the longest interview being 120 minutes in length. The individual interview schedule was designed to elicit data across seven overarching themes, (1) initial experiences of higher education; (2) experiences of teaching and learning; (3) learning approaches and strategies; (4) articulating needs and interests; (5) relationships with peers; (6) relationship with teachers; (7) student identity. Questions and sub-questions were formulated to guide the interview but not to structure it rigidly in order to enable the participants' responses to also shape the direction of the interview. The interviews were designed to create a space for critical reflection for the students about their pedagogical identities and experiences, as well as their relationships with others during the pedagogical encounters they experienced at university. Dr. Barbara Read, Jo Peat, Julie Hall, Professor Gill Crozier and Professor Penny Jane Burke conducted the 64 individual interviews and focus group interviews. The students were either undertaking courses under the six main programme areas and/or were Programme Representatives. The interviews were audio recorded and then transcribed verbatim. The students were reminded of the ethical guidelines, with which they had already become familiar through the recruiting and consent process. All of the students were given pseudonyms and their subject of study is not included in the data extracts to help ensure anonymity.

The focus groups were undertaken at the start of the following academic year (between September 2011 and January 2012) with the Executive Student Consultants:

Table A1.2 Overview of student participants

Student group interviews	Number of student participants
1. English & Creative Writing	3
2. Sports Science	4
3. History/Business/Philosophy	4
4. Programme Representatives	3
4 GROUP INTERVIEWS	**14 STUDENT PARTICIPANTS**

Methods of data collection: focus group discussions with staff

Twelve focus groups were conducted with staff across the six programme areas. All of the programme teams, except for Dance, participated in two focus group discussions. The Dance programme team was unable to find a time to meet again as one of the key members was away on sick leave. The focus group discussions were facilitated by a member of the team but designed to be interactive and not too rigidly structured, enabling the perspectives of the participants to influence the shape the discussion took. However, the focus group discussions were supported by material emerging from the project to stimulate discussion in relation to the key research questions.

The first set of discussions was supported by data extracts from the individual interviews with students, as well as questions formulated to help generate a

Table A1.3 Summary of staff focus groups

Subject	Number of focus groups held
Classics & History	2
Sports Science	2
Philosophy	2
Business Studies & Management	3
English & Creative Writing	2
Dance	1
TOTAL	**12 FOCUS GROUPS HELD**

discussion. The second set of focus group interviews consisted of data extracts from their first discussion, so that they had the opportunity to critically reflect on their original contributions and also to build further on that discussion. Below is a summary of the number of focus group discussions that took place (NB: an additional focus group discussion was held with Business Studies staff to ensure that as many of the team could participate in a discussion as possible).

Method of data collection: observations of classroom practices

We conducted 20 observations of classroom practice to deepen our data in relation to the aim to gain a detailed understanding of pedagogical practices and relations and the ways these might be gendered.

We developed an observation schedule, which aided the focus of the observations in relation to our key research questions. Key themes guiding the observations included: (1) teaching space and context; (2) pedagogical practices; (3) pedagogical relations; (4) formations of gender, with more detailed prompts also included in the schedule to help focus the observation process. Jo Peat, Dr Barbara Read, Professor Gill Crozier, Julie Hall and Professor Penny Jane Burke, conducted the observations. Hand-written notes were taken by the observer against the observation schedule and then typed up. A summary of the observations is included below.

Methods to enhance participation: overview

As described above, a key aim of the research was to create a reflexive space for participants to discuss and exchange their experiences, ideas and recommendations for developing inclusive pedagogies and considering the ways social identities shape pedagogical experiences, practices and relations.

Table A1.4 Summary

Subject	Number of staff observations
Sports Science	3
Philosophy	4
Business Studies & Management	4
Classics & History	4
English & Creative Writing	4
Dance	1
TOTAL	**20 STAFF OBSERVATIONS CARRIED OUT**

Methods to enhance participation: executive student consultants

In order to enhance student participation in the project and develop a closer relationship with our student participants, we identified a smaller group of Executive Student Consultants (ESCs). The ESCs were drawn from our group of 64 student participants and were selected in relation to the following criteria: (1) they were able and willing to participate actively in the second stage of the research and (2) they represented the diversity of the student group particularly in terms of programme of study, gender, social class and ethnicity. In order to induct the ESCs, we held a Student Forum on 13 October 2011 and 16 of the 18 chosen students attended this event. During the first part of the session, we explained to them in some detail the different activities they would participate in as ESCs and gave them each an information sheet to further clarify what being an ESC would entail. We also explained the benefits of participation including the receipt of a certificate of participation, extracurricular experience for their CV, experience of taking part in a national research project and contributing to discussions about developing HE pedagogies plus a small voucher as a token of appreciation for their contribution.

Following the induction and an overview of the concepts of 'gender' and 'pedagogies', the students then took part in small group discussions to explore the relationship between gender and pedagogies. From their discussion, they produced posters of their key points and perspectives, which we included as part of the data.

Two additional ESCs, who were unable to attend the student forum, met with the Project Leader for an induction later.

A key activity for some of the ESCs was to take part in the planning, organisation and facilitation of our National Student seminar on HE pedagogies. We also worked with the NUS and the case study university Student Union to encourage their interest and participation in the project – the University Student Union supported and participated in the student forum held in October 2011, and the NUS and Riverside University SU contributed to our National Student seminar event held on 21 February 2012.

Five of the ESCs took responsibility for organising the student seminar, with the support of Carolyn Gallop, Professor Penny Jane Burke and Julie Hall. The ESCs identified a title for the seminar and helped to promote it through their networks. The title of the seminar was 'Un-I-versity Uncovered' and the aims of the seminar were to bring students together from across the country to:

- Uncover what it means to be a student in the 21st century
- Share ideas for creating more inclusive higher education
- Contribute to a national research project
- Advise policy-makers how to make a difference to teaching and learning.

Further to these aims we also wanted to provide students a space to voice their perspectives and through the GaP project to feed these perspectives to policy-makers, senior managers and HE lecturers. A keynote lecture was given by the Vice President of the National Union of Student, Usman Ali, encouraging students to exercise their right to a voice in higher education.

Methods to enhance participation: enhancing staff participation

Staff were involved in formal and informal discussions throughout the life of the project. In the initial recruiting phase of the project, all staff teaching on the six identified programme areas were invited to attend an informal meeting to hear about the project and its aims and to begin a process of critical dialogue about their own experiences of teaching and learning in higher education in relation to questions of gender and other social identities. The focus group discussions, although a formal part of the data collection for the project, also served to provide staff with a space for critical reflection and discussion about issues not usually explored. A key theme emerging from the data was the significance that staff placed on having such a space which was not normally available but of great value given the continual changing nature of higher education, placing increasing pressure on their time, and the impact of this on pedagogical practice and relations.

Those staff observed were also invited to have an informal follow up meeting with the researcher who carried out the observation. This meeting was not structured but allowed further reflection on pedagogical practice following the experience of being observed for the research. In the section below on findings, we have not included the subject of study affiliated with individual lecturers to help ensure anonymity.

A number of dissemination events have provided further spaces of critical reflection for staff to explore questions about pedagogies and identity formations.

Methods to enhance participation: GaP workshops

Two intensive workshops were held at King's College London, organised by Professor Louise Archer. The workshops sought to develop further the project's participatory methodological approach by creating reflective spaces for staff and students to engage with emergent findings and data from the main study.

The workshops were also designed to enable wider groups of staff and students (from a range of other HEIs and disciplinary backgrounds) to add their voices and experiences to the project and to help contextualise (and contest or substantiate) the main project findings.

The first workshop (with HE teaching staff) was held on 10 February 2012.

Twenty-two lecturers attended, representing over 10 universities and 11 disciplinary backgrounds (including medicine, sciences, arts, social sciences, business and humanities). The second workshop (with students) was held on 7 March 2012, and 17 students attended, representing 6 different types of universities from across England and over 8 disciplinary backgrounds (including Nursing, History, Business, Law, Technology and Classics). A further two National Union of Student representatives also participated in the workshop. Students and lecturers from Riverside were not invited to participate in these workshops, which were designed to extend the project beyond the case study institution and to 'check' the data by engaging new participants with it.

Each workshop was structured in three main sections:

- 'Changing students, changing pedagogies?'
- 'Gender and other identities' and
- 'Developing equitable and effective pedagogies'.

Each section reflected a core concern within the project, to enable a focused yet in-depth exploration of the breadth and diversity of participant views. In each section, participants were engaged through interactive and participatory methods and were invited to work with anonymised data extracts and provisional analyses from the main project data set. Participants worked mostly in small groups and all group discussions were recorded (with their formal consent). As such, the sessions not only provided a form of 'triangulation' (contextualising the main project findings) but also generated additional original data for the project (about 17 hours of recorded discussions) plus posters.

The sessions aimed to (i) prompt reflection on how HE is changing and how these changes (in structure and identities) shape experiences of teaching, teacher and learner identities and pedagogical relations, (ii) introduce the substantive focus on gender, race, class and stimulate discussion/reflection on these axes and (iii) stimulate reflection on how to translate this into pedagogy and change within HE.

The workshops not only generated rich data but also received very positive feedback from staff and student participants. Both groups commented after the workshops that they had found the experience interesting and engaging. They particularly valued the opportunity to reflect on teaching and learning in HE and to share views with peers from other institutions and disciplines.

Methods of data analysis

All the data collected were analysed in relation to the research questions, collaborative reflections with research participants and the research team, drawing on theoretical perspectives from the body of literature on formations of gender and intersections with other aspects of social identity (e.g. Butler, 1990; Mac an Ghaill, 1994; Brah, 1996; Francis and Skelton, 2002; Brah and Phoenix, 2004), as well as literature on HE pedagogy, diversity and inclusion (e.g. Ellsworth, 1996; McLean, 2006; Burke and Jackson, 2007; Crozier, Reay, Clayton and

Colliander, 2008, 2010; Hockings et al., 2008; Reay et al., 2009, 2010). The data were read and reread, and then discussed in detail in research team analysis meetings. Through this collaborative approach, we looked across the interview transcripts and observation notes and identified key themes emerging from the data. We then used NVivo to facilitate the analytical process, by reducing the data into NVivo nodes, into the key themes we identified collectively. Through our critical and analytical discussions of emergent themes, the analysis embedded a reflexive approach to consider the impact of the research team's standpoints and identities and the perspectives and values we brought to the research. Each team member was allocated an overarching research theme to explore in more detail in relation to the project research questions and the emergent themes from the data. Drawing on the NVivo data we developed through these preliminary methods, we each developed a working paper on the overarching theme for which we were responsible. This involved developing the initial analysis we had undertaken collectively in relation to the overarching theme being explored and going through a process of data complication, by further conceptualising the themes in relation to our research questions (Coffey and Atkinson, 1996).

Appendix two
Fulbright

From December 2012 to March 2013, Dr. Lauren Ila Misiazek carried out nine focus groups with 44 academics (31 women and 13 men) in nine Higher Education Institutions (HEIs) (eight public, one private) in the 4 countries – Portugal, Spain, Italy and the USA. The participants ranged from 25 years to 80 years of age and represented eight major disciplines. Following university ethics approval, colleagues from each of the countries' Paulo Freire Institute networks recruited the academics.

Using semi-structured focus group questions adapted from the GaP project, participants were asked about strategies, inequalities and control and autonomy as they related to their teaching, as well as how their teaching related to their other work in HE and about opportunities to challenge any structures, policies or practices that negatively affected their teaching and/or relationships with students. Focus groups were utilised for both practicality – allowing for the participation of many participants during limited visits to the participating universities – and because of focus groups' effectiveness in cultivating rich discussions around the topic. In fact, many of the participants had never met each other, or discussed these topics with each other, and the space provided for interesting interuniversity discussions.

Lauren conducted the focus groups in the host languages of the country (working in Italy with bilingual colleagues to confirm my translations). She translated, transcribed and coded the interviews. To protect participants' identities, names have not been used.

This research does not pretend to be a cross-country study; it cannot answer questions about differences in culture between the different countries. We recognise differences between countries (and of course, at all levels both more macro [European Union] and more micro [a particular faculty at a particular institution]), but in the data, we can see the ways in which the participants highlight some similarities of the effects of neo-liberalism on HE. Thus, the comparisons here are between individual participants of the focus groups. And, although in the focus group, participants spoke of politics, practices and politics at the local, regional and national levels, and this is reflected in some of the conversation, based on our methodology we would not attempt to make any generalisations about broad cultural differences, not least because we do not want to homogenise those cultural differences.

Appendix three

Table of student information
(GaP project)

Table A3.1 Table of student information (GaP project)

Pseudonym	Gender	Year	Young/ Mature student	Student rep	Age	Self-identified social class	Home/ International	School type	Father's occupation	Mother's occupation	Bursary/ Scholarship
Mark	M	1	Young	R	19		Home	Comp, Mixed	Retired	Social worker	Y
Stephanie	F	2	Young	R	19	mc	Home	Comp, Mixed	Stock broker	Training manager	N
Laura	F	1	Young	R	17	mwc	Home	Comp, Mixed	Firearms instructor	Nurse	N
Emily	F	2	Young	R	19	mwc	Home	Comp, Mixed	Compressed air engineer	Housewife	Y
Sameera	F	3	Mature	R	33	wc	Home	Comp, Mixed	Business owner	Chef	Y
Michelle	F	2	Young	R	21	umc	Home	Independent, All-Girls	Chartered surveyor	Nurse	N
Angelika	F	1	Young	R	22	mc	International	Norwegian, unknown	Engineer	Nurse	Y
Sam	M	3	Young	R	23	mc	Home	Comp, Mixed	"Aviation" (?)	Nurse	N
Agda	F	2	Young	R	22	mc	International	Norwegian, unknown	Military engineer	Social worker	Y
Christopher	M	3	Young	R	21	mc	Home	Trust, Mixed	Sales person	Hospital manager	N
Pat	M	1	Mature	R	27	mc	Home	Comp, Mixed	"Vice president" (?)	Administration assistant	Y
Ariella	F	3	Mature	R	26	wc	Home	Comp, Mixed	Retired	Retired	N
Robert	M	3	Young	R	23	wc	Home	Comp, Mixed	Farmer	Nursery teacher	Y
Claire	F	3	Young	R	21	wc	Home	Comp, Mixed	Avionics engineer	Warden (sheltered housing)	Y

(Continued)

Table A3.1 (Continued)

Pseudonym	Gender	Year	Young/Mature student	Student rep	Age	Self-identified social class	Home/International	School type	Father's occupation	Mother's occupation	Bursary/Scholarship
Nova	F	1	Young	R	22	umc	International	Norwegian, unknown	Engineer	Doctor	Y
Doreen	F	3	Young	R	21	mc	International	German, unknown	Shop owner	Shop owner	N
Aaina	F	2	Young	R	20	mc	Home	Private school	"Professional" (?)	"Professional" (?)	N
Natalie	F	1	Young	R	19	wc	Home	Comp, Mixed			
Arlene	F	1	Young	R	19	mc	Home	Comp, Mixed	Social worker	Director, Consultancy	N
Jackie	F	2	Young	R	20	wc	Home		IT	Sales person	Y
Larissa	F	2	Mature	R	48	mc	Home	Comp, Mixed	"Blue collar worker" (?)	Business owner	N
Jonathan	M	3	Mature	R	49	wc	Home	Comp, Mixed	Engineer	Nurse	Y
Lorena	F	3	Young	R	20	wc	Home		Unemployed	Unemployed	N
Nic	M	2	Young	X	19	wc	Home	Comp, Mixed		Student	
Adora	F	2	Young	X	19	wc	Home	Comp, Mixed			
Sheryl	F	2	Young	X	20	mc	Home	Voluntary-Aided, Faith, Mixed	Banker	Teacher	N
Timothy	M	2	Young	X			Home				
Daniel	M	2	Young	X	19	mc	Home	Comp, Mixed			
Barbara	F	2	Young	X	21	mwc	Home	Comp, Mixed	Driving instructor	Nursery school manager	N

Name	Sex	No.	Age group		Age	Class	Residence	School			Y/N
Diana	F	2	Young	X	21	no view	Home		Business manager	PA to financial director	N
Ria	F	2	Mature	X	29	mwc	Home	IPTA (Italian), unknown	Pharmacist	Nurse	N
Simon	F	2	Young	X	21	wc	Home	Comp, Mixed		Civil servant	Y
Stephen	M	2	Young	X	23	mc	Home	Independent, mixed	Teacher	Teacher	
Alexia	F	2	Young	X	20	wc	Home	Grammar, Mixed			
Greg	M	3	Young	X	20	wc	Home	Comp, Mixed	Black cab driver		
Lalitesh	M	1	Young	X	19	wc	Home	Comp, Mixed	Unemployed	Unemployed	Y
Mark	M	3	Young	X	22	mc	Home	Independent, mixed	Company director	Administration	N
Alan	M	2	Mature	X	25	wc	Home	Comp, Mixed	Pub landlord	Data analyst	Y
Julie	F	3	Mature	X	41	mc	Home	Comp, Mixed	Teacher	Teacher	Y
Kalini	F	3	Young	X	21	wc	Home	Comp, Mixed			
Chandana	F	3	Young	X	20	wc	Home	Comp, Mixed	Lorry driver	Laundrette	Y
Tony	M	2	Young	X	19	mc	Home	Comp, Mixed	Self-described in interview as 'business-oriented family' (!)		
Erika	F	3	Young	X	22	mc	Home	Comp, Mixed	Dentist	Manager	N

(Continued)

Table A3.1 (Continued)

Pseudonym	Gender	Year	Young/Mature student	Student rep	Age	Self-identified social class	Home/International	School type	Father's occupation	Mother's occupation	Bursary/Scholarship
Ronald	M	3	Young	X	21	wc	Home	Comp, Mixed	Unemployed	Unemployed	Y
Elina	F	3	Young	X	20	mc	Home	Academy, All-girls	Self-employed	Unemployed	Y
Elizabeth	F	3	Young	X	22	wc	Home	Comp, Mixed	Retired	Unemployed	N
Petra	F	3	Young	X	21	mwc	Home	Academy, Faith, Mixed	Financial advisor	Secretary	U
Audun	F	3	Mature	X	25	mc	International		Nurse (unspecified)	Nurse (unspecified)	N
Sohpie	F	3	Young	X			Home				
Rebekka	F	2	Young	X	20	mc	International	Latvian, unknown			
Susy	F	2	Young	X	19	mc	Home	Comp, Mixed			
Gerald	M	2	Young	X	21	mwc	Home	Comp, Mixed	Operations manager	Retail manager	Y
Christian	M	2	Young	X	19	mwc	Home	Grammar, Mixed			
Abdul	M	2	Young	X	19	mwc	Home	Independent, All-Boys	Auditor	General manager	Y
Maria	F	2	Young	X			Home				
Michael	M	2	Young	X	20	mc	Home				
Kate	F	2	Mature	X	31	mc	Home	Comp, All-girls	Self-employed	Unemployed	N
Ian	M	2	Young	X	20	wc	Home	Comp, Mixed			

Damien	M	2	Young	X	22	mc	Home	Independent, Mixed	Architect	Volunteer	Y
Bradley	M	2	Young	X	20	mc	Home	Comp, Mixed			
Jim	M	2	Young	X	20	wc	International	Comp, Mixed			
Mary	F	2	Young	X	21	mc	Home	Comp, Mixed			
Andrew	M	2	Young	X	19	mc	Home	Comp, Mixed			
Dennis	M	2	Mature	R	28	wc	home	Comp, Mixed	Sales person	Manager, WHSmith	Y

References

AAUW. (2016) *The Simple Truth about the Gender Pay Gap*. http://www.aauw.org/research/the-simple-truth-about-the-gender-pay-gap/. Accessed 27 March 2016.

Ahlefeld, H. (2009) *Evaluating Quality in Educational Spaces: OECD/CELE Pilot Project*. OECD. http://www.oecd.org/education/innovation-education/centreforeffectivelearningenvironmentscele/43904538.pdf. Accessed 20 July 2015.

Ahmed, S. (2004) *The Cultural Politics of Emotion*. New York: Routledge.

Alexander, C. (2000) *The Asian Gang*. Oxford and New York: Berghahn Books.

Anderson, C. and McCune, V. (2013) 'Fostering Meaning: Fostering Community', *Higher Education* 66: 283–296.

Anderson, V. (2014) '"World-Travelling": A Framework for Re-Thinking Teaching and Learning in Internationalised Higher Education', *Higher Education* 68: 637–652.

Archer, L., Hollingworth, S., and Halsall, A. (2007) '"University's Not for Me—I'm a Nike Person": Urban, Working-Class Young People's Negotiations of Style, Identity and Educational Engagement', *Sociology* 41 (2): 219–237.

Archer, L., Hutchings, M., and Ross, A. (2003) *Higher Education and Social Class*. London: RoutledgeFalmer.

Ashwin, P. (2015) *Going Global – Opportunities and Challenges for HE Researchers Valuing Research into Higher Education: Advancing Knowledge, Informing Policy, Enhancing Practice*. SRHE 50th Anniversary Colloquium, 26 June 2015.

Astin, W.A. (1999) 'Student Involvement: A Developmental Theory for Higher Education', *Journal of College Student Development* 40 (5): 518–529.

Baldwin, G. and James, R. (2000) 'The Market in Australian Higher Education and the Concept of Student as Informed Consumer', *Journal of Higher Education Policy and Management* 22 (2): 139–148.

Ball, S.J. (1993) 'Education Markets, Choice and Social Class: The Market as a Class Strategy in the UK and US', *British Journal of Sociology of Education* 14 (1): 3–19.

Ball, S.J. (2001) 'New Youth, New Economies, New Inequalities', *Studies on Education and Society* 11: 11–19.

Ball, S.J. (2003) 'The Teacher's Soul and the Terrors of Performativity', *Journal of Education Policy* 18 (2): 215–228.

Ball, S.J. (2012) 'Performativity, Commodification and Commitment: An I-Spy Guide to the Neoliberal University', *British Journal of Educational Studies* 60 (1): 17–28.

Ball, S.J. (2014) *Universities and the Economies of Truth*. Paper presented at the Governing Academic Life Conference, London School of Economics, London, 26 June 2014.

Barnett, P. (2011) 'Discussions across Difference: Addressing the Affective Dimensions of Teaching Diverse Students about Diversity', *Teaching in Higher Education* 16 (6): 669–679.

Batchelor, D.C. (2006) 'Vulnerable Voices: An Examination of the Concept of Vulnerability in Relation to the Student Voice', *Educational Philosophy and Theory* 38 (6): 787–800.

BBC. (2015) 'Four in 10 Students Say University Not Good Value – Survey', http://www.bbc.com/news/education-33204691. Accessed 17 May 2016.

Bekhradnia, B. (2009) *The Academic Experience of Students in English Universities*. http://www.hepi.ac.uk/2009/05/07/the-academic-experience-of-students-in-english-universities-2009-report/. Accessed 17 May 2016.

Bennett, S. (2006) 'First Questions for Designing High Education Learning Spaces', *The Journal of Academic Librarianship* 33 (1): 14–26.

Bernstein, B. (2000) *Pedagogy, Symbolic Control and Identity*. New York and Oxford: Rowman and Littlefield Publishers.

Bhabha, H. (1994) *The Location of Culture*. London and New York: Routledge.

Bhopal, K. (2010) *Asian Women in Higher Education: Shared Communities*. Stoke-on-Trent: Trentham Books.

BIS. (2015) *Fulfilling Our Potential: Teaching Excellence, Social Mobility, and Student Choice*. London: Department for Business Innovation & Skills. https://www.gov.uk/government/uploads/system/uploads/attachment_data/file/474227/BIS-15–623-fulfilling-our-potential-teaching-excellence-social-mobility-and-student-choice.pdf. Accessed 15 November 2015.

BIS. (2016) *Success as a Knowledge Economy: Teaching Excellence, Social Mobility and Student Choice*. London: Department for Business Innovation & Skills. https://www.gov.uk/government/uploads/system/uploads/attachment_data/file/523546/bis-16–265-success-as-a-knowledge-economy-web.pdf. Accessed 20 May 2016.

Boler, M. (1999) *Feeling Power: Emotions & Education*. New York: Routledge.

Boler, M. and Zembylas, M. (2003) 'Discomforting Truths: The Emotional Terrain of Understanding Difference', in P. Trifonas (Ed) *Pedagogies of Difference: Rethinking Education for Social Change*. New York: Routledge, 110–136.

Bonilla-Silva, E. (2003) *Racism without Racists: Color-Blind Racism and the Persistence of Racial Inequality in the United States*. Lanham, MD: Rowman & Littlefield.

Bourdieu, P. (1986) 'The Forms of Capital', in Richardson, J.G. (Ed) *Handbook of Theory and Research for Sociology of Education*. New York: Greenwood Press, 241–258.

Bourdieu, P. (1990) *In Other Words: Essays towards a Reflexive Sociology*. Cambridge: Polity Press.

Bourdieu, P. (1992) *An Invitation to Reflexive Sociology*. Cambridge: Polity Press.

Bourdieu, P. (2000) *Pascalian Meditations*. Cambridge, UK: Polity Press.

Bourdieu, P., Passeron, J.C., and De Saint Martin, M. (1994) *Academic Discourse*. Cambridge: Polity Press.

Brah, A. (1996) *Cartographies of Diaspora: Contesting Identities*. London and New York: Routledge.

Brah, A. and Phoenix, A. (2004) 'Ain't I A Woman: Revisting Intersectionality', *Journal of International Women's Studies* 5 (3): 75-86.

Brown, P., Lauder, H., and Ashton, D. (2011) *The Global Auction: The Broken Promises of Education, Jobs and Incomes*. Oxford: Oxford University Press.

Brusoni, M., Josep Grifoll Sauri, R., Jackson, S., Komurcugil, H., Malmedy, M., Matveeva, O., Motova, G., Pisarz, S., Pol, P., Rostlund, A., Soboleva, E., Tavares, O., and Zobel, L. (2014) *The Concept of Excellence in Higher Education. European Association for Quality Assurance in Higher Education*. Occasional Paper. http://www.enqa.eu/indirme/papers-and-reports/occasional-papers/ENQA%20Excellence%20WG%20Report_The%20Concept%20of%20Excellence%20in%20Higher%20Education.pdf. Accessed 26 November 2015.

Burke, P.J. (2002) *Accessing Education: Effectively Widening Participation*. Stoke-on-Trent: Trentham Books.

Burke, P.J. (2012) *The Right to Higher Education: Beyond Widening Participation*. Milton Park, Abingdon, Oxon, and New York: Routledge.

Burke, P.J., Bennet, A., Burgess, C., Grey, L., and Southgate, E. (2016) *Capabilities, Belonging, and Equity in Higher Education*. Curtin: National Centre for Student Equity in Higher Education.

Burke, P.J. and Crozier, G. (2013) *Teaching Inclusively: Changing Pedagogical Spaces*. https://www.heacademy.ac.uk/sites/default/files/projects/teaching_inclusively_resource_pack_final_version_opt.pdf. Accessed 17 May 2016.

Burke, P.J. and Crozier, G. (2014) 'Higher Education Pedagogies: Gendered Formations, Mis/Recognition and Emotion', *Journal of Research in Gender Studies* 4 (2): 52–67.

Burke, P.J., Crozier, G., Read, B., Hall, J., Peat, J., and Francis, B. (2013) *Formations of Gender and Higher Education Pedagogies Final Report (GaP)*. Higher Education Academy: York, UK.

Burke, P.J. and Jackson, S. (2007) *Reconceptualising Lifelong Learning: Feminist Interventions*. London and New York: Routledge.

Burke, P.J. and Kuo, Y. (2015) 'Widening Participation in Higher Education: Regimes and Globalizing Discourses Policy', in J. Huisman, H. de Boer, D. Dill, and M. Souto-Otero (Eds) *The Palgrave International Handbook of Higher Education Policy and Governance*. Hampshire and New York: Palgrave Macmillan, 547–568.

Burke, P.J., Stevenson, J. and Whelan, P. (2015) 'Teaching "Excellence" and Pedagogic Stratification in Higher Education.' *International Studies in Widening Participation* 2 (2): 29–43.

Butler, J. (1990) 'Gender Trouble, Feminist Theory, and Psychoanalytic Discourse.' *Feminism/postmodernism*, 327.

Butler, J. (1993) *Bodies that Matter: On the Discursive Limits of 'Sex'*. London: Routledge.

Butler, J. (2014) *Speaking of Rage and Grief: A Progressive Voice*. Leigha Cohen Video Production. http://www.leighacohenvideo.com/. Accessed 29 April 2016.

Campbell, C. (1996) 'Detraditionalisation, Character and the Limits to Agency', in Heelas P., Lash, S. and Morris P. (Eds) *Detraditionalisation: Critical Reflections on Authority and Identity*. Oxford: Blackwell.

Caress, A.L. (2014) *Public Involvement and the REF 'Impact' Agenda: Squaring the Circle?* http://www.invo.org.uk/public-involvement-and-the-ref-impact-agenda-squaring-the-circle/. Accessed 10 May 2016.

Carvalho, M. (2014) 'Gender and Education: A View from Latin America', *Gender and Education* 26 (2): 97–102.

Case, K.A. (2013) *Deconstructing Privilege: Teaching and Learning as Allies in the Classroom.* New York: Routledge.

Charlesworth, S.J., Gilfillan, S., and Wilkinson, R. (2006) 'Living Inferiority', *Soundings* 33: 76–88.

Chawla, D. and Rodriguez, A. (2007) 'New Imaginations of Difference: On Teaching, Writing, and Culture', *Teaching in Higher Education* 12 (5): 697–708.

Clayton, J., Crozier, G., and Reay, D. (2009) 'Home and Away: Risk, Familiarity and the Multiple Geographies of the Higher Education Experience', *International Studies in Sociology of Education* 19 (3–4): 157–174.

Clegg, S. (2008) 'Academic Identities under Threat', *British Educational Research Journal* 34 (3): 329–345.

Clegg, S. (2011) 'Cultural Capital and Agency: Connecting Critique and Curriculum in Higher Education', *British Journal of Sociology of Education* 32 (1): 93–108.

Clegg, S. (2014) *Translations and Contradictions: On Making a Difference and Critical Distance.* Paper presented at the Society For Research into Higher Education's Higher Education Close Up, Lancaster, UK. http://www.lancaster.ac.uk/fass/events/hecu7/abstracts/clegg.htm. Accessed 15 April 2016.

Clegg, S. (2015) 'Adventures in Meaning Making: Teaching in Higher Education 2005–2013', *Teaching in Higher Education* 20 (4): 373–387.

Clegg, S., Stevenson, J., and Burke, P.J. (2016) 'Translating Close-up Research into Action: A Critical Reflection', *Reflective Practice*, doi:10.1080/14623943.2016.1 145580

Coffey, A. and Atkinson, P. (1996) *Making Sense of Qualitative Data: Complementary Research Strategies And Social Thought.* London: Sage Publications.

Collini, S. (2012) *What Are Universities For?* London: Penguin Books.

Collins, P.H. (1998) 'The Tie that Binds: Race, Gender and US Violence', *Ethnic and Racial Studies* 21 (5): 917–938.

Crozier, G. (2013) 'CHEER Seminar Presentation on Formations of Gender and HE Pedagogies Project Findings.' University of Sussex, March 20.

Crozier, G., Burke, P.J., and Archer, L. (2016) 'Peer Relations in Higher Education: Raced, Classed, and Gendered Constructions and Othering', *Whiteness and Education* 1 (1): 39–53.

Crozier, G. and Davies, J. (2006) 'Family Matters: A Discussion of the Role of the Extended Family in Supporting the Children's Education, with Specific Reference to Families of Bangladeshi and Pakistani Origin, in the UK.' *Sociological Review* 54 (4): 677–694.

Crozier, G. and Davies, J. (2008) '"The Trouble is They Don't Mix": Self-segregation or Enforced Exclusion? Teachers' Constructions of South Asian Students', *Race, Ethnicity and Education* 11 (3): 285–301.

Crozier, G. and Reay, D. (2008) *The Socio-Cultural and Learning Experiences of Working Class students in Higher Education.* ESRC End of Award Report. www.societytoday.ac.uk. Accessed 2 May 2016.

Crozier, G. and Reay, D. (2011) 'Capital Accumulation: Working-class Students Learning How to Learn in HE', *Teaching in Higher Education* 16 (2): 145–155.

Crozier, G., Reay, D., and Clayton, J. (2010) 'The Socio-Cultural and Learning Experiences of Working Class Students in Higher Education', in M. David (Ed) *Widening Participation through Improving Learning*. London and New York: Routledge, 62–74.

Crozier, G., Reay, D., Clayton, J., and Colliander, L. (2008) 'Different Strokes for Different Folks: Diverse Students in Diverse Institutions – Experiences of Higher Education', *Research Papers in Education* 23 (2): 167–177.

Davies, B. (2006) 'Subjectification: The Relevance of Butler's Analysis for Education', *British Journal of Sociology of Education* 27 (4): 425–438.

DCSF. (2010) *Identifying Components of Attainment Gaps*. Research Report RR17. London: HMSO.

Deem, R. and Brehony, K. (2005) 'Management as Ideology: The Case of "New Managerialism" in Higher Education', *Oxford Review of Education* 31 (2): 217–235.

Delgado, R. and Stefancic, J. (2000) *Critical Race Theory: The Cutting Edge*. Philadelphia: Temple University Press.

Doughty, S. (2007) '£40 Million Waste of the "Mickey Mouse" Degrees', *Mail On-Line*. http://www.dailymail.co.uk/news/article-476620/40m-waste-Mickey-Mouse-degrees.html. 20 August 2007.

Ellsworth, E. (1996) 'Why Doesn't this Feel Empowering? Working through Repressive Myths of Critical Pedagogy', *Harvard Educational Review* 59 (3): 297–324.

Flax, J. (1995) 'Postmodernism and Gender Relations in Feminist Theory', in M. Blair, J. Holland, and S. Sheldon (Eds) *Identity and Diversity: Gender and the Experience of Education*. Avon: Open University, 143–160.

Foucault, M. (1977) *Discipline and Punish: The Birth of the Prison*. trans. A. Sheridan. New York: Pantheon Books.

Foucault, M. (1982) 'The Subject and Power', in H. Dreyfus and P. Rabinow (Eds) *Michel Foucault: Beyond Structuralism and Hermeneutics*. Brighton: Harvester, 208–228.

Francis, B., Burke, P.J., and Read, B. (2014) 'The Submergence and Re-emergence of Gender in Undergraduate Accounts of University Experience', *Gender and Education* 26 (1): 1–17.

Francis, B. and Skelton, C. (2002) *Investigating Gender: Contemporary Perspectives in Education*. Buckingham: Open University Press.

Fraser, N. (1997) *Justice Interruptus: Critical Reflections on the "Postsocialist" Condition*. New York: Routledge.

Fraser, N. (2003) 'Social Justice in the Age of Identity Politics: Redistribution, Recognition and Participation', in N. Fraser and A. Honneth (Eds) *Redistribution or Recognition? A Political-Philosophical Exchange*. London and New York: Verso, 7–109.

Fraser, N. (2008) *Scales of Justice: Reimagining Political Space in a Globalising World*. Cambridge: Polity Press.

Fraser, N. (2011) *Transcript of Podcast: Nancy Fraser on Recognition/Interviewer: N. Warburton*. Multiculturalism Bites. London: The Open University.

Fraser, N. and Honneth, A. (2003) *Redistribution or Recognition?: A Political-Philosophical Exchange*. London and New York: Verso.

Freire, P. (1970) *Pedagogy of the Oppressed*. New York: Continuum.

Freire, P. (2009) *Pedagogy of Hope*. London: Continuum.

Froumin, I. and Lisyuktin, M. (2015) 'Excellence-Driven Policies and Initiatives in the Context of Bologna Process: Rationale, Design, Implementation, and Outcomes', in A. Curaj, L. Matei, R. Pricopie, J. Salmi, and P. Scott (Eds) *The European Higher Education Area*. Open Access: SpringerLink, 249–265.

Gaine, C. (1995) *Still No Problem Here*. Stoke-on-Trent, UK: Trentham Books.

Gill, R. (2010) 'Breaking the Silence: The Hidden Injuries of Neo-Liberal Academia', in R. Flood and R. Gill (Eds) *Secrecy and Silence in the Research Process: Feminist Reflections*. London: Routledge, 228–244.

Gill, R. (2014) *The Psychic Life of Neoliberalism in the Academy*. Paper presented at Governing Academic Life conference, LSE and British Library, London, 25–26 June 2014.

Gillborn, D. (2005) 'Education Policy as an Act of White Supremacy: Whiteness, Critical Race Theory and Education Reform', *Journal of Education Policy* 20 (4): 485–505.

Gore, J. (1993) *The Struggle for Pedagogies: Critical and Feminist Discourses as Regimes of Truth*. New York: Routledge.

Gov.uk. (2016) https://www.gov.uk/government/consultations/higher-education-teaching-excellence-social-mobility-and-student-choice.

Grant, B. (1997) 'Disciplining Students: The Construction of Student Subjectivities', *British Journal of Sociology of Education* 18 (1): 101–114.

Hale, S. (2014) 'A Propensity for Self-Subversion and a Taste for Liberation: An Afterword', *Journal of Middle East Women's Studies* 10 (1): 149–163.

Hall, S. and du Gay, P. (1996) *Questions of Cultural Identity*. Los Angeles: Sage Publications.

Harding, S.G. (1991) *Whose Science? Whose Knowledge?: Thinking from Women's Lives*. Ithaca: Cornell University Press.

Harvey, L. (2008) *Jumping through Hoops on a White Elephant: A Survey Signifying Nothing*. Times Higher Education, 12 June 2008.

HEA. (2011) *The UK Professional Standards Framework for Teaching and Supporting Learning in Higher Education*. York, UK: The Higher Education Academy, Guild HE and Universities UK. https://www.heacademy.ac.uk/sites/default/files/resources/ukpsf_2011_english.pdf. Accessed 20 May 2016.

HEFCE. (2003) *The Future of Higher Education. Executive Summary*. www.hefce.ac.uk/pubs/hefce/2003/03_35.htm. Accessed 3 May 2016.

HEFCE. (2005) *Young Participation in Higher Education*. www.hefce.ac.uk/pubs. Accessed 16 February 2010.

HEFCE. (2010) *Trends in Young Participation in Higher Education: Core Results for England*. Bristol: Higher Education Funding Council for England.

HEFCE. (2013) *Trends in Young Participation in Higher Education: Core Results for England*. Bristol: Higher Education Funding Council for England.

HEFCE, SFC, HEFCW, DELNI (2012) *Assessment Framework and Guidance on Submissions* (02.2011 updated version) www.ref.ac.uk/media/ref/content/pub/assessmentframeworkandguidanceonsubmissions/GOS%20including%20addendum.pdf. Accessed 21 March 2016.

HEPI. (2009) *Male and Female Participation and Progression in Higher Education*. Oxford: Higher Education Policy Institute.

Hey, V. and Leathwood, C. (2009) 'Passionate Attachments: Higher Education, Policy, Knowledge, Emotion and Social Justice', *Higher Education Policy* 22 (1): 101–118.

Hockings, C.S., Cooke, S. and Bowl, M. (2008) 'Learning and Teaching for Social Diversity and Difference: Full Research Report ESRC End of Award Report.' RES-139-25-0222. Swindon, ESRC.

Holt, M. and Griffin, C. (2005) 'Students vs Locals: Young Adults Constructions of the Working Class Other', *British Journal of Social Psychology* 44 (2): 241–267.

hooks, b. (1994) *Teaching to Transgress: Education as the Practice of Freedom.* New York: Routledge.

hooks, b. (2003) *Teaching Community: A Pedagogy of Hope.* New York: Routledge.

hooks, b. (2010) *Teaching Critical Thinking: Practical Wisdom.* New York: Routledge.

Hotson, H. (2012) *Big Business at the Heart of the System: Understanding the Global University Crisis.* Keynote Lecture at Society for Research into Higher Education Annual Conference, Newport, South Wales.

Hunter, C.P. (2013) 'Shifting Themes in OECD Country Reviews of Higher Education', *Higher Education* 66: 707–723.

International Labour Organisation. (2016) *Women and the Future of Work. Beijing + 20 and Beyond. Gender, Equality and Diversity Branch.* Conditions of Work and Equality Department, Geneva, Switzerland.

Jackson, C. (2006) *Lads and Ladettes in School: Gender and a Fear of Failure.* Maidenhead: Open University Press.

Jamieson, P., Fisher, K., Gilding, T., Taylor, P., and Trevitt, A.C.F. (2000) 'Place and Space in the Design of New Learning Environments', *Higher Education Research and Development* 19 (2): 221–236.

JISC. (2006) *Designing Spaces for Effective Learning: Guide for the 21st Century Learning Design.* Higher Education Funding Council for England. http://www.webarchive.org.uk/wayback/archive/20140616001949/http://www.jisc.ac.uk/media/documents/publications/learningspaces.pdf. Accessed 24 July 2015.

Keevers, L. and Abuodha, P. (2012) 'Social Inclusion as an Unfinished Verb: A Practice-Based Approach', *Journal of Academic Language and Learning* 6 (2): 42–59.

King, J. (1991) 'Dysconscious Racism: Ideology, Identity, and the Mis-education of Teachers', *The Journal of Negro Education* 60 (2): 133–146.

Ladson-Billings, G. (1998) 'Just What Is Critical Race Theory and What's It Doing in a Nice Field Like Education?', *International Journal of Qualitative Studies in Education* 11 (1): 7–24.

Lareau, A. (2003) *Unequal Childhoods: Class, Race and Family Life.* Berkley, LA and London, UK: University of California Press.

Lather, P. (1991) *Getting Smart: Feminist Research and Pedagogy with/in the Postmodern.* New York and London: Routledge.

Leathwood, C. (2006) 'Gender, Equity and the Discourse of the Independent Learner in Higher Education', *Higher Education* 52: 611–633.

Leathwood, C. and Hey, V. (2009) 'Gender/ed Discourses and Emotional Sub-texts: Theorising Emotion in UK Higher Education', *Teaching in Higher Education* 14 (4): 429–440.

Leathwood, C. and Read, B. (2009) *A Feminised Future? Gender and the Changing Face of Higher Education.* London: SRHE & Open University Press.

Lehman, W. (2009) 'Becoming Middle Class: How Working Class University Students Draw and Transgress Moral Class Boundaries', *Sociology* 43 (4): 631–647.

Leibowitz, B. and Bozalek, V. (2016) 'The Scholarship of Teaching and Learning from a Social Justice Perspective', *Teaching in Higher Education* 21 (2): 109–122.

Lester, J. (2011) 'Regulating Gender Performances: Power and Gender Norms in Faculty Work', *NAPSA Journal about Women in Higher Education* 4 (2): 142–169.

Levitas, R. (1998) *The Inclusive Society? Social Exclusion and New Labour*. New York: Palgrave MacMillan.

Levitas, R. (2005) *The Inclusive Society? Social Exclusion and New Labour* (2nd ed.). New York: Palgrave MacMillan.

Lindsay, Brink (2013) *Human Capitalism: How Economic Growth has Made us Smarter – and More Unequal*. Princeton and Oxford: Princeton University Press.

Lingard, B., Rawolle, S., and Taylor, S. (2005) 'Globalising Policy Sociology in Education: Working with Bourdieu', *Journal of Education Policy* 20 (6): 759–777.

Llamas, J. (2006) 'Technologies of Disciplinary Power in Action: The Norm of the "Good Student"', *Higher Education* 52: 665–686.

Luke, C. (1994) 'Women in the Academy: The Politics of Speech and Silence', *British Journal of Sociology of Education* 15 (2): 211–230.

Lynch, K. (2010) 'Carelessness: A Hidden Doxa of Higher Education', *Higher Education* 9 (1): 54–67.

Mac an Ghaill, M. (1994) *The Making of Men: Masculinities, Sexualities and Schooling*. Buckingham, UK: Open University Press.

Macdonald, H.M. (2013) 'Inviting Discomfort: Foregrounding Emotional Labour in Teaching Anthropology in Post-Apartheid South Africa', *Teaching in Higher Education* 18 (6): 670–682.

Majors, R. and Billson, J.M. (1992) *Cool Pose: The Dilemmas of Black Manhood in America*. New York: Lexington Books.

Mann, S. (2001) 'Alternative Perspectives on the Student Experience: Alienation and Engagement', *Studies in Higher Education* 26 (1): 7–19.

Mann, S. (2005) 'Alienation in the Learning Environment: A Failure of Community?', *Studies in Higher Education* 30 (1): 43–55.

Mann, S. (2008) *Study, Power and the University*. UK: McGraw-Hill Education.

Marginson, S. (2015) *The Landscape of Higher Education Research 1965–2015 Equality of Opportunity: The First Fifty Years*. Keynote Address. Valuing Research into Higher Education: Advancing Knowledge, Informing Policy, Enhancing Practice. SRHE 50th Anniversary Colloquium, Friday 26 June 2015.

Mayuzumi, K., Motobayashi, C., Nagayama, A., and Takeuchi, M. (2007) 'Transforming Diversity in Canadian Higher Education: A Dialogue of Japanese Women Graduate Students', *Teaching in Higher Education* 12 (5–6): 581–592.

McArthur, J. (2010) 'Achieving Social Justice within and through Higher Education: The Challenge for Critical Pedagogy', *Teaching in Higher Education* 15 (5): 493–504.

McLean, M. (2006) *Pedagogy and the University: Critical Theory and Practice*. London: The Continuum International Publishing Group.

McLeod, J. (2011) 'Student Voice and the Politics of Listening in Higher Education', *Critical Studies in Education* 52 (2): 179–189.

McNay, L. (1999) 'Gender, Habitus and the Field Pierre Bourdieu and the Limits of Reflexivity', *Theory, Culture & Society* 16 (1): 95–117.

McNay, L. (2008) *Against Recognition*. Cambridge: Polity.

Miller, J. (1995) 'Trick or Treat? The Autobiography of the Question', *English Quarterly* 27 (3): 22–26.

Mills, D. and Spencer, D. (2011) 'Teacher or Anthropologist? Pedagogy and Ethnographic Sensibility', *Teaching Anthropology* 1 (1): 1–2.

Mirza, H.S. (2009) *Race, Gender and Educational Desire*. London and New York: Routledge.

Misiaszek, L.I. (2015) '"You're Not Able to Breathe": Conceptualizing the Intersectionality of Early Career, Gender, and Crisis', *Teaching in Higher Education* 20 (1): 64–77.

Morley, L. (2003) *Quality and Power in Higher Education*. Berkshire: Society for Research in Higher Education and Open University Press.

Morley, L. (2010) *Imagining the University of the Future*. Professional Lecture. University of Sussex, 25 May 2010.

Mountz, A., Bonds, A., Mansfield, B., Loyd, J., Hyndman, J., Walton-Roberts, M., Basu, R., Whitson, R., Hawkins, R., Hamilton, T., and Curran, W. (2015) 'For Slow Scholarship: A Feminist Politics of Resistance through Collective Action in the Neoliberal University', *ACME: An International E-Journal for Critical Geographies* 14 (4): 1235–1259.

Murray, J. (2006) 'Constructions of Caring Professionalism: A Case Study of Teacher Educators', *Gender and Education* 18 (4): 381–397.

Museus, S.D. and Griffin, K.A. (2011) 'Mapping the Margins in Higher Education: On the Promise of Intersectionality Frameworks in Research and Discourse', *New Directions for Institutional Research* 151: 5–13.

Naidoo, R. (2015) *Transnational Perspectives on Higher Education and Global Well-Being*. Valuing Research into Higher Education: Advancing Knowledge, Informing Policy, Enhancing Practice. SRHE 50th Anniversary Colloquium, Friday 26 June 2015.

National Union of Students. (2014) *Equality Survey*. London.

Neal, M.A. (2013) *Looking for Leroy: Illegible Black Masculinities*. New York: New York University Press.

Neary, M., Harrison, A., Crellin, G., Parkeh, N., Saunders, G., Duggan, F., Williams, S., and Austin, S. (2010) *Learning Landscapes in Higher Education*. http://learninglandscapes.blogs.lincoln.ac.uk/files/2010/04/FinalReport.pdf. Accessed 28 September 2015.

Nevile, A. (2006). 'Is Social Exclusion a Useful Concept for Policy-makers in Australia?' *Public Policy* 1 (2): 83–91.

Nicoll, K. and Harrison, R. (2003) 'Constructing the Good Teacher in Higher Education: The Discursive Work of Standards', *Studies in Continuing Education* 25 (1): 23–35.

Nixon, J. (2013) 'The Drift to Conformity: The Myth of Institutional Diversity', in T. Erkkilä (Ed) *Global University Rankings: Challenges for European Higher Education*. London and New York: Palgrave MacMillan, 92–106.

Nixon, J. (2015) 'Learning to Think Together', *Teaching in Higher Education* 20 (4): 1–11.

Noguera, P.A. and Leslie, T. (2014) 'Intersectionality and the Status of Black Males: Risk, Resilience and Response', in C. Grant and E. Zwier (Eds) *Intersectionality and Urban Education*. Charlotte, NC: Information Age Publishing, 79–96.

OECD. (2012) *Education Indicators in Focus*. http://www.oecd.org/education/skills-beyond-school/49986459.pdf. Accessed 10 April 2016.

Pain, Rachel. (2014) 'Impact: Striking a Blow or Working Together?' *ACME: An International E-Journal for Critical Geographies* 13 (1): 19–23.

Powell, G. (2014) 'In Search of Relevant Learning Spaces', in T. Fitzgeral (Ed) *Advancing Knowledge in Higher Education: Universities in Turbulent Times*. Hershey: Information Science Reference, 99–111.

Puwar, N. (2004) *Space Invaders: Race, Gender and Bodies out of Place*. Oxford: Berghahn Books.

Radcliffe, D., Wilson, H., Powell, D., and Tibbetts, B. (2008) *Designing Next Generation Spaces of Learning: Collaboration at the Pedagogy-Space-Technology Nexus*. The University of Queensland: Australian Learning and Teaching Council Report. http://documents.skgproject.com/skg-final-report.pdf. Accessed 28 September 2015.

Ramirez, F.O. and Tiplic, D. (2014) 'In Pursuit of Excellence? Discursive Patterns in European Higher Education Research', *Higher Education* 67 (4): 439–455.

Read, B., Archer, L., and Leathwood, C. (2003) 'Challenging Cultures? Student Conceptions of "Belonging" and "Isolation" at a Post-1992 University', *Studies in Higher Education* 28 (3): 261–277.

Reay, D. (2009) 'Identity Making in Schools and Classrooms', in M. Wetherell and C. Mohanty (Eds) *The Sage Handbook of Identities*. New York: Sage, 277–294.

Reay, D., Crozier, G. and Clayton, J. (2009) 'Strangers in Paradise: Working Class Students in Elite Universities', *Sociology* 43 (6): 1103–1121.

Reay, D., Crozier, G., and Clayton, J. (2010) '"Fitting in" or "Standing Out": Working-class Students in UK Higher Education', *British Educational Research Journal* 36 (1): 107–124.

Reay, D.M., David, M.E., and Ball, S. (2005) *Degrees of Choice: Class, Race, and Gender in Higher Education*. Stoke-on-Trent: Trentham Books.

Rhoads, R. and Szelenyi, K. (2011) *Global Citizenship and the University: Advancing Social Life and Relations in an Interdependent World*. Stanford, CA: Stanford University Press.

Romão, J.E. (2007) 'Chapter 9: Sociology of Education or the Education of Sociology? Paulo Freire and the Sociology of Education', in C.A. Torres and A. Teodoro (Eds) *Critique and Utopia: New Developments in the Sociology of Education in the Twenty-First Century*. Lanham, MD: Rowman & Littlefield, 131–138.

Said, E. (2003) *Orientalism*. London: Penguin Books.

Scholl, B. (2012) *Higher Education in Spatial Planning: Positions and Reflections*. Zurich: Die Deutsche Nationalbibliothek.

Schulte, B. (2014) *Overwhelmed: Work, Love and Play When No One Has the Time*. New York: Sarah Crichton Books.

Sellar, S. (2013) *Measuring the Unmeasurable: Intensive Human Capital and New Data Infrastructures in Schooling*. Pedagogies for Social Justice Conference, University of South Australia, October 2013.

Sellar, S. and Gale, T. (2011) 'Mobility, Aspiration, Voice: A New Structure of Feeling for Student Equity in Higher Education', *Critical Studies in Education* 52 (2): 115–134.

Sewell, T. (1997) *Black Masculinities and Schooling*. Stoke-on-Trent: Trentham Books.

Shain, F. (2011) *The New Folk Devils*. Stoke-on-Trent: Trentham Books.

Sharrock, G. (2000) 'Why students Are Not (Just) Consumers (and Other Reflections on Life after George)', *Journal of Higher Education Policy and Management* 22 (2): 149–164.

Sharrock, G. (2015) 'Making Sense of the MOOCS Debate', *Journal of Higher Education Policy and Management* 37 (5): 597–609.

Shepherd, J. (2010) '"Stop Funding Mickey Mouse Degrees", Says Top Scientist', *The Guardian*. 10 February 2010.

Sibley, D. (1995) *Geographies of Exclusion*. London and New York: Routledge.

Sin, C. (2015) 'Teaching and Learning: A Journey from the Margins to the Core in European Higher Education Policy', in A. Curaj, L. Matei, R. Pricopie, J. Salmi, and P. Scott (Eds) *The European Higher Education Area*. Open Access: SpringerLink, 325–341.

Six, F. (2005) *The Trouble with Trust: The Dynamics of Interpersonal Trust Building*. Cheltenham. UK and Northampton, MA, USA: Edward Elgar.

Skeggs, B. (2004) *Class, Self and Culture*. London: Routledge.

Souter, K., Riddle, M., Sellers, W., and Keppell, M. (2011) *Spaces for Knowledge Generation*. Final Report: Australian Learning and Teaching Council. http://documents. skgproject.com/skg-final-report.pdf. Accessed 28 September 2015.

Stevens, P. and Crozier, G. (2014) 'Review of Research into Race and Education in England', in P. Stevens, and G. Dworkin (Eds) *The Palgrave Handbook for Race and Ethnic Inequalities in Education*. London and New York: Palgrave MacMillan Publications, 259–307.

Stevenson, J. (2012) *Black and Minority Ethnic Student Degree Retention and Attainment*. York: Higher Education Academy.

Stevenson, J., Burke, P., and Whelan, P. (2014) *Pedagogic Stratification and the Shifting Landscape of Higher Education*. York, UK: Higher Education Academy.

Stromquist, N. (2012) 'The Gender Dimension in the World Bank's Education Strategy', in S.J. Klees, J. Samoff, N.P. Stromquist, and X. Bonal, (Eds.), *The World Bank and Education*. Rotterdam: SensePublishers, 159–172.

Swain, H. (2009) 'A "Hotchpotch" of Subjectivity', *The Guardian* 19 May 2009.

Taylor, C. (1992) *The Ethics of Authenticity*. Cambridge, MA: Harvard University Press.

Tatlow, P. and Phoenix, D. (2015) *Policy Briefing: The Possibilities and Pitfalls of a Teaching Excellence Framework*. London: Million+.

Temple, P. (2008) 'Learning Spaces in Higher Education: An Under-researched Topic', *London Review of Education* 6 (3): 229–241.

Testa, D. and Egan, R. (2014) 'Finding a Voice: The Higher Education Experiences of Students from Diverse Backgrounds', *Teaching in Higher Education* 19 (3): 229–241.

Torres, C.A. (2007) 'Paulo Freire, Education, and Transformative Social Justice Learning', in C.A. Torres and A. Teodoro (Eds) *Critique and Utopia: New Developments in the Sociology of Education in the Twenty-First Century*. Lanham, MD: Rowman & Littlefield, 155–160.

Torres, C.A. (2011) 'Public Universities and the Neoliberal Common Sense: Seven Iconoclastic Theses', *International Studies in Sociology of Education* 21 (3): 177–197.

Torres, C.A. (2014) *First Freire: Early Writings in Social Justice Education*. New York: Teachers College Press, Teachers College Columbia University.

Trowler, P. (1998) *Education Policy*. East Sussex, UK: The Gildredge Press.

Troyna, B. (1993) 'Underachiever or Misunderstood? A Reply to Roger Gomm', *British Educational Research Journal* 19: 167–174.

Westwood, S. (1990) 'Racism, Black Masculinity and the Politics of Space', in J. Morgan and D. Hearn (Eds) *Men, Masculinities and Social Theory*. London: Unwin Hyman, 55–71.

Williams, J. (1997) *Institutional Rhetorics and Realities. Negotiating Access to Higher Education: The Discourse of Selectivity and Equity*. Buckingham: The Society for Research into Higher Education & Open University Press.

Williams, J. (2013) *Consuming Higher Education: Why Learning Can't Be Bought*. London and New York: Bloomsbury.

Whitty, G., Hayton, A., and Tang, S. (2016) *The Growth of Participation in Higher Education in England*. CEEHE Occasional Papers (Co-published with Faculty of Education, Beijing Norma University). Newcastle: Centre of Excellence for Equity in Higher Education. Issue 1. April 2016.

Zembylas, M. and Boler, M. (2002) *On the Spirit of Patriotism: Challenges of a "Pedagogy of Discomfort"*. Teachers College Record. Electronic Document. http://www.tcrecord.org/Content.asp?ContentID11007. Accessed 3 June 2012.

Index

academic governance, decline of 13
academic identity 8; discourses of 60;
    teaching vs. research 26
accommodation, discourses of 38
acculturation 36
age 3, 6, 29, 69, 81–2, 94, 102, 122,
    123, 128, 143, 153; discrimination
    by 82
agency 52, 54, 124, 127
antagonism, discourses of 88
Archer, Louise 56, 143, 150
assessment: criterion 51; measures
    24, 43, 52, 137, 144; modes of 5;
    by peers 70; processes 38; regimes
    24; research 37; by students 16;
    of students 65, 68, 70, 80, 86;
    technologies of 37
assimilation 38; as device of White
    control 113; discourse of 36; vs.
    mimicry 113; strategies of 119; and
    White superiority 113
austerity measures 10, 11, 131
Australia 20, 32, 58; higher education
    in 20–1; 'Indigenous knowledge'
    31; Office of Learning and Teaching
    (OLT) 26
authenticity 67, 77, 108–10, 120; and
    identity formation 110; in- 118
authority 41, 43, 93, 97–9; politics
    of 93

belonging 8, 34–5, 64, 65, 97, 108,
    110, 141; not 32, 97, 103; politics of
    32; see also recognition; representation
Bernstein, B. 33, 35, 76, 77, 134
Black and Minority Ethnic (BME)
    students 8, 60, 67, 72, 77–9, 82,
    84, 89, 108–15, 117–20, 145;

fear of being noticed 114; as 'folk
    devils' 119; living off campus
    113; marginalisation of 119; and
    moral panics 119; and music 114;
    objectification of 110; perception of,
    by White students 112–13, 114–20;
    surveillance of 119; see also student(s)
Black students 65–9, 77, 83, 97, 108–14,
    116, 144, 145; see also Black and
    Minority Ethnic (BME) students
Bologna Process 16, 128
Bourdieu, P. 7, 19, 35, 68, 76, 83, 88,
    123, 126, 134
Britain 59, 109
Butler, J. 35, 39–40, 45, 123, 134

capital: cultural 19, 70, 82, 83, 89;
    intellectual 34; social 19, 31, 82, 83,
    89; see also human capital
capitalism: global 14; human 23;
    predatory 12
casualisation 13, 22, 136
categories 27, 37, 46, 96, 145;
    classification of 33; see also recognition
    rules
categorisation: limitations of 36
China 133
choice 5, 21, 57; discourse of 12, 133–4;
    life 126; student 7, 13, 15–16, 20–1,
    76, 82, 84, 106, 108, 111, 139
class, social 8, 65, 69, 75, 76, 81–2,
    89, 102, 109, 110, 114, 118, 120,
    122, 139, 140, 141, 143, 145,
    149, 151; antagonisms 120; BME
    working-class students 111, 112, 114;
    discrimination by 82; and ECTs 122;
    and fitting in 110; and friendship 84;
    structural inequalities of 56–7; White

middle-class students 108, 110, 112, 114–20; White working-class students 108, 110, 114–20; working-class 31, 67, 97, 109, 117–18, 145
classification 33, 77; technologies of 93
classism 92
collegiality 72
compulsory schooling systems 2
confidence 11, 28; lack of 30, 60; of students 64, 67, 78, 79, 81, 84, 85, 87, 98, 101–2, 106
corporatisation 1, 3, 13
counting culture 24; see also datafication; surveillance

datafication 11, 22, 23, 51, 124, 133
deficit discourse 30, 72, 75, 124, 129–30, 131
deregulation 11
difference 1–6, 9–10, 11–12, 17, 20, 25, 27–8, 29–31, 34–41, 44–8, 50, 53, 54, 55, 92, 97, 102, 110, 116, 119, 131, 134, 135–7, 139, 142, 143; construction of 92; fear of 10, 38–9, 131, 137; formations of 3, 4, 31, 34, 132, 135–41; and pedagogy 11, 28; politics of 17, 37–8, 41; and power 41; recognition of 39, 55; regulation of 29; relations of 92; as resource 138; vs. standardisation 29, 38; surveillance of 138; see also pedagogy(-ies)
disability 31, 81–2, 102: discrimination by 82
disciplinarity 42; inter- 42
disciplinary: canons 56; community 74; culture 6, 59; experts 61, 136; framework 73; identity/identification 70, 86, 136; knowledge 25–6, 34, 41–2, 43, 45, 138, 139, 142; practices 140; spaces 7, 91; subject/contexts/fields 7, 31, 38, 42, 56, 70, 74, 76, 97, 106, 108, 109, 135, 138, 143, 144, 150–1; technologies 37, 39, 92
disconnection 39, 56
distancing 65, 88, 115, 118
diversity 1, 5, 6, 9, 12, 15, 17, 26–7, 34, 37–8, 46, 50, 59, 89, 92, 95, 97, 108, 131, 136, 139, 143, 144, 149, 151; of class 114; colonialist history of 115; of ethnicity 114; and excellence 20; and fear 38; in higher

education 35, 48, 92, 97, 110, 116, 119; as marketing tool 37–8, 131, 138; and pedagogy 11; and power 40; signifiers of 113; see also plurality
'dumbing down' 10, 48, 100, 104, 131; see also standards

economic rationalism 15–16; definition of 15
educational cultivation 70
education market 20, 139
emotion(s) 23, 24, 25, 35, 37–9, 44–7, 60, 61, 71, 91–3, 95, 99, 101, 132, 136, 137; cultural politics of 3; discourse of 64; exclusion of 122; fear as 91; fear of 47, 91, 122; and misogyny 91
employability: competition for jobs 120; of students 1, 16, 21, 40, 59, 64, 134
empowerment 24, 40, 54–5; dis- 140; of students 96, 102
enculturation 64, 70
England 4, 15, 20, 49, 62, 98, 120, 133, 151
equality 130, 134, 140; see also inequality(-ies)
equity 1, 3–5, 11, 15, 31, 36, 41, 43–4, 47, 65, 93, 101, 134, 136, 140–2; discourse of 135; vs. excellence 19, 20; groups 30; in higher education 12, 16, 20–1, 24, 26–8, 35, 43, 95, 97, 102, 133, 134, 139; policies of 3, 140; problematical nature of 45
ethnicity 4, 6, 8, 18, 29, 36, 38, 39, 43, 46, 65, 68, 112–13, 114, 120, 143, 144, 149; and ECTs 122
'evidence-based': discourses 6, 51; policy and practice 15, 93
excellence: academic 1, 7, 11, 26, 51, 76, 136; discourse(s) of 12, 15–20, 37, 47, 133, 135; and diversity 17–18, 20; drive for 11, 36, 47, 88, 92, 139; vs. egalitarianism 18; vs. equity 19, 20; and global competitiveness 16–17; meaning of 16, 36–7; in research 74, 76; vs. social justice 19; of teaching 134; see also Bologna Process
exclusion(s) 1, 2, 4, 5, 7, 10, 27, 29, 34, 36, 42, 44, 47, 77, 83, 93, 104, 122, 131; geographies of 77; in

higher education 11, 30, 50, 92, 111, 138; pedagogical 141

fair access 1, 4, 50
female students 67, 74, 77–82, 84–7, 89, 96, 98, 102–4, 112, 114, 116–17, 143–5
femininity 92, 101, 106, 137; discourses of 93; identity 141; as power resource 99
Formations of Gender and Higher Education Pedagogies (GaP) 4, 6, 7, 8, 22, 33, 49–50, 52, 54–5, 58–64, 66–73, 76, 77, 80, 91, 94, 96–101, 105, 106, 111, 114, 143–52, 153, 154–9
Foucault, M. 8, 35, 39, 42–3, 134; 'docile bodies' 107; and power 55
framing 33
Fraser, N. 3, 30–2, 35, 134, 138
Freire, P. 6, 14, 34, 35, 40, 44, 53, 134; announcement and denouncement, concepts of 55; banking education 44; capacity to dream 40; circle of knowledge 34, 41, 53; concepts of *inédito viável* 14, 54, 123–4, 130; pedagogy of the oppressed 44; project of humanisation 44, 53
friendship(s) 83, 84, 86, 108, 111

gender 2–8, 11, 18, 20, 22, 24, 27, 29, 32, 34, 37–9, 43, 46, 49–53, 55–8, 59–61, 63–5, 69–70, 75–6, 89–90, 91–107, 113, 114, 117, 118, 120, 123, 132, 135, 136–41, 143–4, 148–51; and ECTs 122; and friendship 84–5; hegemonic discourses of 91; marginalisation of 95; structural inequalities of 56–7
gendered subjectivity 5–6, 29, 91
globalisation 1, 5, 16, 132; hegemony of 92
global knowledge economy 1
governance: of education systems 12, 13, 40, 54, 59, 133; frameworks 52, 135; technologies of 54
governmentality 51
Green Paper 15, 17, 18; and economic rationalism 15; Teaching Excellence Framework (TEF) 15–16, 17

habitus 25, 76, 83, 85, 89
higher education: allocative social power of 23; and capacity to dream 40; as

careless culture 92; commodification of 13; competitive space of 116, 118, 129; corporatisation of 1, 3, 13, 92; and drive for excellence 11, 36, 47, 133; effect of data on 14; equity goals of 20; and evaluation and assessment regimes 24; feminisation of 5, 7–8, 61, 91–2, 98, 100–2, 107, 137; governance of 59, 132–3; hierarchisation of 109; high participation system (HPS) of 23; historical masculinity in 93; management orientation of 59; marketisation of 10, 20, 26, 48, 92, 97, 131, 132, 140; men in 50; and neo-liberalism 11–12, 97; parity of participation in 31; as part of global market 5, 11, 12–15, 133, 139; pedagogical relations in 23; and power 43; and profit-making 15; and public investment 13; purpose of 22, 59, 132; reforms in 11; right to 1, 2, 5, 20, 77, 132, 134, 138, 150; spaces of 34–5, 57, 73, 132, 135; standardisation in 35; stratification of 20, 109, 133–4, 136, 139; structural inequalities of 36; and subordination to transnational corporations 13; and teaching quality 16, 26; and technologies of measurement 21–2, 23, 131; *see also* casualisation; corporatisation; datafication; performativity; social justice; social mobility
homogenisation 47
hooks, bell 9, 121–2, 129, 134; presence 124–5; wholeness 121–2
human capital 23, 37, 134, 138; techno-rationalist discourses of 37, 92; theory of 15, 23
humanisation 44, 53–4; *see also* Freire

identity(-ies) 37, 46–7, 64, 110, 132, 146, 150, 151; academic 8, 26, 60, 74, 82; and authenticity 110; and autobiography vs. biography 53; categories of 46; disciplinary 86, 136; formation of 5–6, 7, 9, 29, 39, 40, 41, 42, 50, 53, 54, 55, 76, 105, 122–3, 125, 124, 127–30, 140, 141, 150; gendered 8, 84, 91, 99, 140; in higher education 74; as learner 76, 77, 81, 84, 88–9; pedagogical

2, 3, 29, 54, 55, 76, 89–90, 146;
and personhood 22, 30, 32, 39–40,
42, 53, 138; politics of 43; positions
of 92; professional 8, 74, 130, 136;
reimagining 46–7; social 49, 76, 82,
84, 105, 148, 150, 153
imaginaries: classist 131; racist 10, 131;
sexist 10
impact, concept of 51–2; definition of 51
inclusion(s) 2, 4, 8, 34, 35, 74,
107, 139, 151; definition of 45;
environment of 64; hegemonic
discourse(s) of 27, 29–30; in higher
education 11, 24, 27–8, 48, 92,
95, 134; material 76; problematical
nature of 45; social 5, 9, 10, 76, 131;
structural 76
Indigenous students 31
individualism 20, 134, 137; culture of
54; individual responsibility 92; as
neo-liberal concept 37
inequality(-ies) 1–2, 3–4, 5, 6, 9, 10n1,
12, 41, 42, 44, 95, 131, 135, 138,
139; classed 120, 135, 140; cultural
20, 132, 134, 138; dynamics of 138;
and ECTs 122, 123; experience
of 24, 93, 134, 136; gendered 7,
93, 106, 120, 135, 137, 140; in
higher education 40, 43, 50, 104;
institutional 5, 20, 134; material
32, 35, 53, 135, 138; patterns of 9,
93, 123; and pedagogy 11, 30, 141;
racialised 5, 115, 120, 135, 140;
relations of 92; social 3, 12, 52, 53,
132–3, 138, 140–1; structural 7, 20,
36, 38, 40, 43, 76, 133, 134–6, 139;
symbolic 35, 45, 123, 138
injustice(s) 3, 6, 12, 29, 91, 137, 142;
cultural 132, 141; material 141; social
132, 133, 141; symbolic 141
interdisciplinarity 42; among subjects 108,
109; 'Mickey Mouse' subjects 108
International Doctoral and Post-
Doctoral Network on Gender, Social
Justice and Praxis (The Network) 51
International Gender Network 58
international students 81, 84
intersectionality, concept of 134
Italy 4, 50, 63, 153

knowing 35, 41, 53, 70; academic forms
of 138; not 82–3, 117, 119; politics
of 35; women's ways of 98

knowledge: forms of 5, 29, 33–4, 41–3,
56–7, 93, 138, 142; hierarchies of
89; politics of 35, 142; production of
64, 138

'laddishness', discourses of 105–6
language 2, 40, 55, 78, 79, 98, 115,
119, 153; body 32; as mechanism of
power 68; polished 68–9; reductive 5,
29; social 66
learning 4–6, 8, 10, 12, 16, 17, 21,
23–8, 29, 33, 34, 38–43, 45, 47, 52,
53, 54, 59–67, 70–2, 75, 78, 84, 85,
88–9, 97–101, 106, 110, 118, 120,
125, 131, 135, 138–41, 143, 146,
149–51; critical transformatory 89;
emotionality of 64, 71; experience
120; feminisation of 100; hegemonic
discourses of 25, 29; and importance
of peer groups 84; independent 67,
78; instrumentalist discourses of
29; passion for 10, 131; as play 99;
process of 21, 25, 65; reflective 67;
see also student(s)
learning communities 27–8, 65, 75
legitimate pedagogic code 34

male students 67–9, 80, 83–4, 87, 89,
97, 102–3, 105–6, 111, 113, 115–18,
143–5
managerialism 13, 37, 54; new 1;
technologies of 92
marginalisation 2, 34, 44, 95, 119, 138,
141
marketisation 15, 23, 24, 60, 120;
discourses of 134, 138; impact of 59;
of higher education 10, 20, 26, 48,
131, 140
masculinity(-ies) 4, 8, 50, 91–3, 96,
98, 137; Black 97, 116, 117, 137;
characteristics of 101; classed 97;
crisis of 5, 7, 106–7; discourses of
93, 106–7; formations of 107, 137;
hegemonic 102, 105, 107; hegemonic
discourses of 91, 107; hyper- 96;
identity 141; racialised 97, 116, 117;
White 106; working-class 137
massification 97
mature students 31, 78, 79, 81, 88
meaning-making 10, 41, 42, 45, 53–4,
101, 132, 135, 138–9, 142
mentoring: cross-institutional 137;
cross-regional 137; see also teacher(s)

meritocracy 5, 15, 20, 105, 134;
discourses of 105, 133; hegemony
of 92
misogyny 15, 92, 105, 133, 134;
discourses of 5, 20, 93
misrecognition(s) 1, 10n1, 20, 27, 40,
42, 44, 92, 96, 101–2, 103, 129–30,
134, 136, 138, 140, 142; causes
of 46; challenges to 45; classed 96;
cultural 53; experience of 11, 24, 32,
91, 121, 137; as mis/recognition
5, 9, 29, 30, 32, 35, 121, 127; and
pedagogical space(s) 35; politics of 5,
10, 29, 30, 32, 37, 43, 47, 91, 92,
93, 121, 131, 137; racialised 96,
119; symbolic 53; among teachers
73, 121, 123
mis/representation 32, 129–30, 138;
politics of 32; see also misrecognition;
representation
multiculturalism, discourses of 38

neocolonialism 1, 5, 12, 92; neocolonial
gaze 31
neoconservatism 1, 132
neo-liberalism 8, 11–12, 13, 14, 23,
37, 39, 53, 54, 64, 88, 92, 105–6,
110, 132–3, 134, 138, 141, 153;
discourses of 56, 60, 132; global
1, 3–4, 8; hegemony of 92; see also
austerity measures; datafication;
deregulation; governmentality;
marketisation; patriarchy; privatisation
neo-liberal opportunity bargain 22
neopatriarchy 1; see also patriarchy
newness 9, 121–4
non-standard student 2–3

OECD 16, 91
oppressions 12, 34, 44, 82; anti- 55;
social 133
Other, the 39, 46, 48, 82, 91, 97, 114–19,
131, 137, 142

panoptic device 25; see also Foucault
participation 1–9, 11, 16, 17, 20, 22–4,
27, 29, 31–3, 36, 42, 43, 96, 97;
collective 47; parity of 3, 31, 52;
pedagogical 2, 3, 33, 134–5, 137; and
student engagement 102; and voice
96, 98–9, 102–4; see also widening
participation (WP)
part-time students 31

patriarchy 5, 7, 12, 37, 92, 105, 106;
discourses of 93; and discourses
of gender 107; and discourses of
masculinity 8; see also neopatriarchy
pedagogical experience(s) 2, 4, 7, 9,
10, 25, 39, 47, 50, 52, 54, 55, 76,
84, 86, 91, 110, 122, 123, 127, 132,
135, 143–4, 148
pedagogical identity(-ies) 2, 3, 29, 54,
55, 76, 146
pedagogical methodology (PM) 6,
49–58, 60, 93, 135, 140, 142,
144; frameworks 135; and parity of
participation 52
pedagogical space(s) 3–8, 10, 13, 15,
17, 22, 29–30, 32, 34–5, 38, 41, 43,
45, 47, 50, 53–5, 91, 93, 95, 102–3,
106–7, 122, 131–42; disempowering
69; gendering of 136; racialisation of
136; of refusal 15; transformative 131
pedagogic stratification 134
pedagogies for social justice 3, 27–8, 30,
35, 49, 134; see also social justice
pedagogy(-ies) 32–3, 53, 125, 129–30,
134; classed 132, 138; collective
engaged 9, 122–3, 129–30, 136,
149, 151; critical 10, 18, 46, 57, 73,
87–9; of difference 28, 29, 34, 35,
41, 46, 49, 138, 139; of discomfort
45–6; engaged 9, 121–2, 126, 129; of
exclusion 76; forms of 64; gendering
of 8, 91, 132, 138; hegemonic 9,
35, 131; higher education 92; and
identity 73; of inclusion 76, 139;
inclusive 27, 34, 50–1, 135–6, 140,
141, 142, 148; invisible 33, 85;
liberatory 53; of the oppressed 44;
and pedagogical relationships 53,
55, 97, 135; and power 29, 32,
41, 134–5; racialised 132, 138; as
relational 134; student-centred 72,
74; transformatory 27, 134
performance management 22, 24, 92;
culture of 54
performativity 5, 11, 12, 17, 22–4, 26,
32, 37, 48, 54, 60, 64, 104, 124,
132, 134, 136, 137; age of 12, 37,
48, 132, 137; culture of 24, 36–7;
and excellence 17
plurality 38; vs. diversity 38
Portugal 4, 50, 103, 153
poststructuralism (post/structuralism)
6, 45, 53

poverty of aspiration 22
power 42–3, 44, 45, 47, 54–5, 77,
  135, 143; dynamics of 55, 57, 67,
  89; gendered relations of 98; and
  maternalism 99–100; politics of 93;
  unequal relations of 64, 69, 88–9, 95,
  104, 137, 139; webs of 42
praxis 6, 24, 28, 41–2, 44, 47, 53,
  54, 123, 135; communities of 58;
  concept of 44, 140; critical 88;
  framework of 6, 28, 141, 142; spaces
  of 49, 53, 135
precariousness 9, 121–3, 126, 129–30,
  136; and newness 123
prestige cultures 19
privatisation: of public sphere 12
protectionism: and higher education 12

quality 1, 7, 15–16, 18–19, 25–6, 41,
  51, 68, 74, 76, 133, 135; discourse of
  37, 74, 76

race 6, 8, 22, 29, 36, 39, 43, 46,
  50, 56–7, 65, 68, 69, 75, 76, 84,
  85, 89–90, 102, 112, 114, 118,
  120, 122, 133, 139–41, 143, 151;
  antagonisms 120; and ECTs 122; and
  friendship 84; structural inequalities
  of 56–7
racism 5, 38, 69, 92, 116, 120; fear
  of 111; global 38; institutional 1,
  12, 37, 92, 104–5, 131–2; racial
  segregation 119; and surveillance
  119; in university sector 120
raising aspirations 1, 4, 50
realisation rules 33–4, 77; definition
  of 77
recognition 3, 5, 9, 17, 26, 29–33,
  38–9, 43, 47–8, 53, 55, 64, 65, 77,
  93, 104, 113, 116, 121–2, 127, 130,
  132, 134, 135, 138; discourses of
  127; and parity of participation 31;
  politics of 31, 38, 39, 43, 93; see also
  misrecognition(s)
recognition rules 33, 77; and
  classification 77; definition of 77; and
  power 33, 77
redistribution 3, 10, 30, 33, 34, 36, 41,
  132, 138; politics of 31
reflexivity 39, 42, 60, 64, 117; critical
  28, 49, 53, 54, 123, 140; ethical 44;
  frameworks of 142; nature of 46;
  spaces of 6, 9, 50, 52, 122, 135, 136

regulation 11, 17, 18, 23–5, 29, 54,
  88, 92, 124, 128, 131, 136–8;
  de- 11; and excellence 17; self- 3;
  technologies of 54, 92
regulatory control 88
representation 3, 19, 30–2, 34, 39, 43,
  47, 57, 113, 129–30, 132, 134, 135,
  138, 142, 144; politics of 142
research 136; assessment exercises of 37;
  commercialisation of 13; pedagogic
  vs. academic 26; as pedagogy 53
'research that makes a difference',
  concept of 49, 51–2, 58
Riverside University 8, 59, 65, 68, 81,
  83, 89, 108, 111–15, 144, 149, 151

self, construction of 7, 76
social capital see capital
social justice 3, 9, 40, 43, 48, 51, 52,
  55, 57, 123, 127, 134, 140, 142;
  approaches 37, 92; discourse of 51;
  framework 27–8, 39, 138; in higher
  education 6, 10, 12, 19, 22, 23, 24,
  28, 30; imperatives of 24, 27, 34,
  132, 138; and praxis/praxis of 44, 58;
  networks 58; as social mobility 23;
  spaces of 57; see also pedagogy(-ies)
social mobility 23; discourse of 12; and
  higher education 22
social networking 108
social privilege 19, 34, 139
social schizophrenia 125–6
space(s) 135, 141; academic 113, 136;
  of critical reflexivity 140; cultural 119;
  geographies of 89; interventionist
  10, 132; participatory 135; see also
  pedagogical space
Spain 4, 19, 50, 62, 63, 80, 94, 95,
  103, 104, 153
spirituality 122; and mind-body-spirit
  122, 128
standardisation 9, 29, 35, 38, 47, 131
standards 19, 25, 36; academic 36, 120;
  discourse of 37; lowering of 5, 8,
  41, 48, 97, 101–2, 107, 131, 137;
  maintaining of 104; strengthening of
  41–2
stratification 11, 33, 105; of higher
  education 109, 133, 136; of
  institutions 20, 133, 139; pedagogic
  134; social 18, 109
structuralism 6, 53; see also
  poststructuralism

student(s) 41, 43, 44, 46, 50, 52, 55–6,
60–75, 76–90, 91, 92, 95–107,
110–20, 131, 132, 135, 137, 139,
140, 141, 142, 143–50, 151, 153;
the bad 67; as choice-maker(s)
20–2, 139; as consumer(s) 5, 13,
15–16, 20–2, 25, 40, 97, 134, 139;
as dangerous 69; difficult 88; with
disabilities 31, 81; evaluation of 24–5;
as evaluators of teachers 25, 37; and
fear of inauthenticity 118; and fear of
university experience 110; feminised
101–2; the good 67, 80, 118;
infantalisation of 61; living off campus
82–4; living on campus 82–3; mature
78, 79, 81, 88; the non-standard 2,
67; the non-traditional 17, 67, 101–2;
as passive recipients 44, 47, 62, 67,
69, 72, 78, 99, 101, 102; and peer
antagonisms 110; and peer assessment
70; retention 9, 60, 61, 88, 100, 136;
and silence 9, 66–7, 77, 96, 98–9,
102–4; success 9, 23, 26, 37, 88; voice
24, 40, 68–9, 85–6, 96, 98, 99, 102,
104, 150; 'Widening Participation'
(WP) 61, 67, 72, 76; working-class 8,
77, 79, 81–3, 85, 87, 108–10, 114–15,
117–20; see also Black and Minority
Ethnic (BME) students; Black students;
class; female students; Indigenous
students; international students; male
students; mature students; part-time
students; students of colour; White
students; working-class students
student-as-consumer model see student
student deficit discourse 61, 70, 100;
see also deficit discourse
students of colour 31, 112
subjectivity(-ies) 4–7, 11, 18, 22–3,
29–33, 36–9, 41–3, 45, 48, 54, 91–3,
104–5, 132, 135–6, 138; concept of
39; embodied 93; formation of 54;
gendered 93
surveillance: culture 5; and excellence
17; in higher education 21, 25, 119,
136; self- 24; of teachers 60, 88;
technologies of 131, 138
sustainability 44, 58
symbolic violence 2, 8, 27, 29, 32, 44,
91, 101, 129, 137

teacher(s) 41, 43, 44, 46, 50, 52, 55–6,
59, 60–75, 78–9, 85–9, 92, 94–107,

110, 118, 121–2, 131, 132, 135–7,
139, 140, 141, 142, 143–8, 150–1;
authority of 41, 93, 97–9; and auto-
independence 127; autonomy of
126–7; and co-mentoring 129–30,
136; continuing professional
development (CPD) opportunities
for 140, 141, 143; as controllers 69,
97; disempowerment of 140; early
career teachers (ECTs) 121–30,
136; feelings of isolation among 74,
126, 127; maternalistic 99–101;
and performance management 22;
as researchers 72, 122, 128, 139;
as service providers 13, 40; student
evaluations of 25, 37, 60, 64, 88;
see also casualisation; precariousness
teaching 43, 47, 60, 97, 131, 135, 136,
139, 140, 146, 149, 150, 151, 153;
critical 56; didactic 56; direct 56;
emotionality of 60, 71; excellence
17, 26, 134; feminisation of 100;
hegemonic discourses of 25, 29,
135; instrumentalist discourses of
29; as interdisciplinary field 41–4;
as play 99; practical 56; professional
development of 26–7; professionalism
of 26; and staff time 56; and student
engagement 33, 34, 102; valuing of
133; see also teacher(s)
temporality(-ies): and ECTs 9, 123–6,
129; and newness 123; and space
123; and trance 125
tolerance 122; discourses of 38
transformation 4, 13, 27, 30, 41,
44–5; cultural 3, 132; in higher
education 12; of individual student
27; intellectual process of 21; of
knowledge 57; learning as 25;
pedagogical 135; reflexive 126; self-
3; social 3, 22, 132; spaces of 42, 135
trust, in pedagogical settings 16, 46

UNESCO 16
United Kingdom 4, 15, 17, 18, 38, 50,
51, 56, 58, 83, 110, 120n1, 133;
British National Student Survey 77;
HE/FE Education Act 109; Higher
Education Academy (HEA) 26,
49, 59; Higher Education Funding
Council for England (HEFCE) 49;
Professional Standards Framework
(UKPSF) 26; University of

Roehampton's Centre for Education Research in Equalities, Policy and Pedagogy (CEREPP) 49; 2014 Research Excellence Framework (REF) 51
United States 4, 50, 69, 119, 133, 153
utopistics, concept of 54

vocationalisation 13
vocationalism 59

White Paper 18; Office for Students (OFS) 18; and Teaching Excellence Framework (TEF) 15, 17, 18, 59–60

White students 8, 65–6, 74, 110, 112–14, 118, 144
White supremacy 57
widening participation (WP) 1–9, 11, 15, 17, 20, 22–4, 31, 36, 49–50, 59–62, 64, 76, 96–7, 101–2, 104, 108–10, 118–20, 131, 133–4, 139–41, 143
working-class students 8, 31, 77, 79, 81–3, 87, 108, 110, 114–15, 117–20
World Bank 16
World Economic Forum (WEF) 13

youth culture 81, 82